ACADEMIC POWER

The Praeger Special Studies
Series in Comparative Education
General Editor Philip G. Altbach

Comparative Perspectives on the Academic Profession
edited by
Philip G. Altbach

The Changing Japanese University in Comparative Perspective*
edited by
William K. Cummings
Ikiro Amano
Kazayuki Kitamura

*forthcoming

ACADEMIC POWER:

Patterns of Authority in Seven National Systems of Higher Education

John H. Van de Graaff
Burton R. Clark
Dorotea Furth
Dietrich Goldschmidt
Donald F. Wheeler

PRAEGER

PRAEGER SPECIAL STUDIES • PRAEGER SCIENTIFIC

Library of Congress Cataloging in Publication Data

Main entry under title:

Academic power.

(Praeger special studies series in comparative education)
1. Comparative education. I. Van de Graaff, John H.
LA132.A265   370.19'5   78-17172
ISBN 0-03-045531-6

**Praeger Special Studies Series in Comparative Education
Series Editor: Philip G. Altbach
Published in cooperation with the
Center for Comparative Education,
State University of New York at Buffalo**

Published in 1978 by Praeger Publishers
CBS Educational and Professional Publishing
A Division of CBS, Inc.
521 Fifth Avenue, New York, New York 10017 U.S.A.

© 1978 by Praeger Publishers

0123456789   038   98765432

Printed in the United States of America

Preface
Burton R. Clark

This book began in an interdisciplinary seminar held during the academic year 1973–74 as part of a new Program of Comparative and Historical Studies of Higher Education in the Institution for Social and Policy Studies (ISPS) at Yale. The seminar was devoted to comparative analysis of organization and control in national systems of higher education. The Yale faculty, visiting scholars, postdoctoral fellows, and graduate students grouped around the table provided expertise on France, West Germany, Italy, Japan, and the United States, and we fell to the task of intensively comparing these five countries. The countries seemed so different in their experiences that, at the time, we were not at all sure we could find ways of comparing them. But in worldwide view we were at least restricting our "sample" to relatively similar countries in the sense that they were all industrialized nations with democratic political regimes. We presented our preliminary impressions at a panel session of the annual meeting of the Comparative and International Education Society held in Washington, D.C., in March 1974. Increasingly persuaded that our work had merit, we decided to continue our joint effort and commit a book-length report to which we would add chapters on Great Britain and Sweden in order to provide greater coverage of important Western nations. During the following two years, we developed materials on those two nations, exchanged numerous drafts of the various chapters, and met together on several occasions in the United States, Great Britain, and Europe to discuss and debate the results. In the process, our prolonged cooperative effort came to span two continents and three organizations. Three of us, Burton R. Clark, John H. Van de Graaff, and Donald F. Wheeler, were part of the Yale Program during most of the preparation of the manuscript, the first as Chairman and the other two as Postdoctoral Fellows. Dorotea Furth, a Visiting Research Associate in the program during 1973–74, completed her efforts from her staff position in the Organisation for Economic Cooperation and Development (OECD) in Paris. Dietrich Goldschmidt, Visiting Professor in the Program during 1973–74, returned to his directorship in the Max Planck Institute of Education in Berlin. Mrs. Mechthild Engert, who prepared the statistical appendices, is also a member of the Berlin Institute. Since Van de Graaff coordinated our efforts, he became the first-listed author of this volume.

The Yale Program (renamed in 1977 as the Higher Education Research Group) plans to publish a number of intensive studies of individual countries in order to strengthen the basic literature on academic organization and control. One book-length study of this nature is already in print: *Academic Power in Italy: Bureaucracy and Oligarchy in a National System of Higher Education*, by Burton R. Clark. Article-length discussions of individual countries are available in the Working Papers Series of the Yale Group. Comparative studies will also be prepared, of which this volume is the first in book-length form. Neither the country studies nor the comparative statements attempt to cover all aspects of higher education, because such efforts pay a high price for their comprehensive scope in superficiality and conceptual disarray. Instead, the studies concentrate on the major institutional forms that carry higher education over time and the systematic connections that link the forms into state, provincial, and national systems. Our intent is to improve the scientific and general understanding of: (1) the common and unique features of the general organization of higher education in whole nations, particularly in regard to the location of power and group interest; (2) the historical evolution of the national structures; (3) the effects of those structures on educational practice and performance; and (4) the ways in which the structures condition reform and are in turn altered by the demands and trends of contemporary decades.

What has been done in the comparative study of the structure and development of the economic and political sectors of society ought to be done for the educational sector. From practical and theoretical quarters, a new demand for knowledge clearly exists: how do we comprehend higher education? On this large task, there is a long way to go even to make an effective beginning. Lacking a disciplinary base, the literature on higher education is small in nearly all countries. In bulk alone, it is of some magnitude only on the United States and secondarily on Great Britain. And on fundamental aspects of academic power, the literature on higher education remains particularly weak: general statements on higher education in a country, taking up such disparate topics as admissions, curriculum, and personnel, commonly skim over the authority structure in a page or two; focused work on governance, now acquiring some momentum, commonly concentrates on a single country at a time, and then either on authority within the university or on the relation of "higher education to the state," the one to the exclusion of the other. At the same time, numerous observers and participants make grand statements about the exercise of power in the academic sector of modern society without the benefit of intensive knowledge of more than one country and from viewpoints that are more normative than empirical.

Much detailed descriptive work on various countries is required, as well as the accumulation of international data and analyses that are directly comparative. As will be seen, we present our materials primarily in a case-study fashion. This approach, often thought old-fashioned in modern social science, is still a useful tool of comparative research, especially when a research sector is undeveloped and more in need of intensive exploration and some insight than of hypothesis-testing and validation. It encourages a mode of comprehension in which the investigator attempts to understand the pattern of an organic whole, the relations among its constituent parts, and the principles by which the parts consistently fit together. This configurational approach is comfortable with the multiplicity of particularities that are nested in the whole of a national system. It inclines investigators to describe what is unique as well as to pursue features that may be widely found. And when country case studies are placed side by side, as we do in this volume, modest generalizations about similarities and differences can be attempted from the newly-strengthened descriptive base. It is our hope that our own first approximation to a crossnational comprehension of academic organization and control will help stimulate and guide the needed additional work.

Acknowledgments

The authors are indebted to the National Science Foundation, the National Institute of Education, and the Lilly Endowment for support of the research program within which this effort was generated and sustained. The Yale Institution for Social and Policy Studies also assisted this work, especially with fellowship aid and general support during 1973–74. In addition, the authors wish to thank the Organisation for Economic Co-operation and Development (OECD) in Paris and the Max Planck Institute for Educational Research in Berlin for personnel leaves and other support afforded this study, and the International Institute for Educational Planning for providing office facilities for research conducted in Paris.

Many individual scholars aided the study by their comments on early drafts, particularly in the countries where the authors' own knowledge was least well rooted in detailed earlier research on academic governance. Special thanks are due Roger Geiger, Bertrand Girod de l'Ain, Jean-Louis Quermonne, and Thierry Malan, for their comments on the chapter on France; Henry Egidius, Ludwig Fischer, Torsten Husen, Sixten Marklund, and Carl G. Sköld, on Sweden; Lord Eric Ashby, Harold Perkin, A. M. Ross, David Eversley, David R. Jones, and Rowland Eustace, on Great Britain; and Ikuo Amano and Ulrich Teichler, on Japan.

Finally, the authors wish to thank Margaret Anbar and Mary Hyson (Yale) and Linda Charest (Editorial Associates) for typing drafts and final copy of the manuscript; and Barbara Baird Ryan, director, Editorial Associates, for editing the manuscript.

John Van de Graaff
Burton R. Clark

Calgary (Canada)
New Haven (U.S.)
December, 1976

Contents

PREFACE
Burton R. Clark   v

ACKNOWLEDGMENTS   viii

LIST OF ACRONYMS   xii

1
INTRODUCTION
John Van de Graaff and Dorotea Furth   1

Characteristics of Authority Structures   2
Levels of Organization   3
Policies and Policy Making   6
Basic Forces in the Recent Development of
   Higher Education   7
Organization of the Study   10
Notes   11

PART I: SEVEN COUNTRIES

2
FEDERAL REPUBLIC OF GERMANY
John Van de Graaff   15

Introduction   15
Traditional Structures   19
Legislative Reform of University Structure   25
Notes   32

3
ITALY
Burton R. Clark   37

Levels of Organization   40
Reform and Change   44
Notes   47

4
FRANCE
John Van de Graaff and Dorotea Furth   49

Administrative Centralism   52
Traditional Structure: Professorial Autonomy and
*   Ministerial Authority*   53
Centrally Administered Structural Change   57
Notes   64

5
SWEDEN
Dietrich Goldschmidt   67

Traditional Structures and Early Reforms   70
Recent Structural Reforms   74
Conclusion   79
Notes   81

6
GREAT BRITAIN
John Van de Graaff   83

Levels of Control   89
Structural Evolution and Policy Transformation   95
Notes   99

7
UNITED STATES
Burton R. Clark   104

Levels of Organization   109
Change   118
Notes   121

8
JAPAN
Donald F. Wheeler 124

Development of the University System 124
Types of Institutions 127
Levels of Organization 129
*Characteristics of Decision Making: Consensus and
    the Containment of Conflict* 135
Crisis and Change 138
Notes 143

PART II: CONCLUSIONS

9
SYSTEMS OF HIGHER EDUCATION
Dietrich Goldschmidt 147

Characteristics of the National Systems 147
Comparisons 153
Changes in the Pattern of Decision Making 159
Concluding Perspectives 161

10
ACADEMIC POWER: CONCEPTS, MODES,
AND PERSPECTIVES
Burton R. Clark 164

Concepts of Academic Authority 164
Modes of Academic Authority 174
Analytical Perspectives 179
Notes 187

APPENDIX 191

ABOUT THE AUTHORS 219

List of Acronyms

AUT	Association of University Teachers	
BAK	Bundesassistentenkonferenz	(Federal Assistants Conference)
BLK	Bund-Länder Kommission für Bildungsplanung	(Federal-State Commission for Educational Planning)
CAT	College of Advanced Technology	
CCE	Central Council of Education	
CDU	Christlich Demokratische Union	(Christian Democratic Union
CNAA	Council for National Academic Awards	
CNESER	Conseil National de l'Enseignement Supérieur et de la Recherche	(National Council for Higher Education and Research)
CNRS	Centre National de la Recherche Scientifique	(National Center for Scientific Research)
CSU	Christlich-Soziale Union	(Christian Social Union)
CVCP	Committee of Vice-Chancellors and Principals	
DES	Department of Education and Science	
DFG	Deutsche Forschungsgemeinschaft	(German Research Association)

DGB	Deutscher Gewerkschaftsbund	(German Union Federation)
ENSI	Ecoles Nationales Supérieures d'Ingénieurs	(Higher National Engineering Schools)
ERIC	Educational Resources Information Center	
FDP	Freie Demokratische Partei	(Free Democratic Party)
FNYS	Försöksverksamhet med nya samarbetsformer	(Experiments with new forms of participation)
GCE	General Certificate of Education	
GEW	Gewerkschaft Erziehung und Wissenschaft	(Education and Science Union)
ISPS	Institution for Social and Policy Studies	
IUT	Instituts Universitaires de Technologie	(University Institutes of Technology)
KBS	Kokusai Bunka Shinkokai	
KMK	Kultusministerkonferenz	(Standing Conference of State Ministers of Education)
MIT	Massachusetts Institute of Technology	
NASDAP	Nationalsozialistische Deutsche Arbeiterpartei	National Socialist German Workers Party (Nazi Party)
NUS	National Union of Students	
OECD	Organisation for Economic Co-operation and Development	
ÖTV	Gewerkschaft Öffentliche Dienste, Transport und Verkehr	(Public Service and Transport Union)
SAP	Sveriges Socialdemokratiska Arbetareparti	(Swedish Social Democratic Labor Party)
SCB	Statistika centralbryan	(Central Office of Statistics)
SDS	Sozialistischer Deutscher Studentenbund	(Socialist German Students League)
SKÖ	(probably the same as SO)	(National Board of Education

SÖ	Skolöverstyrelsen	(National Board of Education)
SOU	Statens offentliga utredningar	(government publication)
SPD	Sozialdemokratische Partei Deutschlands	(Social Democratic Party of Germany)
UER	Unité d'Enseignement et de Recherche	(Unit of Teaching and Research
UHÄ	Universitets-och Högskoleämbetet	(National Board of Universities and Colleges)
UKÄ	Universitetskanslersämbetet	(Office of the Chancellor of the Universities)
UKAS	Universitetskanslerämbetets arbetsgrupp för fasta studiegangar m.m.	(Working group for curriculum planning attached to the office of the chancellor of the universities)
VDS	Verband Deutscher Studentenschaften	(Association of German Students' Unions)
WRK	Westdeutsche Rektorenkonferenz	(West German Rectors Conference)

ACADEMIC POWER

1
INTRODUCTION
John Van de Graaff
Dorotea Furth

The flood of polemical and scholarly writing produced during the past decade of change and turmoil in higher education has seldom directly confronted the problem of power. To be sure, academics have been quick to lament their lack of power. The more conservative are eager to reassert their traditional autonomy against students, administrators, or government officials; the more liberal seek to redefine that autonomy in a socially progressive vein. Politicians, civil servants, and administrators—often with economic concerns uppermost in mind—attempt to keep the universities in line with the government policies of the day. Students are often joined by junior staff and a sprinkling of their senior colleagues in decrying their lack of power, which the more radical among them interpret as an inevitable consequence of the university's subservience to the economic elite and its role as a bulwark of the capitalist system.

Amidst such polemics, reasoned analyses and empirical studies of academic power are rare indeed.[1] This book takes aim at that gap, focusing on a topic central to classical social science—power—and investigating it in a particular institutional setting—higher education. Using modes of analysis characteristic of a number of social science subfields, such as sociology of organizations, comparative politics, and public administration,[2] the structure of power is compared in seven national systems of higher education: the Federal Republic of Germany, Italy, France, Sweden, Great Britain, the United States, and Japan. Each country chapter begins with historical background, a review of important contextual features, and basic data on the system of higher education. The core of each case then focuses on power relationships within the traditional, prereform university sector as it existed in the 1950s and early 1960s and, in some countries, even to this day. In this section of each chapter six levels of organization are covered, from the professor or department at the academic grass roots up to the national government, analyzing both the overall distribution of power and influence as well as the locus of decision making for specific policy areas. Finally, a concluding section assesses the recent reform and evolution of these power structures from the perspective of higher education as a whole, in a broad socioeconomic context.

CHARACTERISTICS OF AUTHORITY STRUCTURES

Two basic concepts are employed to analyze structures at the various levels of organization: the degree of structural hierarchy and the extent of unity or cohesion in decision making.

The first concept, degree of hierarchy, is used to characterize the steepness or flatness of organization for an authoritarian structure at one extreme and a collegial or democratic one at the other. In the former case, power is concentrated sharply at the peak of the structure, whereas in the latter it is spread evenly among different units encompassed at a given level. Power is accorded through either formal authority or informal status, or sometimes both. The head of an academic department, for example, may have extensive formal authority which he cannot fully exercise because his informal status among his colleagues is low. Conversely, a department head with limited formal prerogatives may enjoy enormous respect and therefore be able to exercise great power. In assessing hierarchy at a given level, both the degree to which individuals, groups, and organizational units participate in decision making, and the relationship among those who do govern, are considered. To the extent that "the basic rule in academia is equality among full members,"[3] academic government is formally collegial. Yet there are always certain groups of academic staff with less than full rights of participation, and the proportion of staff in those groups, as well as the extent of their exclusion from decision making, represents an element of hierarchy.

The other structural characteristic analyzed is the degree of unity or cohesiveness of decision making, the extent to which a level of organization can adopt, implement, and enforce a coherent or uniform policy. In a typology proposed by Roland T. Warren, structures can be characterized as, at one extreme, highly cohesive, through the intermediate categories of federative and coalitional, to those exhibiting free social choice at the other extreme.[4] The important criteria are the extent to which decisions are made in terms of goals that are inclusive (for a given level), the extent of inclusive organization for decision making, and the locus of both actual decision making and formal authority. In a unitary decision-making context, the units forming a given level have an inclusive formal organization that possesses formal authority and actually makes binding decisions for all units. In a federative context, there is an inclusive formal organization, but it shares authority and decision-making powers with the constituent units, which pursue their individual goals as well as inclusive ones. In a coalitional context, there is no formal organization; there is informal collaboration, but authority and decision-making powers rest with the units, which are committed primarily to their own goals. Finally, in a social-choice context, the units pursue their own goals; consensus is the only means of keeping to any sort of common path. In the organization of academic life, federative structures assume a special importance, especially at middle levels, since they permit the academic departments and institutes to pursue their primary concerns of teaching and research in relative freedom, while preserving a degree of coordination and pursuit of common goals.

Although related, these two aspects of structure, hierarchy and cohesive decision making, are distinct. Hierarchical structures may be more likely than collegial or democratic ones to exhibit unitary decision making, but collegial bodies like the U.S. academic department are quite capable of reaching cohesive decisions that their members accept. Conversely, hierarchical bureaucracies such as the French or Italian or the German state ministries are not necessarily capable of following coherent overall policies.

LEVELS OF ORGANIZATION

The present classification includes six levels, not all of them found in every system. From bottom to top, in the same order as they are covered in the country chapters, the levels are the institute or department, the faculty (in the European sense, as the unit of organization for a professional training or a cluster of disciplines), the university, the multicampus system, state government, and national government. The first three are encompassed by the traditional university, and the last three lie above it.

The first level of the institute or department is normally the locus of teaching and most research. Its basic orientation is toward the pursuit of an academic discipline. In Europe the typical form is that of an institute built around a professorial chair, whereas in England a similar structure has been called a department. Generally, however, the term department is used in the American sense of an academic unit encompassing a number of professors, usually of different rank and status. The U.S. department is structured more collegially than the typical European institute, which has traditionally been under the absolute authority of the chair-holding professor as its director. In general, departments and institutes are becoming less clearly distinguishable as the numbers of staff of all ranks increase and as collective decision-making organs become more prevalent. Traditionally the unit of department or institute was very small, including one full professor and one or two junior staff; today a typical small department may include at least a dozen teaching staff, and the large ones many dozens, servicing several hundreds of students.

The next level is traditionally called the faculty, except in the United States, where the term college or school is more common. The division into faculties goes back to the Middle Ages, when the four faculties of theology, law, medicine, and arts or philosophy were established. The European universities largely retained that fourfold structure through the nineteenth century, whereas England, Japan, and the United States varied from the pattern relatively early. The traditional role of the faculties has been mainly that of preparation for learned professions. However, since the early nineteenth century, the mission of disinterested scholarship and research has been located in one of the faculty-level units: the faculty of philosophy in Europe and especially Germany, and the graduate school of arts and sciences—usually closely linked with the undergraduate liberal arts college— in the United States. Historically, the two patterns of chair-based institute and department at the lowest level have been associated with two distinct patterns of authority structures at the next level. In Europe (including England) the faculty was controlled by the assembly of all full professors, which selected a largely honorific dean from among their number. In the United States, in contrast, the administrators at the school or college level have significant authority and are responsible for a substantial bureaucratic apparatus. Size varies greatly at this level and has tended to increase sharply, sometimes giving rise to reforms that create small units, such as *Fachbereiche* in Germany and *unités d'enseignement et de recherche* in France.

The university itself is the next level of organization, in its traditional sense of an institution limited to a single locality. According to the traditional ideal, the university embodied the unity of the higher learning. Even today, when faith in such unity has ebbed, the university is still viewed as the locus for a comprehensive conception or interpretation of knowledge and its uses. The university is probably the highest administrative level at which all its members can participate in policy making, although universities with 10,000 or 20,000 students may have passed the upper boundary, wherever it may precisely lie. Universities vary greatly in their heterogeneity. Some include hardly more than the disciplines traditionally found within the four medieval faculties, whereas many have become the multiversities that Clark Kerr celebrated and Abraham Flexner, over 30 years before Kerr, already deplored.[5] In this study, the full-fledged universities are dealt with primarily; specialized technical and professional schools, as well as other postsecondary institutions of less than university rank, are considered only as part of the overall system of higher education.

The most common organs at the university level are a chief executive (rector or president), a small executive council, and a largely advisory assembly, usually supplemented by specialized committees. Where the institute system permits chair-holding professors to wield great power, the rector is largely a figurehead, chairing an academic senate with limited powers. In contrast, the department system permits more bureaucracy and power at the university level, as can be seen in the American university president with his administrative entourage, and (to a much lesser extent) in the English vice-chancellor. Again, the distinction is becoming blurred, as the chair-based systems implement reforms to strengthen the faculty and, above all, the university level.

The fourth level consists of multicampus institutions of higher education. This is the least sharply defined of the six levels, because it is still emergent. Indeed, among the seven countries, it is now significant only in the United States, although most of the others are introducing it in one form or another. It includes institutions that are much more dispersed and usually larger than the conventional local or single-campus university. Thus it is not synonymous with the comprehensive university, as that term is used in West Germany, for example, where it can mean a university that includes training institutions previously not considered to be of university status. This level does include large-scale municipal, regional, and statewide organizations or coordinating boards, insofar as they are distinct from regular state government. In practice, organization at Level 4 is always public; private institutions are almost always single-campus universities.

There are four principal types of organization at Level 4. The first is a statewide coordinating body for all of higher education, which has been attempted in some German states, or even for all of education, as in the case of the New York State Board of Regents, which has been referred to as a fourth branch of state government.[6] Second, there are statewide coordinating boards for separate sectors of higher education, as in California's three boards for the university, the state colleges, and the community colleges. Third, countries such as Sweden, France, and Italy are forming regional boards that have some jurisdiction over higher education; they are somewhat analogous to the English federal universities of the nineteenth century or the present-day University of Wales. Finally, there are large municipal systems of higher education, such as the City University of New York and London University.

The fifth level is state government, which among our countries exists only in the United States and West Germany. This level includes regular state ministries of education or higher education, as in the eleven German *Länder*, and the state education departments of the fifty U.S. states. In France, an analogous level is the *académie*, which, although it has jurisdiction only over education, is in every other way an integral part of the French governmental structure. Even where this level of government exists, the need for marshaling sufficient expertise for planning and coordinating higher education has led to the creation of organs at Level 4, distinct from state government and more suited to working closely with the universities while safeguarding their autonomy.

Finally, at the sixth level is the national government. Here there is an important distinction between the federal systems—West Germany and the United States—which assign constitutional responsibility for higher education to state governments, and other countries, where the national level has direct authority over higher education. Nevertheless, the role of the federal governments in higher education in Germany and to a lesser extent the United States has grown substantially over the past two decades. In both Japan and the United States, it is partly because of the involvement of the national government that the private universities may be considered a part of the national system of higher education.

For each of these levels, various policy-making organs and their composition, the groups involved, the extent of bureaucratic structures, and the degree of hierarchy and cohesiveness are analyzed. The structure and performance of a given level of university government cannot be fully understood without investigating patterns of power and influence at all levels and the interrelationships between them.

POLICIES AND POLICY MAKING

The importance of these interrelationships is confirmed by a further undertaking of the study—to analyze the pattern of decision making in six policy areas: overall planning and policy making, budget and finance, student admissions and access, curricula and examinations, appointment of senior and junior teaching staff, and research. In the first two areas, governments are usually directly involved, at least in state systems, whereas the last four have traditionally been matters more often decided within the university. However, authority for a given policy area rarely lies exclusively at a particular level. Typically, one level will initiate or propose a measure, and higher ones will approve it, veto it, send it back for further consideration with or without amendments, and so forth. The relationship of power among the different levels can be delicate and subtle; in fact, the important maneuvering may take place informally and behind the scenes, so that when a matter comes up for formal consideration at a given level, the outcome is a foregone conclusion.

To the extent feasible, not only the patterns of policy making which prevail in the six areas, but also how variations in structure affect the quality of the policies, will be assessed. The criteria used necessarily vary according to the level of organization. The institute or department will normally be concerned with making satisfactory progress within its academic discipline and with preserving what it sees as a healthy balance between teaching and research. Higher levels of governance must keep wider perspectives and criteria in view. The university, whether at the single or multicampus level, bears responsibility for seeing that disciplinary boundaries do not become barriers in research and teaching, and for encouraging innovation. In shaping its policies, the university stands to gain in the long run by taking a comprehensive view of its needs and priorities and those of society, reconciling them where possible. At the levels of state or national government, the difficulties in setting priorities are compounded, especially in federal systems and those with a significant private sector. The latter may have to rely extensively on mechanisms of social choice. Beyond maintaining some support for every discipline, the questions of which disciplinary and interdisciplinary endeavors to nurture will, for governmental authorities, inevitably be linked with problems of social need.

BASIC FORCES IN THE RECENT DEVELOPMENT OF HIGHER EDUCATION

Contextual forces such as demographic, political, economic, and social trends impinge strongly on the contemporary development of higher education. These forces are by no means confined to national borders, and indeed they can impose a common developmental framework on otherwise highly diverse nations. It is striking to note, for example, the extent to which the so-called university crisis of the middle and late 1960s was common to industrialized countries. Any comparative analysis of recent structural changes in countries such as the seven treated in this volume, given the reality of their common university crisis, must probe for common explanatory factors. The most general one is certainly economic growth, together with its various consequences. However, a number of more specific forces have placed traditional university structures under steadily increasing strain, thereby furthering pressures for reform. Six such factors are outlined below.

Expansion of Student Body and Teaching Staff

The most important single pressure bearing on institutions of higher education has been the well-known and generalized phenomenon of the "explosion of numbers." Enrollments doubled or even trebled in the course of the late 1950s and early 1960s, and policy makers and academics became aware that emerging problems could not be solved merely by enlarging institutions and by following the past policies of providing "more of the same." Quantitative expansion generated new, qualitative problems; the institutional framework that had evolved for a small minority of the age group was unsuited for the wide range of abilities, interests, and motivations of the expanding student population. This expansion itself led directly to a massive increase of teaching personnel, mainly of junior staff members whose subordinate position vis-à-vis established professors created conflicts and tensions that could not easily be alleviated within traditional structures strongly influenced by the chair system and its hierarchical staff relationships. A further consequence of this growth in numbers has been the development of academic bureaucracy. In the past few years, in most countries, a slowing of enrollment growth—or in the case of Sweden an actual turn downwards—has occurred.[7] In such cases, the need for planning, which was largely but by no means universally accepted by the early 1970s, has become even more acute.

The fundamental importance of enrollment expansion resulting from consumer demand cannot be underestimated. Yet two other forces have extended and mediated the impact of expansion on the structure of higher education. The first is the demand for highly trained manpower by both the public service and private employers. The second is egalitarianism.

Labor Market Demand

Although no Western industrialized country can claim that the structure of its universities has been principally determined by manpower requirements, their influence has nonetheless been significant. In the early 1960s universities faced criticism for their inability to provide the increased range of skills and qualifications—especially at middle levels—required by modern economies, while students were dropping out in large numbers without any vocational training and even graduate unemployment was becoming a problem. The resulting emphasis on close linkage between postsecondary education and employment needs, compounded by scarcity of resources and a growing governmental concern with efficiency and accountability, has been a strong force for diversification of higher education in the sense of developing new types of professionally and vocationally oriented institutions outside the traditional university sector, often with shorter programs of study and under closer government control.[8]

Egalitarianism

A concern for equality of opportunity, stemming from a growing mass of evidence that enrollment growth has at best modestly diminished disparities in educational participation rates according to social or regional origin. sex, or race,[9] has created strong pressures on universities to ensure access and educational opportunities to groups that had been underrepresented in the past. Egalitarianism focused attention not only on problems of access to higher education but also on the need to adapt it so as not to disadvantage the newcomers. To that extent it fostered diversity in higher education. But because of the oft-cited tendency of short-cycle, nonuniversity, vocational institutions to deflect their students from going on to further studies—the "cooling-out" function [10]—advocates of egalitarianism sometimes oppose, as they did in Germany, too sharp diversification into institutions with different purposes, lest the chances of the students in the lower-status units be unduly restricted.

In any case, manpower requirements and egalitarian values have both led to a greater emphasis on teaching and training and have fostered such trends as the divorce between undergraduate and graduate programs and (as in Sweden) the employment of staff whose only formal duties are to teach, with no participation in research.

Since the late 1960s, with the changing economic situation, the slowdown in the demand for personnel within the educational sector itself, and the consolidation of many internal reforms, certain of these trends have become stronger and others have emerged. Above all, universities are becoming more responsive to outside pressures, as can be seen in their increasing concern with lifelong or continuing education.

The Knowledge Explosion

The exponential growth of science and the central role of knowledge in the total development of society have imposed increasing responsibilities and conflicting tasks on higher education. Pressures from within universities led to a growing differentiation of knowledge along disciplinary lines, to specialization, and to rapid development of postgraduate education. Research was increasingly drawn away from teaching and in some cases even left the universities altogether. In recent years, however, to counteract the dangers of extreme fragmentation of knowledge and excessive specialization, a demand for multidisciplinary and interdisciplinary forms of study and for problem- or project-oriented research and teaching has grown. Underlying this development is a search for new ways of organizing knowledge to make it more useful and relevant to society's needs and problems.

Rising Costs

All of these developments—expansion of student numbers and above all staff, institutional diversification, separation between research and teaching, growth of postgraduate training—are highly expensive. Indeed, in the majority of the industrialized countries, during the last decade recurrent and capital expenditures on higher education have grown faster than total educational expenditures, total public spending, and gross national product. In the current context of budgetary stringency, strong political pressures are being exerted to counter rising unit costs. Pressed to increase productivity and to make better use of available resources, the universities feel squeezed between their need for autonomy and the demand by government and public opinion for greater accountability.

Politicization

In its most fundamental sense, politicization means the "arrival" of higher education as a key element in economic and social policy and thus implies the need for structural diversification and the promotion of novel or hitherto neglected institutions within the postsecondary sector as a whole. The principle that the performance of higher education, as a national institution of paramount importance, must be gauged according to national needs and societal standards is now widely accepted.

In a narrower sense, politicization serves to legitimize the involvement not only of parties, politicians, and government officials in policy making for higher education, but also of hitherto uninvolved groups both within the universities (students, junior staff, nonacademic staff) and outside them (trade unions, employers' associations). This participation, whether informal or instituted through the formal democratization of decision making, can be linked to the occurrence of sharp ideological and partisan conflicts in higher education. Any far-reaching assessment of the mission and structure of higher education, especially under political and group pressure, is bound to be highly unsettling, not least for the universities. Having remained so long at the pinnacle of the educational system, the universities have to adapt the most and therefore have potentially the most to lose.

The convergence of these six major forces, and other derivative ones which have been less crucial, has strongly affected patterns of power and organization in higher education. Traditional decision-making processes, most often based on interplay between government bureaucracies and the collegial, guild-like units of senior professors, have been challenged on grounds of both legitimacy and efficiency. Where such policy-making structures have persisted in conjunction with inflexible institutional patterns that were not sufficiently diverse to handle growing manpower needs and the floods of new student clienteles, as in Germany, France, and Italy, the crisis has been most dramatic and has led simultaneously to a reassessment of the mission of higher education and to attempts to reform governing patterns. At the other extreme, the United States has historically possessed unparalleled institutional diversity together with dispersed, flexible policy-making structures. Which systems will eventually weather the buffeting, emerging with renewed vigor, is quite another matter; such tentative prognoses as this study can hazard must be left to the conclusion.

ORGANIZATION OF THE STUDY

The country-by-country organization of the study brings out characteristic features of the various systems. This volume deals first with the four relatively pure state systems—Germany, Italy, France, and Sweden—and concludes with three under more mixed authority—England, the United States, and Japan. Germany comes first of all, as the classic case of a chair-based state system (although administered by the several *Land* governments), whose universities were widely regarded as the best in the world until well into the present century. Italy resembles Germany in its dependence on the chair structure, although its universities are nationally administered. Next is France, with a system as nationalized as Italy's, but with more commitment to central planning and control. Top rank in national planning effort goes to Sweden, with centralized but pragmatic consultative procedures. A pragmatic political style also characterizes England, which has a traditionally autonomous university sector, now much strained by central policies aimed at a more thoroughly articulated system than before. The United States, as the second Anglo-Saxon nation, possesses a largely market system, partly under loose government control at the state level and partly in private hands. The only non-Western nation is Japan, featuring a steep national pyramid of institutions which shades from state-sponsored autonomy at the peak to a state-subsidized private sector at the base. This sequence permits an evolving treatment of our main themes: state versus market system, hierarchy versus collegiality in structure, cohesion versus social choice in decision making, and autonomy versus public accountability.

NOTES

1. Bibliographical references have been provided for the different countries in the various chapters. However, no systematic attempt has been made to provide references for the more general sections of the study, because the literature on higher education tends to deal peripherally with questions of organization and power. For studies that do treat the topic bibliographically, see Burton R. Clark and Ted I. K. Youn, *Academic Power in the United States: Comparative, Historical and Structural Perspectives*, ERIC/Higher Education Research Report No. 3, (Washington, D.C.: American Association of Higher Education, 1976); and Jacques Fomerand, John H. Van de Graaff, and Henry Wasser, *Higher Education in Non-Communist Industrial Societies: An Annotated Bibliography* (forthcoming).

2. The approach here is convergent with the broad appeal for a more "scientific" approach to the comparative study of education in Harold J. Noah and Max A. Eckstein, *Toward a Science of Comparative Education* (New York: Macmillan, 1969). The use of the social sciences in such comparisons is a major theme of Reginald Edwards, Brian Holmes, and John Van de Graaff, eds., *Relevant Methods in Comparative Education* (Hamburg: Unesco Institute for Education, 1973).

3. Gerald M. Platt and Talcott Parsons, "Decision-Making in the Academic System: Influence and Power Exchange," in *The State of the University: Authority and Change*, ed. Carlos E. Kruytbosch and Sheldon L. Messinger (Beverly Hills, Calif.: Sage Publications, 1970) p. 137.

4. Roland T. Warren, "The Interorganizational Field as a Focus for Investigation," *Administrative Science Quarterly* 12 (December 1967):396–419.

5. Clark Kerr, *The Uses of the University* (New York: Harper Torchbooks, 1966); Abraham Flexner, *Universities: American, English, German* (New York: Oxford University Press, 1930).

6. For a discussion of the various types of statewide coordinating agencies in the United States and their historical evolution, see Robert O. Berdahl, *Statewide Coordination of Higher Education* (Washington, D.C.: American Council on Education, 1971).

7. Since these words were written, the slowdown in enrollment growth has become more pronounced, with consequences that have been barely touched upon here.

8. *Short-Cycle Higher Education: A Search for Identity* (Paris: Organisation for Economic Co-operation and Development, 1973).

9. For an extended comparative analysis of this phenomenon, see Raymond Boudon, *Education, Opportunity, and Social Inequality: Changing Prospects in Western Society* (New York: Wiley, 1974).

10. Burton R. Clark, "The 'Cooling-Out' Function in Higher Education," *American Journal of Sociology* 65 (May 1960):569–76.

PART I
SEVEN COUNTRIES

2
FEDERAL REPUBLIC OF GERMANY
John Van de Graaff

INTRODUCTION

The reputation of the German universities reached its height around 1900; they were widely regarded as the best in the world. Lord Ashby, like most contemporary observers, considers the German model as "*the* nineteenth century idea of a university."[1] This ideal inspired admiration and emulation from Sweden to the distant United States and Japan. In many scientific disciplines, a period of study in Germany was an essential prerequisite to a successful career. The traditional German university organization is a classic case of the research institute built around the professorial chair with the professor as scholar. This structure effectively promoted the development of scientific research in the latter part of the nineteenth century, although it would later prove too inflexible for an ever more massive and complex scientific enterprise.[2]

The first universities established in the German-speaking world were Prague (1348), Vienna (1384), and Heidelberg (1385). Unlike the earlier Italian, French, and English universities, which evolved gradually from loose associations of students or masters, the German universities were planned and founded by territorial governments. As state institutions serving the needs of their government sponsors, they were less international in outlook than universities elsewhere. Later universities were founded in waves[3] and, in fact, every major period of German history has produced new institutions of higher education.

Often the foundation of new universities provided significant innovations and adaptations. A dramatic example of this evolutionary process occurred at the beginning of the nineteenth century, when the quality of German higher education was at a low ebb: an increasingly outmoded, virtually medieval scholasticism persisted in teaching and learning, and the

15

instability of the French Revolution and Napoleonic Wars forced half of the 42 German universities that existed in 1792 to shut down by 1818. Prussia's foundation of Berlin in 1809, as an effort to regain in intellectual strength what it had lost in material resources through military defeat by Napoleon in 1806, exercised a symbolic spell far beyond Berlin's considerable scholarly achievements. Although Berlin inherited much of its structure from the medieval past, it engendered a novel dedication to research as the preeminent mission of the university. During the first half of the nineteenth century, the ideal of the unity of research and teaching, as propounded by Wilhelm von Humboldt and others,[4] was newly combined with an increasing reliance on specialization and empirical research methods. This "research imperative"[5] fostered the dramatic scientific progress that the German universities had achieved by the end of the nineteenth century. It integrated research and teaching in the full professor, reinforcing his dominance as director of his research institute and as part-time policy maker at other levels of university administration.

Even after the unification of Germany under Bismarck in 1870, the separate German states retained responsibility for higher education, although Prussia continued to exert a certain centralizing influence. Depending on the ability and influences of the responsible state officials, government control could be quite direct.[6] The universities were state institutions in other ways as well. Professors and other salaried staff were civil servants, and the four classical faculties of theology, law, medicine, and philosophy trained their students largely for state examinations. The majority of graduates entered government employment.

Upon taking power in 1933, the Nazi regime attempted to centralize university control for the first time. They appointed rectors and deans and stripped academic bodies of all decision-making authority. Although the Nazis drove large numbers of Jewish and politically dissident professors into exile, with devastating consequences for the scientific productivity of the universities, they ultimately had only partial success in indoctrinating students and subjugating research to political goals.[7]

After 1945, the occupation powers in the three Western zones permitted the restoration of traditional academic structures to their pre-1933 state. The state governments, however, were distinctly weaker than they had been before the Nazi regime. State boundaries were redrawn, leaving most of the 11 constituent states with no cohesive political or administrative tradition. Officials in the new state ministries of education were largely inexperienced and inferior in status to the senior professors who spoke for the universities. Moreover, state control had been discredited by the political extremes to which it had been carried under the Nazi regime. Therefore, although in theory many of the states' powers persisted, in practice the universities easily asserted their independence. They also easily resisted proposals to establish organs representing outside groups or individuals, aimed at rendering them more formally responsible to the economic and social expectations of a newly democratized society. Together, these developments left the German universities more autonomous than ever before.[8]

The sectors of German higher education have shifted with time, as nonuniversity institutions have gained university status or were absorbed into them. During the nineteenth century, polytechnical schools for technological training, modeled on the Ecole Polytechnique in Paris, evolved into full-fledged technical institutes (*Technische Hochschulen*), which by 1899 had been formally recognized as of university quality. By the early 1960s, there were nineteen universities and seven Technische Hochschulen. A typical university comprised four to six faculties: theology (Catholic or Protestant, and occasionally both), law, medicine, philosophy, natural science, and social sciences, including economics. There were also a few other specialized colleges for mining, forestry, agriculture, and the like, which could confer doctorates and were therefore considered as *wissenschaftliche* Hochschulen, belonging to higher education, as well as a large number of teacher-training colleges without such degree-granting status. Of still lower rank were *Ingenieurschulen* and other technical schools (enrolling 48,000 students in 1960, as compared with 203,000 in the universities, Technische Hochschulen, and specialized colleges, and 33,000 in the teacher-training colleges).[9] Apart from a few small divinity schools (enrolling less than 3,000 students), private institutions played no role whatever in higher education.

During the 1960s, the higher education system underwent other substantial changes. Student enrollment accelerated after a brief slowdown around 1965, and between 1960 and 1974, 18 new universities were established. Some of these were upgraded specialized institutions. In 1969, the technical schools gained technical college status (as *Fachhochschulen*). During this period, the teacher-training colleges were receiving the right to grant academic degrees or, in a few cases, were being fully integrated into the universities. A few states established comprehensive universities (*Gesamthochschulen*), which integrated Fachhochschulen, teacher-training colleges, and university-level courses. By the fall of 1974 there were 533,000 students in universities (including Technische Hochschulen), 160,000 in technical colleges (including art colleges), and 93,000 in teachers colleges.[10]

Politicization

German society tends to be strikingly politicized, and its institutions are governed in highly legalistic fashion. The politicization of the German universities stems from their very origins as institutions of the states. The university has provided trained personnel for the government bureaucracy and for state-sponsored occupations such as teaching and medicine; through the nineteenth century it also contributed to territorial self-sufficiency, however modestly, simply by providing higher education within the states' borders. Repeatedly, military and political crises have unleashed efforts toward university reform.[11] The relatively modest political crisis of the late 1960s is likely to have far-reaching consequences, for it galvanized both the federal and state governments to reassert their traditional role of oversight in higher education.

During the eighteenth and nineteenth centuries, the German states demanded increasing political allegiance from university staffs. This requirement remained largely implicit, although government authorities sporadically enforced conformity. With reference to political and religious restrictions on academic appointments, Max Weber argued in 1908 that it would be hypocritical "to act as if we [German academics] possess an 'academic freedom' which someone could infringe."[12] Nevertheless, open political conflict between governments and universities remained rare, at least until the Nazis actively enforced racial purity and political conformity. Indeed, the professors so directly and widely accepted state control and expectations that they considered themselves, very much in abstract Hegelian terms, as symbiotically linked with the state in a higher realm, transcending the primarily material interests of society.[13] Under Hitler, chauvinistic dedication to German education and scholarship—*Deutsche Bildung*—reached a new high.[14]

Throughout most of its history, the German university maintained a striking aloofness to nongovernmental social and economic pressures and demands.[15] Even today, most academics view the state as the only legitimate patron of scholarly enterprise and stoutly resist any effort to give private individuals or outside groups a voice in university affairs. This attitude coexists with the traditional assumption that the university's basic role is not vocational, that it is the pursuit of pure research and scholarship. Although most students do prepare for later employment, professional preparation traditionally has been considered a secondary concern of the university. Lectures and seminars have usually reflected professors' research interests rather than students' vocational requirements. Ultimately, research has been considered the best way to prepare for practical life.

Legalism

German political life traditionally has heavily stressed laws and rules, from the constitution at the most fundamental level to more detailed laws, government decrees, and bureaucratic regulations at the "circumstantial" level.[16] Individuals and institutions commonly go to court to gain status or treatment that they feel the law guarantees them. In this process, the constitution is repeatedly invoked and its principles elaborated and interpreted in exhaustive detail. Such legalism channels the recurrent conflicts among political or ideological factions in many institutions.

This legalism historically extended to the administration and organization of universities, which were decreed by government statute. Statutes were drawn up by ministerial officials, who sometimes consulted with the universities or even proceeded on the basis of university proposals. In the post-1945 democracy, with the state governments weakened, primary responsibility for the drafting of statutes shifted to the universities, although the Land ministries retained the final say. Nevertheless, except for the mostly temporary measures of the Nazi regime, the statutes changed relatively little between the 1800s and the early 1960s and tended to lag decades behind actual administrative practice. Moreover, the statutes left many gaps, and thus while the body of university law grew steadily, it relied increasingly on unwritten conventions and mutually accepted procedures.[17]

Such an unsystematic approach is unusual in German administrative law, and its persistence into the mid-1960s can best be explained by continuing acceptance of the traditional, Humboldtian idea of the university and its associated administrative structure. The university as both state institution (*Staatsanstalt*) and an autonomous corporation of scholars, dominated by the full professors, had functioned well, at least up to the early decades of the twentieth century, and the dominant aim after 1945 was to restore and refine it. Shared by professors and civil servants alike, this powerful consensus regarding the validity of the traditional concept of the university preempted reform initiatives. Only after 1967, as new and conflicting concepts of the university gained wide acceptance in the wake of student protest, did the political authorities assert their long-dormant prerogatives by drafting extensive university reform legislation.

TRADITIONAL STRUCTURES

Until the late 1960s German university organization remained much as it had been in the nineteenth century.[18] The full professor, or *Ordinarius*, at level 1 in the system, was the building block of the university.[19] Traditionally the only chair holder in his field at a university, and normally the sole head of an institute, the Ordinarius was in charge of research and teaching in that field.[20] The functional equivalent in the United States would be the department. However, the German institute was usually smaller in scope, often representing what Americans would call a subfield, such as ancient history or theoretical physics, and was a self-contained teaching and research unit, containing all necessary personnel and facilities, such as laboratories, a library, and lecture and seminar rooms. The term 'institute' was most commonly used for such units in the natural sciences; in the humanities and social sciences they were traditionally called seminars; in the medical faculty they were termed clinics and included hospital facilities. As student numbers grew, two or more professors sometimes shared the directorship of an institute, each heading a division within it. Often, however, when a second professor was appointed in a field, a separate institute was established for him.[21]

The institutes were the main source of professorial power. They were hierarchical, with intricate, formal gradations of status and function. Below the Ordinarius were two groups of teachers and researchers. Entry into the higher-status group of those not holding chairs, or *Nichtordinarien*, usually required a postdoctoral qualification called the *Habilitation*, which gave this group the right to lecture independently within the university as *Privatdozenten*. However, they were seldom tenured and often unsalaried; they depended on the professor for access to research facilities in his institute.[22] The second main category of staff was the assistants, who lacked the Habilitation and sometimes even the doctorate. Untenured, they were appointed to short-term contracts by the minister on the recommendation of the individual professor and were entirely subject to his authority. They were not considered as formal members either of the faculty or of the university. The formal complexity of this steep personnel hierarchy is unparalleled in any of the other countries in this study.[23]

The next level of academic organization, the faculty, was equivalent to a school or college within an American university; the typical postwar German university had four to six. The faculty as a whole (*weitere Fakultät*) included all full professors and Nichtordinarien. It rarely assembled, however, and its powers were advisory. The only real decision-making organ was the inner faculty (*engere* Fakultät), which had between 15 and 40 members. It included all full professors, a few of those not holding chairs, and, occasionally, students or assistants. The inner faculty was responsible for general curricular matters, academic examinations and degrees, and, most significantly, recommendations to the minister of candidates for vacant chairs and Nichtordinarien appointments. Structurally, the inner faculty was "both a parliament and a club" for the professors,[24] a loose collegial gathering of high-status equals. The position of the nominal executive of the faculty, the dean, fitted this pattern. In contrast to a U.S. deanship, it involved only routine administrative duties and little power, rotating each year to a new professor chosen by his peers in the inner faculty.

The inner faculty generally gave professors freedom to manage their institutes, their course offerings, examinations (at least through the doctorate), and research in their own fields. In granting the Habilitation, however, the faculty was more active; candidates therefore did not depend solely on the support of the responsible professor. Similarly, the inner faculty usually kept a tight rein on proposals to fill vacant chairs, seldom permitting a departing professor much influence in naming his successor. These practices served somewhat to mitigate particularistic domination by professors of their academic realms. Otherwise, the faculty rarely infringed on the domain of its professorial members. Its nonhierarchical, collegial structure predisposed it to conservatism, and it often responded negatively to active policy initiatives. The faculties resisted the establishment of chairs in new fields, especially those of an interdisciplinary nature, and discouraged cooperation across faculty lines. Borders between faculties were sharp and arbitrary, so that many overlapping fields were neglected while some were represented by chairs in more than one faculty.[25]

At the university level (Level 3), the academic senate was ordinarily the chief policy-making organ. Just as each faculty was a club of professors, so the senate was a club of the faculty deans and one other full professor elected from each faculty by his peers for a limited term. There were also two or three represenatives of the Nichtordinarien and sometimes, more frequently than in the faculties, a like number of assistants and students.[26] The jurisdiction of the senate was normally limited to academic matters, such as guidelines for curricula and examinations, although it was less powerful than the faculties. For example, in most universities proposals for professorial appointments were communicated by the faculties directly to the ministry and were not handled by the senate at all.

Most universities also possessed a large professorial assembly, called the council or large senate (*Grosser Senat*), whose only significant function was the election of the rector. In certain South German universities, however, its power was superior to that of the academic senate, which remained responsible for day-to-day affairs.

The rector, who was a professor, served as chairman of the senate and academic head of the university. An assembly of all professors and representatives of Nichtordinarien elected him for a one-year term; reelection for a second term was fairly common. Traditionally, the rector was a respected senior scholar, chosen less for his administrative competence than to symbolize the dignity and academic eminence of the university. This executive structure, the so-called rectoral constitution, was a formal characteristic of the full-fledged institution of higher education (wissenschaftliche Hochschule).

In assessing the relative distribution of power among the three intra-university levels of organization, one sees that the great power of professors at Level 1 was directly related to the powerlessness of faculty- and university-level organs. The hierarchical, unitary institutes at the lowest level coexisted with loose, federal organizations at the next two levels. Of these, the faculty was more powerful than the senate because of the faculty's direct responsibility for the curriculum as a whole, the Habilitation, and proposals for appointments. The collegial bodies (inner faculty and academic senate) closely controlled the nominal executives (dean and rector) who handled routine administrative matters and carried out their colleagues' decisions.

The administrative and bureaucratic apparatus at faculty and university levels was not extensive. A division between academic matters and other affairs was traditional in German universities. Academic affairs were largely the responsibility of the university and its academic organs; in contrast, "general" affairs—especially fiscal affairs, including budget, physical plant, personnel—were the responsibility of the state governments, which administered them partly through separate organs and partly by delegation to the academic authorities.

This formal division was particularly significant at the institute and university levels. The professor was subject to the authority of faculty and senate only in academic matters, as a chair holder, and then only to a limited extent. The institute, however, was treated as a state institution, within the realm of general administration. The professor as institute director had full charge of budget, facilities, and personnel, subject only to the authority of the ministry. Such nonacademic matters were usually not discussed in the faculty or senate but were handled at university level by a civil servant (curator or chancellor). Although this official was sometimes supervised by a small administrative committee of professors (separate from the senate), he was directly responsible to the ministry and not under the authority of the rector.[27]

Thus, what little bureaucracy existed within the university was partly under government authority and administered by civil servants. Having normally received only standard training in German administrative law, these officials tended to handle university affairs in the same routine, legalistic style prevalent in the rest of the civil service.[28] Such legalism was frequently reinforced by a university counsel (*Universitätsrat*), usually a judge or a professor of law serving full time, who provided the academic authorities with legal advice.[29] Similarly, the most important subcommittee of the academic senate was usually that responsible for legal matters and in particular for drafting and amending the university statutes and other regulations. As a result, professorial experts on university law consistently exerted a conservative influence on the development of higher education.[30] More effective modern administrative techniques had no chance to develop.

A multicampus level of organization did not exist in the traditional system, and so the role of state government, at Level 5, is considered next. Because the universities and institutes were considered state institutions, governmental authority extended downward through the official in charge of general administration at university level to the professors as civil servants and institute directors. In this way government ministries in each state supervised the administration of nonacademic matters in the universities, including the capital and operating budget, personnel, and general services.[31]

The process by which professors were appointed illuminates these relationships. The inner faculty commenced by sending its list of proposed candidates, containing three names, directly to the ministry. The ministry then took over, negotiating with the prospective chair holder not only his salary but also the research funds, facilities, and personnel with which it would equip his institute. An incumbent professor negotiated both with his home ministry and with the ministry that sought to recruit him. Historically, as Helmut Schelsky has observed, this system of face-to-face bargaining was "the sole driving motor for the expansion of the universities," but the responsible ministers seldom used their leeway to plan systematically, especially after 1945.[32] The system reinforced the power of individual professors, and the ministries reacted in piecemeal, incremental fashion to their salary, budgetary, and personnel demands.

At the national level, the Constitution of 1949 assigned the federal government no responsibility for education except the power to legislate support for scientific research.[33] Although federal authorities have gradually increased their role, higher education remains predominantly the domain of the states. Even so, the educational system is substantially uniform—more so, for example, than in the United States. Legalism reinforces this trend, for not only do Germans accept extensive government regulation of social institutions as a matter of course, but they expect a certain uniformity and equity of treatment from state to state.[34] Most of the teaching staff are civil servants, and although their situation varies somewhat from state to state, their salaries are linked to those negotiated nationally for higher civil servants, and the basic conditions of service are quite uniform, under federal legislation. Similarly, standards and conditions of study are quite comparable among universities in different states.

In 1948, the states established the Standing Conference of State Ministers of Education (*Kultusministerkonferenz* or KMK). In the early postwar period, the KMK was the only structural instrument for the coordination of higher education policy among the states. The KMK has no formal constitutional authority and considers itself a voluntary group that helps the states "coordinate themselves."[35] The KMK is a collegial body of 11 equals whose decisions do not have the power of law. To have effect, its recommendations to the state governments must be enacted by law or ministerial decree. From the outset, the matters on which the ministers have reached agreement have been largely administrative and procedural. Although the KMK thereby has contributed to the formal uniformity of the higher education system, it has neither stimulated structural change nor made any effort at systematic planning.

Because of these inadequacies, the state and federal governments established the Science Council (*Wissenschaftsrat*) in 1957, after prolonged negotiations. The council is made up of two commissions of equal status. One consists of 16 academics and 6 other persons (mainly industrialists), and prepares the recommendations. The other commission includes 11 state representatives and 6 from the federal government (with 11 votes). The two commissions, separately and together, must approve the council's proposals. Unlike the KMK, which requires a unanimous vote, the Science Council can act by a two-thirds majority and this may have contributed to the greater influence which its recommendations have generally had. Even so, the proposals must be enacted by the responsible state or university authorities in order to take effect.

Although the Science Council's mandate includes both science and higher education, it has dealt mainly with the latter. Its first bulky set of recommenations, issued in 1960, entailed hardly more than a sharp increase in the teaching staff at most levels.[36] All sides conceded the need for such quantitative expansion to handle the rising number of students, and the targets were quickly reached in most of the states. Only later did the Science Council confront issues of qualitative reform and engage in comprehensive planning.

Until the late 1960s, the role of the federal government itself was limited. It enacted legislation in such limited areas as the civil service, participated with the states on the Science Council in matters such as student grants, and shared in funding these and other areas, notably research. It directly administered a number of its own research institutes. Constitutional amendments in 1969 vested authority in the federal government for general educational planning and for the overall development and structure of higher education, and a full-fledged Ministry for Education and Science was established for the first time.[37] Thus the federal government now assumes an active role in higher education. However, the states remain dominant and jealous of their prerogatives.

Many interest groups, often with divisions at the state level which mirror the federal structure, have traditionally been concerned with higher education. Most notable is the West German Rectors Conference (WRK), in which the universities are represented by their chief executives. Because the rectors were bound to their professorial senates, which were reluctant to entrust authority to a national organization, the WRK found it difficult to take firm stands on policy issues. When it spoke at all, the WRK spoke first for the professors and only after that for the universities as institutions. Similarly, the University Association (*Hochschulverband*), the main organization of university staff, was restricted to senior faculty (professors and Nichtordinarien), and tended to represent chiefly the professors.[38] The conservatism of both the WRK and the University Association lent legitimacy to student reform efforts. The official Association of German Students (VDS) and the Socialist German Students League (SDS) wanted primarily to reorganize research and teaching and to democratize decision-making structures.[39]

Two national institutions, each overseen by federal and state officials and represenatives of the universities, industry, and other sectors of society, deal exclusively with research. The Max Planck Association administers about fifty research institutes in all areas of scholarship, although it concentrates on the natural sciences. The institutes are outside the universities, yet many of their researchers hold part-time academic appointments. In contrast, the German Research Association (DFG) supports university research through project grants and subsidies for long-term programs. The DFG works primarily through committees in the various disciplines, each consisting of academics elected by their peers. These committees are the

378.101 Ac12v

closest German equivalent to the national committees of professors which are so powerful in French, and especially Italian, higher education. However, the DFG committees have authority only over research funds, which merely supplement the resources allocated by the states to the professors' institutes. The DFG system of peer review, therefore, did not weaken the institutes as the main source of professorial power in the traditional German system.

LEGISLATIVE REFORM OF UNIVERSITY STRUCTURE

By the early 1960s, several state governments had begun to draft limited university-reform legislation. Ministerial officials recognized that the ad hoc, piecemeal process by which individual universities had amended their statutes since the war had left gaps and inconsistencies in their legal foundations, and they at first tended to be more concerned with closing these gaps than with substantive reform.[40] At the time a short-term drop in enrollments seemed possible,[41] while rapid implementation of the Science Council's 1960 recommendations for increased teaching staff had reduced pressures from previous growth.

Aside from proposals from student groups such as VDS and SDS, substantial organizational changes were not widely propounded or seriously discussed until 1967. A visit from the Shah of Iran provoked student demonstrations in Berlin, where the Free University had experienced recurrent unrest for more than two years, and when a student was shot and killed by a plainclothes policeman on June 2, 1967, protests spread to the universities in the Federal Republic proper.[42] The reform debate intensified overnight, questioning the very foundations of the traditional university and putting its advocates on the defensive for the first time. Groups and policy makers at all levels, including state and national political parties, set to work drafting comprehensive measures for structural change.

Student groups and their allies pressed the university to take up societal issues and problems; they now also sought greater participation in its decision making. By the end of 1967, most student groups were demanding one-third parity (*Drittelparität*), or one-third of the seats in all decision-making organs for students, a third for assistants, and a third for senior staff (professors and Nichtordinarien).[43] In contrast, other reformers, including many professors, wanted the higher education system to meet more effectively the manpower and research needs of Germany's highly technological economy. They argued for strengthening university administration with full-time, long-term president-managers and close state supervision to ensure that the university fulfilled its economic mission. These technocrats, as the students called them, could not oppose expanded participation, so sharply had the climate shifted in its favor, but insisted that the degree of participation should vary according to the function and expertise of the various groups and the task of the particular organ. Under such plans senior faculty would maintain control in most cases.[44] A distinct polarization between the major political parties accentuated the political overtones of the controversy. The Social Democrats (SPD) and Free Democrats (FDP), who won the national election in 1969 and also formed coalition governments in a number of states, sympathized with the students and junior faculty, to the point of advocating one-third parity in a number of cases. In contrast, the Christian Democrats (CDU/CSU) favored the technocrats' proposals.

From 1968 on, legislation has been generally far more extensive and represented a turning away from the traditional concept of the university to new ideas about the university's mission and structure. This legislative activity in the states went through two phases. The first phase extended through 1971. Nine states enacted laws emphasizing greater autonomy for the university and broader participation for students and junior staff. By 1972, the climate of reformist optimism had turned more cautious, and the second group of measures, enacted in 1973–74, reduced the degree of student and junior staff participation and reasserted state authority over the university.[45]

A constitutional amendment adopted in 1969 had empowered the federal government to enact legislation determining "the general principles of higher education." Under the SPD-FDP coalition government, the federal Ministry of Education and Science set about drafting a Framework Law (*Rahmengesetz*) in 1970 and, although its actual enactment took nearly six years, the successive drafts substantially influenced the legislative efforts of the states. This escalation of the higher education policy debate to the federal level accentuated not only tensions between the federal authorities and the states, but also the confrontation between political parties. The CDU and CSU states, aided by the more conservative political climate from 1972 on, used their majority in the *Bundesrat*, the second chamber of the federal parliament, to force the SPD to yield on important aspects of the bill. The eventual compromise, which became law in January 1976, struck a balance among the interests of federal and state authorities. Virtually all of the more progressive aspects of the bill had been dropped or diluted at earlier stages. Most university groups had sharply criticized the successive versions of the Framework Law. They were, and continue to be, particularly skeptical of the detailed regulation of the universities which the state laws have already brought and which the further state legislation needed to implement the Framework Law will reinforce. University structure has already been altered considerably and it will continue to change for some time. The following summary of the changes indicates certain important differences among the states and analyzes the probable impact of the Framework Law.

By 1973, all of the states had extended participation to all intra-university groups, including nonacademic staff, at all levels of the university. The SPD-governed states, which had led the way between 1969 and 1971, on the whole went further than the CDU states. This difference was most evident in the councils, which were conceived as universitywide parliaments, although their powers were quite limited. In SPD states, the councils were constructed on modified one-third-parity lines; senior staff (with Habilitation and tenure) held between 27 and 33 percent of the seats, with the rest shared among the other groups. The five CDU/CSU states gave senior staff a majority of 55 to 67 percent in every state except Rhineland-Palatinate, where they held 38 percent. The academic senates and the newly formed departments (Fachbereiche) at Level 2 were generally less democratized. In most states, senior staff held a majority of just over 50 percent to 62 percent. Three states, however, gave them a minority of 40 to 47 percent: Berlin and Lower Saxony, both Social Democratic, and Rhineland-Palatinate, again more liberal than its CDU brethren. Within most institutes, collegial government replaced professorial autarchy although there was a general proviso that senior staff hold a majority.[46]

Because by the late 1960s the full professors, or Ordinarien, were outnumbered within the senior staff as a whole, many of them perceived their loss of power as extreme. Hundreds of scholars joined in constitutional suits against several of the state laws, and in May 1973 the federal constitutional court, reflecting the more cautious political climate, rejected major aspects of Lower Saxony's provisions for participation and set guidelines for other states. In essence, the court ruled that senior staff (*Hochschullehrer*) must have half the seats in any organ dealing directly with matters of instruction, and a clear majority in matters of research and appointments.[47] The Framework Law of 1976 not only requires the senior group to hold over half the seats in all such organs, but also permits a majority of professors both to exercise a veto in appointments and research affairs on an initial ballot and to impose its own decision on the second ballot. However, the ranks of senior staff have been greatly expanded in recent years and internal differences of function and status reduced, which has entailed a substantial sharing of power.[48] The provisions of the Framework Law will reinforce this homogenization of the senior staff, all of whom will now carry the prestigious title of professor.

An important administrative reform has been the creation of departments (Fachbereiche) to replace the unwieldy faculties at Level 2. The usual five or six university faculties have been divided into 15 to 25 departments, with greater authority over the allocation of personnel, funds, and equipment. Therefore, although the institutes at Level 1 remain, they no longer receive resources independent of faculty or university authorities, and some have been consolidated. In a few states, the departments formally had the option of dissolving the institutes as distinct administrative units—an alternative that was exercised substantially only in Hesse but that has now been eliminated for most fields even there.[49] The Framework Law requires the formation of departments but leaves open the matter of institutes at the lowest level.

Measures have also been taken to strengthen administration at the university level. The Framework Law requires either a full-time executive elected for at least four years, or a small executive committee with a full-time chairman. Most states have already instituted a full-time president, elected by the council for a fixed term of from six to nine years.[50] The president directs both the academic and the general or financial administration of the university. He is not required to be a professor or to come from the university which he is to head. In fact, the first three presidents elected, at Hamburg and the two Berlin universities in 1969–70, were assistants; they garnered the great majority of students' and assistants' votes in councils in which senior staff were outnumbered. Since then, however, the great majority of elected presidents has come from the ranks of the professoriate. Nearly all are supported by liberal or even conservative coalitions led by senior staff rather than by leftist coalitions dominated by junior staff or students.

Under this system, there are one or two part-time vice-presidents, who ordinarily must be elected from the professoriate. The president heads an administrative staff that is small by U.S. standards but large compared to that of the rector; usually it includes mostly younger persons chosen more for their substantive skills rather than for a traditional background in administrative law. In addition to the council and senate, small standing committees often deal with particular policy areas, such as planning and budget, research, and curriculum. In some cases these committees have formal decision-making authority.[51] The president does not have much formal power to make decisions on his own, but his staff usually does the preparatory work for all of the central university bodies, and this is a major source of power. Moreover, the president is usually the central figure in a complex system of checks and balances; he (or a central decision-making body) usually has authority to review decisions made by organs at lower levels and if necessary to refer them to the minister for final decision. These changes strengthened the university's policy-making capacity, at both the department and university levels. A distinct class of academic administrators, the university presidents and their staff, is emerging.

At Level 4, a minority of the states has established comprehensive universities. The aim is to create a common administrative umbrella for professional or technical nonuniversity institutions (Fachhochschulen) and university programs. Such amalgamations are intended to broaden student options, to expand transfer possibilities at each curriculum level, and thus to reduce attrition and duplication of offerings. The Framework Law requires the formation of comprehensive institutions; it leaves the dual option of integrating the constituent units (favored by the SPD) or retaining their independence and linking them in 'cooperative' fashion (the preference of the CDU). Thus the diversity of linkages will doubtless continue, and even the SPD has become reluctant to establish further comprehensive institutions.[52]

When they began drafting reform legislation, government policy makers intended to give the university, with its stronger administrative structure, greater autonomy from state tutelage. To some extent they were successful. States such as Berlin and Hesse have granted the universities authority to allocate their funds internally as they see fit. The initiative in establishing new departments and institutes resides with the university. Indeed, the universities have been active at every stage in the intensive deliberations that the entire process of reform has required. Yet the state either has made most of the decisions or its blessing has been required. The laws themselves have been very much government products, with ministerial officials generally dominating the legislative process. Those same officials, at the state level, then oversee every step in the university's implementation of the laws, which are even more detailed than traditional university statutes. As each side has sought recognition for its interpretation of a law or governmental decree, court actions have been frequent. Yet another round is due as the states amend their laws to conform to the federal Framework Law and the universities in turn amend their statutes.[53]

Increased government influence is apparent in several policy areas. State ministries have been cautious in appointing leftist or Marxist scholars to academic posts and have rejected several such candidates, evidently hoping to keep the departments that proposed them from tipping further to the left. The exercise of this long-dormant state prerogative illustrates the continuing tension between the political and bureaucratic system, determined to defend its postwar stability, and left-wing academics, the source of a pervasive ideological critique of the very foundations of contemporary German society.[54]

Admission to the universities—traditionally automatic with an academic secondary-school-leaving certificate (*Abitur*)—has become a volatile political issue. After a 1972 decision by the federal constitutional court insisted on more systematic regulation of the admission process, and as more and more fields of study restricted admissions through a *numerus clausus*, the 11 states adopted a formal state covenant establishing a jointly administered central admissions agency. Admission was on the basis of the overall grade on the Abitur, with a state-by-state adjustment according to the average grade level in each state. In a complex decision, the Bavarian constitutional court ruled that the covenant was unfair to Bavarian students, whose marks received the largest downward adjustment, and was therefore contrary to the Bavarian constitution. A new interstate covenant was impossible; it would have required unanimous agreement among the 11 states. Federal authorities helped to insert a compromise in the Framework

Law, which set state-by-state admissions quotas for each field of study and permitted achievement tests in the most crowded fields.[55]

The Framework Law provides for the states and universities to cooperate in establishing curriculum reform commissions at both state and national levels; government representatives will form the majority on most commissions, and the state ministries will be able to make the universities' programs conform to the commissions' recommendations.

As noted earlier, federal authorities have been involved in planning higher education through the Science Council since the 1960s, and the 1969 constitutional amendments increased this involvement. Within a year the amendments led to the establishment of a joint federal-state planning committee for construction and of the federal-state Commission for Educational Planning (BLK).[56] The planning committee is charged with producing a general plan (*Rahmenplan*) for all construction projects in higher education; the plan covers four years and is revised and extended annually. In contrast, the BLK has the global mandate of preparing a general plan for the development of the education system, which it did first in 1973. In each body the federal government has as many votes as the Länder; all proposals require three-quarters of the votes for adoption. Even then, however, the BLK's recommendations bind only those states that vote for them. The planning committee is more powerful because the federal and state governments must include the necessary funds in the budgets they submit to the *Bundestag* and the state legislatures. The Science Council advises both bodies. A major part of its work each year is devoted to preparing recommendations for the general construction plan to be adopted by the planning committee. Every spring the states submit requests to the council, whose subcommittees cooperate closely with ministry officials in developing recommendations.[57] The committee usually accepts the council's recommendations with few changes. Under the federal Framework Law, both the universities and the states must draw up extended plans; thus the annual reviews at the university, state, and national levels will be an important part of the planning process.

A striking increase in the activities of groups concerned with higher education accompanied the beginnings of legislation in 1967. Students led the way; other groups changed their stands and their tactics as the reform climate evolved. New organizations coalesced; others faded from view or even disbanded. As the progressive student groups, particularly the SDS and the national VDS, rapidly became more radical after 1967, their leadership of the reform movement was assumed by the Federal Assistants Conference (BAK), founded in 1968 as the first national organization of junior staff. As part of a comprehensive reform of staff structure, the BAK urged creating a category of untenured but independent assistant professors, somewhat on U.S. lines. But as this reform proved unattainable, the political climate for change became increasingly inhospitable, and BAK dissolved itself at the end of 1974, recommending that its members join the Education and Science Union (GEW)—the largest national teachers' union and a member of the German Union Federation (DGB). Another DGB member, the public worker's union (ÖTV), enjoys some support among the nonacademic staff. The still-conservative University Association, which has recently become more unionist in orientation, remains the official organization for professors. The Federation for the Freedom of Science has militantly opposed the students' and assistants' agitation. It was formed in 1970 by professors, conservative politicians (mainly from the CDU), and industrialists, for all of whom the reforms had gone too far. Its counterpart on the Left is the Federation of Democratic Scholars. After a period of oscillation, the WRK has taken a moderately reformist course under the direction of a large bloc of liberal university presidents and longer-term rectors who themselves owe their positions to reformed structures.

Intense as the activity of interest groups has been over the past decade, their ability to influence legislation has been modest compared to that of the politicians and especially the ministerial officials. The traditional direct dependence of the universities on the state largely excludes nonuniversity groups from regular involvement in university policy making. The Framework Law provides an exception to its inclusion of professional representatives on the curriculum-reform commissions. But they will form an uneasy minority between the majority of state spokesman and the academic representatives.

In conclusion, the state's extension of its grip over the universities, against broad academic opposition, is the most prominent trend of the past decade. Legislative fiat has fundamentally altered traditional structures, replacing the hallowed rectoral constitution dominated by the Ordinarius with the group university dominated by the state bureaucracies. The university's strengthened administrative and decision-making capacities serve at most to make it a more efficient policy-making partner of the state rather than to increase academic autonomy. The sequential process of level-by-level planning certainly allows more effective allocation of resources than the former system of piecemeal negotiations between professors and ministerial officials. But it also tends to defeat the main purpose of expanding participation; the new decision-making organs do not have the authority that reformers of the late 1960s had hoped for. However, the fears of such conservative groups as the Federation for Freedom of Science about the disruption and politicization of the universities have not materialized either. In a 1974 survey of academic staff, most respondents assessed student-staff relations in their departments as generally good, and only 4 percent claimed that teaching suffered substantially from political disruptions.[58] This 4 percent figure may seem high compared to what it would be in other countries, but is probably reflects accurately the extent of politicization. Predictions of the ruin of the German universities in a wave of Marxism seem premature. In the long term it is the ubiquitous legalism of the state, applied in ever more exhaustive rounds of legislation and ministerial regulation, that presents the most serious threat to German scholarship.

NOTES

1. Eric Ashby, "The Future of the Nineteenth Century Idea of a University," *Minerva* 6 (Autumn 1967):3–17. The most comprehensive contemporary German study in this vein is Helmut Schelsky, *Einsamkeit und Freiheit: Idee und Gestalt der deutschen Universität und ihrer Reformen* (Reinbek: Rowohlt, 1963).

2. Joseph Ben-David, *The Scientist's Role in Society: A Comparative Study* (Englewood Cliffs, N.J.: Prentice-Hall, 1971), pp. 108–38; Wolfgang Nitsch et al., *Hochschule in der Demokratie: Kritische Beiträge zur Erbschaft und Reform der deutschen Universität* (Berlin: Luchterhand, 1965).

3. Schelsky, *Einsamkeit*, pp. 17–18, distinguishes foundings under humanistic influence (1450 to 1510) from foundings during the religious conflicts of the Reformation (1520–1670) and Enlightenment impulses (1690–1740).

4. Wilhelm von Humboldt's classic memorandum on the outlines of the university to be founded in Berlin is translated as "On the Spirit and the Organizational Framework of Intellectual Institutions in Berlin," *Minerva* 8 (April 1970):242–50. Along with certain seminal writings by Fichte, Schleiermacher, and others, it is reprinted in Ernst Anrich, ed., *Die Idee der deutschen Universität* (Bad Homburg: Gentner, 1959).

5. R. Steven Turner, "The Growth of Professorial Research in Prussia, 1818 to 1848—Causes and Context," *Historical Studies in the Physical Sciences* 3 (1971):137–82.

6. The classic example is Friedrich Althoff, who administered university affairs in the Prussian Ministry of Education from 1881 to 1907. See Max Weber, in "The Power of the State and the Dignity of the Academic Calling in Imperial Germany: The Writings of Max Weber on University Problems," *Minerva* 11 (October 1973):571–632.

7. Helmut Seier, in "Der Rektor als Führer," *Vierteljahreshefte für Zeitgeschichte* 12 (April 1964):105–46, provides an overview of the Nazis' administrative measures. Recent studies of the situation of students and scholarly research in the Third Reich are provided by (respectively) Geoffrey Giles, "The National Socialist Students' Association in Hamburg 1926–1945" (Ph.D. diss., University of Cambridge, 1975); and Reece Conn Kelly, *National Socialism and German University Teachers: The NASDAP's Efforts to Create a National Socialist Professoriate and Scholarship* (Ph.D. diss., University of Washington, 1973, Xerox University Microfilms).

8. Dietrich Goldschmidt, "Autonomy and Accountability of Higher Education in the Federal Republic of Germany," in Philip G. Altbach, ed., *The University's Response to Societal Demands* (New York: International Council for Educational Development, 1975), pp. 153–56.

9. Dietrich Goldschmidt et al., *Gutachten und Materialien zur Fachhochschule.* Deutscher Bildungsrat. Gutachten und Studien der Bildungskommission, 10 (Stuttgart: Klett, 1974), p. 147; *Empfehlungen des Wissenschaftsrates zum Ausbau der wissenschaftlichen Hochschulen bis 1970* (Tübingen: Mohr, 1967), p. 283. There were an additional 8,000 students in colleges of music and art.

10. Among the latter two categories were some 40,000 students in institutions that had been established or amalgamated as comprehensive universities. *Informationen Bildung Wissenschaft* (Bundesminister für Bildung und Wissenschaft), 9/75, September 27, 1975, p. 131.

11. Besides the founding of Berlin in 1809, notable reform attempts began in 1848 and 1945, in each case without lasting consequences. See Karl Griewank, *Deutsche Studenten und Universitäten in der Revolution von 1848* (Weimar: Böhlaus Nachfolger, 1949), and Rolf Neuhaus, ed., *Dokumente zur Hochschulreform 1945–1959* (Wiesbaden: Steiner, 1961). Analyses of efforts toward administrative reform in the two periods are provided in John H.

Van de Graaff, *The Politics of German University Reform, 1810–1970* (Ph.D. diss., Columbia University, 1973, University Microfilms 74-1521), pp. 85–107, 178–231.

12. Weber, "Writings of Max Weber," p. 587.

13. See especially Fritz K. Ringer, *The Decline of the German Mandarins: The German Academic Community, 1890–1933* (Cambridge, Mass.: Harvard University Press, 1969).

14. Dietrich Goldschmidt and Sibylle Hübner, "Changing Concepts of the University in Society: The West German Case," in *The World Year Book of Education 1971/72* (London: Evans Brothers, 1971), pp. 276–80.

15. This assertion should not be overstressed and may have to be substantially revised in the light of recent research by Bernard H. Gustin, "The Emergence of the German Chemical Profession, 1790–1867" (Ph.D. diss., University of Chicago, 1975), and others. However, it does seem clear that the penetration of the German universities by private industrial interests, as in the development of chemistry described by Gustin, took place initially with little state support and even against state policy insofar as it existed; similarly, such developments were probably opposed by a majority of professors.

16. This paragraph owes much to the discussion in Herbert J. Spiro, *Government by Constitution: The Political Systems of Democracy* (New York: Random House, 1959), pp. 211–36.

17. Alexander Kluge, *Die Universitäts-Selbstverwaltung: Ihre Geschichte und gegenwärtige Rechtsform* (Frankfurt/Main: Klostermann, 1958), pp. 101–102, 213, 216–27.

18. The standard overview of traditional university law was Werner Thieme, *Deutsches Hochschulrecht* (Berlin: Carl Heymanns, 1956); Kluge, *Universitäts-Selbstverwaltung*, provides a somewhat more liberal and developmental interpretation.

19. The classic study of the German professoriate is Helmuth Plessner, ed., *Untersuchungen zur Lage der deutschen Hochschullehrer*, 3 vols. (Göttingen: Vandenhoeck & Ruprecht, 1956). Some of the data are summarized in Dietrich Goldschmidt, "Teachers in Institutions of Higher Learning in Germany," in *Education, Economy and Society*, ed. A. H. Halsey et al. (Glencoe, Ill.: Free Press, 1963), pp. 577–88.

20. Ordinarien were typically appointed in their early or mid-forties, after earning the Habilitation in their thirties, as much as a decade after the doctorate.

·21. As late as 1960, the Science Council still recommended the establishment of parallel institutes for most fields with two or more chairs (*Empfehlungen des Wissenschaftsrates zum Ausbau der wissenschaftlichen Einrichtungen. Teil I: Wissenschaftliche Hochschulen* [Tübingen: Mohr, 1960], pp. 72–73). In 1969, 63 percent of the institutes at the still-unreformed University of Frankfurt had only one professor (Van de Graaff, "German University Reform," p. 135).

22. In a widely regarded analysis, Joseph Ben-David (*Scientist's Role*, pp. 132–33) cites the inflexibility of the institute system as a major cause of the gradual decline of German science in the early decades of this century. Initially, however, the institutes under the direction of professors, together with the mechanism of competition between the German state governments for leading young researchers in new subdisciplines, provided great stimulus for the development of university science, above all in the 1860s and 1870s. However, as the conduct of research increasingly required laboratory facilities, "the competitive mechanism . . . was impaired," for young scholars could not establish themselves without full access to the institute laboratories which their professors controlled, and the latter "had vested interests in keeping new specialties that arose in their fields as subspecialties within their own institutes rather than allowing them to become separate chairs with claims for new institutes." Thus the system became inflexible and hindered the spread of new experimental fields. The founding of the Kaiser Wilhelm Society (later the Max Planck Society) in 1911, to support research institutes outside the universities, may be seen as a response to this.

23. See Council of Europe, Council for Cultural Co-Operation, *Structure of University Staff: Schemes of Academic Hierarchy, Dictionary of Terms* (Strasbourg: The Council, 1966), pp. 78–87, in which the description of the German structure requires nearly half again as much space as for any other country.

24. Ralf Dahrendorf, "Starre und Offenheit der deutschen Universität: Die Chancen der Reform," *European Journal of Sociology* 3 (1962):263–93, at 283.

25. Ibid., pp. 284–85; Dahrendorf notes that "when political authorities . . . impose [new] chairs, faculties find numerous ways, if not of rejecting the unwelcome gift, then at least of neutralizing it."

26. Students and assistants usually were permitted to attend only sessions dealing with agenda points concerning their interests. On student participation, see Harm Rösemann *Die Beteiligung der Studenten an den Selbstverwaltungsaufgaben der Universität* (Essen-Bredeney: Stifterverband für die Deutsche Wissenschaft, 1961); on the assistants, Werner Müller, "Zur Stellung der Assistenten in der Korporation der Universität: Die Hochschulrechtliche Situation," *Deutsche Universitätszeitung* 21 (October/November 1966):10–13.

27. The organization of nonacademic administration varied greatly in the Federal Republic; other forms were supervision by a "curatorium" of government and university representatives (in the two Berlin universities and the Saar) and delegation of general affairs by the state to the academic organs (rector and senate, at certain South German universities).

28. Although the jurists' monopoly of the civil service is no longer as pronounced as in the past, the higher positions still are held predominantly by jurists; cf. Renate Mayntz and Fritz Scharpf, *Policy-Making in the German Federal Bureaucracy* (Amsterdam: Elsevier, 1975), p. 53.

29. Thieme, *Deutsches Hochschulrecht*, pp. 182–85.

30. Ludwig von Friedeburg et al., *Freie Universität und politisches Potential der Studenten: Über die Entwicklung des Berliner Modells und den Anfang der Studentenbewegung in Deutschland* (Neuwied: Luchterhand, 1968), documents the key role of the Constitutional and Legal Committee of the Free University's Academic Senate in neutralizing the reform efforts embodied in the founding of that university in Berlin in 1948; see especially p. 109 ff.

31. Government ministries were usually in charge of all education. Some states—including Berlin, Hamburg, Bremen, and North Rhine-Westphalia—separated the responsibility for higher education and research.

32. Helmut Schelsky, *Abschied von der Hochschulpolitik oder die Universität im Fadenkreuz des Versagens* (Bielefeld: Bertelsmann Universitätsverlag, 1969), p. 88.

33. Article 74 (13) of the Basic Law gave the federal government power to legislate concurrently to support scientific research; as specified in Article 72, such concurrent legislative power was to be exercised when legislation by single states would be ineffective or prejudicial to the interests of others, or in order to preserve "legal or economic unity" among the states. No such law in support of research has ever been enacted, although the provision did serve as the constitutional foundation for the federal support given research and the universities (through agreements with the states) prior to 1969.

34. As noted in the preceding footnote, "the preservation of legal or economic unity" was the main justification for concurrent legislation on the part of the states (Article 72 of the Basic Law), and this was the basis of the constitutional amendment of 1969 which authorized federal framework legislation for higher education.

35. Kurt Frey, "Über die Zusammenarbeit der Kultusministerien der Länder in der Bundesrepublik Deutschland," *Bildung und Erziehung* 20 (February 1967):6.

36. Wissenschaftsrat, *Empfehlungen zum Ausbau der wissenschaftlichen Einrichtungen. Teil I: Wissenschaftliche Hochschulen* (Tübingen: Mohr, 1960).

37. Until the 1960s the Federal Ministry of the Interior handled many of the national government's responsibilities in higher education. In 1955 a Ministry for Atomic Energy was established and then expanded somewhat into the Ministry for Scientific Research in 1962.

38. Relations between the WRK and the University Association have traditionally been close; indeed, the initiative for founding the latter came from the WRK in 1950, and the rectors continued to play a major formal part in the deliberations of the association. See Hans Gerber, "Entwicklungsgeschichte des Hochschulverbandes," *Mitteilungen des Hochschulverbandes* 11 (April 1963):52–54.

39. The most influential VDS proposal was *Studenten und die neue Universität*. Gut-

achten einer Kommission des Verbandes Deutscher Studentenschaften zur Neigründung von wissenschaftlichen Hochschulen (Bonn: VDS, 1962). Members of the SDS prepared a memorandum in 1961 which was later published in much-expanded form as Nitsch et al., *Hochschule in der Demokratie.*

40. For a case study of the most substantial state-level legislative effort prior to 1967, culminating in the enactment of a still very tradition-bound law, see John H. Van de Graaff, "Legislating German University Structure: The Politics of Tradition in Hesse, 1960–1966." Working Paper, January 1975, Higher Education Program, Yale University.

41. For the enrollment projections—soon outdated—see Wissenschaftsrat, *Abiturienten und Studenten. Entwicklung und Vorschätzung der Zahlen 1950 bis 1980* (Tübingen: Mohr, 1964). The first significant reforms proposed by the Science Council were contained in its 1966 recommendations on the reform of studies (*Empfehlungen zur Neuordnung des Studiums an den wissenschaftlichen Hochschulen*) and its 1968 proposals for the universities' structure and administrative organization (*Empfehlungen zur Struktur und Verwaltungsorganisation der Universitäten*).

42. For analyses of the Berlin situation, see Richard L. Merritt, "The Student Protest Movement in West Berlin," *Comparative Politics* 1 (July 1969):516–33, and Ludwig von Friedeburg et al., *Freie Universität.*

43. The initial proposal for one-third parity was drafted by student representatives in Hamburg, and after it ran through three printings locally, the national VDS published it in revised form as Detlev Albers, *Demokratisierung der Hochschule: Argumente zur Drittelparität* (Bonn/Beuel: Verlag Studentenschaft, 1968).

44. For more detailed discussion of the views of the two groups, see John H. Van de Graaff, *Democracy and Technocracy in German Higher Education* (forthcoming).

45. The two phases are elaborated by Peter Dallinger, "Ein guter Kompromiss: Zum Inkrafttreten des Hochschulrahmengesetzes," *Deutsche Universitätszeitung vereinigt mit Hochschuldienst*, 2nd January edition 1976, pp. 34–41. A broader study of the Federal Framework Law of 1976 and its political context is Guntram von Schenck, *Das Hochschulrahmengesetz: Hochschulreform in der Gesellschaftskrise* (Bonn-Bad Godesberg: Verlag Neue Gesellschaft, 1976). Hesse's first law of 1966 was too traditional in substance to be classified with later legislation. The state laws covered in the following analysis, with the main responsible party and date of parliamentary enactment, are: Baden-Württemberg, CDU, 1968 (amended 1973); Hamburg, SPD, 1969; Berlin, SPD, 1969 (amended 1974); North Rhine-Westphalia, SPD, 1970; Hesse, SPD, 1970 (amended 1974); Rhineland-Palatinate, CDU, 1970; Saar, CDU, 1971; Lower Saxony, SPD, 1971 (covering participation only); Schleswig-Holstein, CDU, 1973; Bavaria, CSU, 1973. (Bremen enacted only brief laws facilitating the founding of its new university, in 1967 and 1970.)

46. Hesse's law of 1970, prior to its amendment in 1974, was the only one permitting nonprofessorial majorities in some cases at the institute level. The new University of Bremen went furthest in expanding participation (without formal legislative authorization), by creating (in 1971) organs at both the university and department levels consisting of one-third academic staff (all levels), one-third students, and one-third nonacademic staff—a unique, extreme form of one-third parity which has made Bremen the object of conservative wrath ever since. For a sympathetic analysis of the functioning of the new structures, see Frederick F. Abrahams and Ingrid N. Sommerkorn, "The Planning Process for the University of Bremen," in OECD, *Participatory Planning in Education* (Paris: OECD, 1974), pp. 195–213; also Thomas von der Vring, *Hochschulreform in Bremen: Bericht des Rektors über Gründung und Aufbau der Universität Bremen während seiner Amtszeit von 1970 bis 1974* (Frankfurt/Main: Europäischer Verlagsanstalt, 1975). For reports and analysis of the implementation of participation, see Dietrich Goldschmidt, ed., *Demokratisierung und Mitwirkung in Schule and Hochschule: Kommissionsbereicht* (Braunschweig: Westermann, 1973), esp. pp. 72–73, 160–76 and A172–266.

47. In characteristically legalistic fashion, the court stipulated that in organs with a membership of exactly half senior staff, provisions had to be made for breaking any deadlock.

48. Compared to 4,800 chairholders in 1966 (with 2,800 other senior staff) the combined total of senior staff reached 13,400 in 1971 and 16,500 in 1972. See Wissenschaftsrat, *Empfehlungen zum Ausbau der wissenschaftlichen Hochschulen bis 1970* (Tübingen: Mohr, 1967), p. 323; *Empfehlungen zum dritten Rahmenplan nach dem Hochschulbauförderungsgesetz* (No imprint [Verabschiedet am 11. Mai 1973]), p. 20.

49. The Hessian provision (in the amendments of 1974) effectively requiring the maintenance (or formation) of institutes in most fields appears to have been influenced by a corresponding clause in the then-current draft of the federal Framework Law which was subsequently modified to leave the matter open. The annual reports submitted by the president of Frankfurt University to its council from 1972 on provide information on the vacillating policy of the Hessian Ministry of Education in the matter and on the university's responses.

50. By summer 1973, among the 43 full-fledged member institutions of the WRK, according to its tally (excluding Pädagogische Hochschulen and the new comprehensive universities in North Rhine-Westphalia), 13 had instituted a presidential administration, and at least two more had long-term rectors (Konstanz and Bremen). This proportion has been increasing since and will continue to do so under the Framework Law.

51. These small committees normally include members of all groups, and in some cases they have worked very well, as, for example, in Hesse.

52. For a critique of internal strains in North Rhine-Westphalia's new comprehensive universities (partly due to rigidities in certification for the labor market), see Gerhard Brinckmann, "Aufstieg zwischen Stufen: Erfahrungen mit der integrierten Gesamthochschule," *Die Zeit* (U.S. edition), No. 33, August 15, 1975. A recent review of the situation of the Fachhochschulen is provided by Goldschmidt, *Fachhochschule* (note 9). Attempts in certain states to establish "superboards" for coordinating purposes at state level (more accurately equivalent to level four in our scheme) do not appear to have met with much success as yet. For a critical analysis of this and other planning measures in the CDU-controlled state of Baden-Württemberg, see Kalus-Dieter Heymann, and Wolfgang Karcher, eds., *Das Scheitern der Hochschulreform: Fallstudie zur Gesamthochschulplanung in Baden-Württemberg 1968-1975* (Weinheim: Beltz, 1976).

53. However, not all state legislation thus far has succeeded in bringing about structural changes in the universities. In North Rhine-Westphalia, universities ignored the mandate of the 1970 law to enact new statutes within two years. Not one had done so as of 1976.

54. See, for example, Kenneth H. F. Dyson, "Anti-Communism in the Federal Republic of Germany: The Case of the 'Berufsverbot'," *Parliamentary Affairs* (Winter 1974–75):51–67.

55. For a detailed analysis of this compromise, see Dallinger, "Guter Kompromiss," pp. 38–39. The setting of enrollment limits in each field is to be closely tied to the time limits for the length of studies in each field to be set by the government, as part of curriculum reform. A further judgement by the Constitutional Court, in February 1977, has reaffirmed that access to higher education must be geared to individual demand as well as manpower needs.

56. See Ständige Konferenz der Kultusminister, *Handbuch für die Kultusministerkonferenz 1974* (Bonn: KMK, 1974), for the law establishing the planning committee and the agreement setting up the BLK, as well as other documents and constitutional provisions.

57. For assessments of the work of the Science Council by two of its chairmen, see "Bericht über die Arbeit des Wissenschaftsrates von 1957 vis 1967," in *Wissenschaftsrat 1957–1967* (Tübingen: Mohr, 1968), pp. 23–38; and "Bericht des scheidenden Wissenschaftsratsvorsitzenden," *Deutsche Universitätszeitung vereinigt mit Hochschuldienst*, 1st February edition 1976, pp. 76–82.

58. See Intratest Sozialforschung, *Hochschulbarometer: Befragung von Lehrenden an Hochschulen Sommersemester 1974*, Vol. 3, p. 5; in general, teachers and students showed striking agreement on the importance of the various functions of higher education (p. 12). For an especially gloomy appraisal of the extent of politicization, see German Universities Commission, *Report on German Universities* (New York: International Council of Future of the University, 1977).

3
ITALY
Burton R. Clark

The great age of university development in Italy took place between the twelfth and fifteenth centuries. Bologna was begun in 1158; Padua, Naples, Rome, and other universities of the present system had developed into substantial, recognized institutions before 1400; and more than two-thirds of the universities extant in the mid-twentieth century had been established by 1600. Only a few new universities, now mainly peripheral seats of learning, were started between the seventeenth and twentieth centuries.[1] The university is among the very oldest major social institutions of Italy, its antiquity surpassed only by the church and the communes. It existed long before a modern national state was created in the mid-nineteenth century.

Formed when guilds were the primary form for organizing urban work, the early universities were themselves guilds and guild federations, collective efforts by students and faculty to sustain self-regulating clusters of people with shared interests to control a small domain of activity and defend themselves against other groups.[2] Italy was notable between the twelfth and the fifteenth centuries for the power of student guilds. As alien residents of city-states, students from other parts of Italy as well as other countries needed to band together in self-defense. At the same time, like the professors, they felt free to move the university from one city to another: "Townsmen and professors alike stood in awe of a body [the university of students] which by the simple expedient of migration could destroy the trade of the former and the incomes of the latter."[3]

But townsmen and professors no longer had to stand in awe once they learned to make the university stand in place. By the fifteenth century, through the erection of permanent buildings, the entry of professors onto city payrolls, and the recruitment of home-town boys as students, city fathers and professors had established dominance over the students, and the most important chapter in the history of student power was at an end.[4] Henceforth, the important power struggles pitted faculty guilds against the encompassing chartering and administrative frameworks of church and state, particularly the latter, which funded and often attempted to regulate the academic guilds as they did the many craft and merchant guilds on whom, in turn, they were dependent. In their significant ties to city-states and provincial rulers, Italian universities may be considered 'state universities' from the fifteenth century onward.

The ancient Italian universities were originally centers for professional studies and, like their counterparts in France and Spain, continued through the centuries to focus primarily on preparation for law, medicine, and public administration, the latter field generally drawing on law graduates. Between 1500 and 1850—centuries of decline for the universities and for the Italian peninsula as a whole—university activity was for long periods reduced virtually to the study of law alone.[5] Its fields of study already diminished, the Italian university became even less open than its counterparts in northern Europe to admitting and developing new fields as a way of adjusting to changing social demands. Science fared especially badly. Internal resistance meshed with a weak interest in scientific advances among Italian ruling circles and with the censorious resistance of the Catholic church mounted in the Counter-Reformation.[6] Conditions at the universities deteriorated further during the eighteenth and early nineteenth centuries, when a venerable institution such as Bologna, which in its earliest centuries attracted students by the thousands from near and far, was reduced to a few hundred students.[7] During this period of university decline, the entire peninsula suffered as it was turned into the battleground and playground of Austrian princes, French kings, and Spanish dukes. Too, the elite of the Italian city-states, unable to form a nation, not only feuded among themselves for three and a half centuries (1500–1850), but remained at the mercy of their more powerful neighbors who had managed to consolidate political control across the large entities that became the nations and empires of modern Europe.[8]

When the Italians finally were able to achieve national unification in the period 1850–70, they began a gradual nationalization of university support and control. The liberal leaders of the new nation, mainly Piedmontese of the Turin area who had been heavily influenced by French forms of governance and administration, began a trend toward both political and administrative centralization, drawing power from the cities and the regions and concentrating it administratively in the central offices of a set of national ministries and bureaus that would grow increasingly unwieldy and Balkanized.[9] They wanted, among other interests, an educational system that would help to make a nation, supporting national identification and unity over the divisive local loyalties of the old cities and provinces, over the disaffection of southern peasants and northern workers, and over the declared opposition of the church to a secular state that had conquered papal territory. An interest in trying to achieve equity and equality through unitary, uniform administration, much like France's, would also develop over time. All education was placed under a national ministry of education. The universities were given a direct, vertical relationship to the ministry, not even formally answering to an area prefect of the national government, much less to local or regional government.

As a result of this trend, which accelerated during the Fascist period (1922–45), the century of development between the 1860s and the 1960s saw the national system achieve a virtual monopoly. In 1960, Italian higher education was conducted at 30 places: 24 universities supported primarily by the state and firmly within the state system, and 6 "free" universities, so called because they were supported mainly by cities, provinces, or private groups. The free universities needed recognition by the national system in order to grant a legitimate degree. Falling under general state supervision, they organized their affairs on the model of the state universities.[10] The 30 universities accounted for 98 percent of enrollment. Thus there were really no higher-education institutions other than the universities, and there were no private-sector institutions truly independent of state authority.

The universities have varied widely in size. In 1960, the University of Rome had 45,000 students, Naples 28,000, while historic Pavia, Perugia, and Parma each had fewer than 5,000, and others such as Camerino and Macerata had only 1,000 or fewer. In the great student expansion of the 1960s, the disparities in size grew larger. By 1970, Rome had doubled to 90,000 students, Naples to more than 60,000, while small and moderately large universities were adding students in much smaller numbers. Disparities among the universities' fields of study were equally striking. A university in Italy can contain up to twelve faculties (*facoltà*). Nine of the faculties cover primarily professional areas: medicine, law, engineering, economics and commerce (mainly the latter), agriculture, teaching, architecture, veterinary medicine, and pharmacy. Three comprise what in the United States would be segments of the liberal arts: letters, science, and political science. The types of faculties are distributed unevenly among the universities. Some universities specialize in only one or two fields, whereas others are comprehensive, covering virtually everything that is recognized within the whole system. In 1960, for example, the University of Rome had all twelve faculties, while Parma had six, Siena three, and Macerata one. A university with a faculty in letters might not have a science faculty. Some have neither.

The types of faculties vary enormously in power, as measured by such simple indicators as the number of chair holders found throughout the national system: for example, in 1960, medicine had about 440 and law 325, compared to about 65 in teaching and 40 in architecture. Each faculty is entered directly from the secondary level and leads to the single degree of *laurea* after four, five, or six years of study, with all graduates assuming the title of *dottore*.

Finally, the Italian universities have been part of a wider structure of elite selection. Universal elementary education did not take hold in Italy until the 1950s; its achievement was a government priority in post-World War II reconstruction and modernization. As elsewhere on the Continent, the secondary level was divided into elite schools (classical and scientific *licei*) that led to automatic admission to the university, and nonelite schools that ended in technical and teacher training. With the secondary schools serving as a screening mechanism, Italian universities as late as 1960 were admitting 5 percent or less of the age group. Mass education at the secondary level in the late 1950s and early 1960s meant that many more students would enter the open doors of the universities after 1965.

LEVELS OF ORGANIZATION

The operating levels of the traditional Italian system are somewhat similar to the German and French, following the Continental style of university organization. At the lowest level, the chair and institute are the organizational units, with the chair holding professor doubling as director of a research institute or as the head of a main section within it. The structure places one man in full charge of both a teaching sector and a research sector, thereby making him a boss and encouraging the personalizing of power. Within his teaching and research domains, the professor personally selects junior personnel and acts as a sponsor in arranging their future careers as well as in deciding their current assignments. The power of the professor is also enhanced by his personal accumulation and filling of a wide network of roles: teaching on several faculties, even in cities far distant from one another, editing and managing a journal, engaging in outside professional practice, advising private organizations and local governments, and serving in posts in the national government, including the legislature and the cabinet. With so many other roles, professors have served only part time as professors. How to make them full-time professors became an issue in the reform efforts of the 1960s and early 1970s. The professor's capacity to accumulate privileges and powers increases his stature in the local cluster, raising him even farther above the *assistenti* and others of lesser rank. Therefore, at the base of the national system, organization tends to be unitary, hierarchical, and particularistic. It may even be said that it is guild-like in vertical authority, with a master having extensive direct control over what are, in effect, journeymen and apprentices.[11]

The second level of academic organization in the Italian system has long been the faculty (facoltà). Numbering about two hundred in the system as a whole, the faculties are the inclusive units to which professors and students belong and hence are organizationally more important than the universities. In internal operation, the faculty is an assembly of chairs, a horizontal grouping of powerful persons who regulate the less powerful at Level 1. The chaired professors, each representing certain subdomains and having one vote, come together in a faculty council (*consiglio di facoltà*) to decide on issues that fall within the collective domain of the faculty. As in Germany, the chairs elect their nominal superior, the dean (*preside*), who has little or no independent administrative power. Thus, the facoltà is not neatly unitary in authority structure, at least not by bureaucratic standards, but is more like a federation. Because it is a collegial body, with strong elements of collegiate monopoly, it is more horizontal than hierarchical. And because the colleagues who come together in the faculty council are fairly autonomous rulers of parts of the organizational countryside, decisions are influenced considerably by academic politics. The professors are much like senators representing different territorial interests, operating in a legislative body that dominates the executive. They must form majorities based on mutual regard for one another's established rights and territorial jurisdiction; senatorial courtesy mixes with bargaining, coalition formation, and occasional power plays. Here, as at the lower level, organization is guild-like, but now in the horizontal relation of a group of masters coming together to vote on common policy. The chair and faculty levels in Italy together place autocracy within collegiality, or, conversely, offer collegial relations among autocrats, having retained the vertical and horizontal relations that together characterize guild authority.[12]

At the next highest structural level, the university as a whole, organization is quite loose. The ruling body, the *senato accademico*, is an assembly of elected deans and certain other elected professors. Before the reforms of the 1970s, there was little or no representation of junior faculty or students. The nominal superior official, the *rettore*, is not bureaucratically appointed but is elected from the ranks of the chair holders to a short term of three years. Without any power base beyond the professors, the rectors have remained amateur administrators, on rotating terms of office and subject to recall.

The bureaucratic side of university organization centers chiefly on the post of the administrative director, who is indeed appointed from on high. This civil servant often has a long stay in office and is expected to serve as an arm of the national government. Traditionally, administrative directors were relatively weak, serving as bookkeepers for faculties and universities run by academic notables. They have grown stronger in recent years as the university system has grown and the need for order and coordination has increased. But local professors have exercised general jurisdiction even over the business affairs of the university through an administrative council, on which they and the rector sit with the administrative director. Thus there are important similarities between the organization of the university and the faculty, most notably the considerable monopoly of collegial power by constituent professors. The main difference between them is the greater looseness of the university structure and the high degree of autonomy of the constituent faculties. As inclusive membership units, the faculties need not be physically grouped but may be scattered around a city. Little horizontal linkage has been needed among them in order to accomplish the necessary work. Thus, the structure of the university is loosely federative, virtually coalitional, with a minimal hierarchy. Constructed around the autocratic powers of its voting members, the university, like the faculty, allows for and even encourages the patronage and favoritism usually found among elected governors.

Above the university level in Italy, in the superstructure of academic control, there has been no major multicampus administration (Level 4 in the comparative scheme), nothing that would parallel the German structure of state control (Level 5), nor even any clustering of universities within regional administration of the national government. The structure connects the university to Rome, the national capital (Level 6), specifically to a division of higher education within the mammoth Ministry of Public Instruction, topped by a minister of education and his staff. Formal lines of authority, as in many other countries, flow upward from the minister to a chief executive and the national legislature. The national system has impressive powers. It decides admission policy. Graduation from one of its approved secondary schools ensures admission to the university system as a whole and the choice of faculty at a particular university. All degrees are awarded by the national system rather than by the individual university. All chair-holding professors and "stabilized" assistants are regular civil service personnel, placed in categories of status and salary that cut across the system. The system finances the universities and has paid up to 80 percent of their costs in recent years, the balance largely made up by student fees and income from a declining base of university-owned property and endowment.

As mentioned earlier, the Fascist period increased educational centralization, thickening the common rulebooks applying to all university personnel. During this period even the curriculum became nationalized, with national codes specifying not only which fields of study would be available in the faculties of the various universities, but also naming the courses that were to be uniformly required throughout the country in each specialty, and listing what additional options were approved for each university. In short, admissions, finance, personnel policy, and curriculum were made uniform and centralized. Especially fascinating is the fact that after the Fascists fell from power, the fat rulebooks were not thrown away or even seriously amended or reduced. The nationally codified rules and laws had become important sources of power for various bureaus of the fragmented national government and thus provided protection and advantage to whichever officials or groups had come to have their interests vested most effectively.

In the higher education sector, the chair-holding professors form a key group. The Italian system is noteworthy for the skill with which the professors have managed to parlay local power into national power. They hold considerable control over what goes on at the center; control is not lodged primarily with bureaucrats or nonacademic politicians. Power flows along lines of professorial networks, nationally as well as locally. These networks connect decision makers within the system. A generalist professor provides more coordination than a specialist professor, and the Italian professor-general in his elaborated and accumulated roles alone can help link parts of the center to one another, the top to the bottom, as well as parts of operating units to each other.

A second structural key is peer election, the wide national use of the elected committee. The center of the national system is interlaced with committees composed of professors, whether in the Ministry of Public Instruction or the National Research Council. One such committee (*Consiglio Superiore dell'Istruzione*), at the apex of the structure alongside the minister, has had, for example, important powers of approval and veto over any changes in the nationalized curriculum. Research monies are given away by committees of professors meeting as segments of the National Research Council. The appointment of another chair holder in the system involves an ad hoc committee of professors working at the center on behalf of the entire system. They must administer a national competition and select three victors, one of whom will get the chair—through often complicated processes of maneuver and exchange among individuals and faculties. In all such national committees, members are not appointed. They are elected by fellow professors, with the voting population usually decided along lines of related disciplines. This democratic procedure operates within a limited electorate, one totaling about 3,000 professors nationally as late as the early 1970s. Coupled with peer election, of course, are peer review and decision.

It has been by means of unusual role accumulation on the part of individual professors and their uncommon peer control that a considerable collegial monopoly at the local level in the Italian structure has been transferred to the highest reaches of the national system. There is some role for bureaucrats in the central ministry, and many rules set forth bureaucratic lines in finance, curriculum, personnel, and other matters. Like states everywhere, the government is particularly concerned about the handling of state-allocated funds. Administrative officials, in the university as well as in the central office, are most likely to assert their bureaucratic position in accounting for the allocation of specifically budgeted monies. But bureaucratic coordination plays only a secondary role, to the point of functioning often as a façade for the professorial oligarchy which rules and coordinates the system. The influence of the professors even extends to important political offices, with chair holders serving in the cabinet and legislature, where they occupy strategic positions on the education committees. Compared to the professors' stature and status, the permanent state officials, including planners, are embedded in a public agency known for the mediocrity of its personnel, within a public administration that in quality and effectiveness is generally ranked lower than that of Germany, France, and Britain.[13] The dullness of the bureaucracy has increased the need for academics to help provide the order mandated by the national-system approach and, while so doing, to write their own privilege into the administrative rules and turn central control to their own advantage. Italians have had reason to speak of the professors as barons (*i baroni*) and, at times, of their country as professor-ridden.

Italian public administration is known for its weak horizontal coordination and its strong verticality, with segmental bureau controls extending downward from the center like stakes driven into the ground.[14] The higher education sector has some of this quality but it has two additional features. First, the top of the stake rests in the hands of those who are supposedly located far down the line, an imposing case of an internally located interest group controlling a segment of government and doing so through guild-like means of autocratic and collegial control; and second, the lowest operating units retain such impressive arbitrary power that the overall bureau, itself a Balkanized sector of the general government, is in turn Balkanized into several hundred faculties and several thousand chairs and institutes.

In the comparative perspective of the six levels of academic organization, the Italian structure is one that has concentrated power primarily at the bottom, secondarily at the top, and only weakly in the middle. The chair holders, rooted in the lowest operating units, occupy not only the first level or organization but also the second and third: The substructure is in their hands, controlled from the bottom up by the guild combination of collegial authority superimposed onto a base of autocratic authority. Little effective supervision by bureaucratic arms of the central state or surveillance by external groups penetrates to these levels. In the secondary concentration of power at the top level, guild and bureaucracy are interwoven. Yet here too the structure is biased toward professorial control. The overall combination of faculty guild and state bureaucracy has finally and most notably meant weakness among a class of administrators whose interests would be vested in effective internal university and faculty coordination and in the linking of the universities to one another in multicampus and regional systems.

REFORM AND CHANGE

As in other nations, recent demands for reform have hit the traditional Italian system hard. By 1960 it was clear that, because of the expansion and widening of access occurring in the 1950s at the lower educational levels, the university system would soon face much larger numbers of students whose social background and educational preparation would vary more widely than before. Such perceptions were articulated in reports in the early 1960s, and proposed university-reform legislation throughout the decade pressed for a number of changes.[15] There seemed so much to be done, on pragmatic as well as ideological grounds, that proponents of reform generally drafted "big bills," some with as many as one hundred clauses. All the political parties entered into prolonged debate; the junior academics, increasing rapidly in number and assuming more responsibilities, lobbied with increasing vigor; and some important scientists joined in, angrily arguing that the traditional structure worked against the development of science and reporting invidious international comparisons and critical external opinion.[16] But the professors as a bloc, together with some of the more conservative politicians, resisted change throughout the 1960s, and none of the big bills, some debated for three to four years, was passed. Exemplifying this lack of movement, throughout the entire postwar period the national government started no new universities until the founding of the University of Calabria in 1972. The old group of 30 universities had to absorb nearly the full impact of an expansion in which unchecked student traffic swelled the large urban universities to gigantic size. Universities that predated 1500, rooted in guild-like organization, now faced ever larger masses of students.

One result of resistance to change was, therefore, a severe overloading of the system. Also overextended was the effectiveness of the full professors themselves at some of the central universities, and particularly at the University of Rome. Having kept their ranks narrow, they were overwhelmed by the number of students and junior staff they had to supervise and somehow manage. A full professor working only part time might face twenty assistants and a thousand students. The old guild ties, heavily dependent on personal intervention, were no longer adequate in such circumstances. By 1970 the system had moved into so deep a stage of institutional insufficiency that it was becoming apparent to groups outside as well as within the structure. Student discontent escalated rapidly after 1967 and helped to dramatize the tribulations of the greatly expanded student body. Their explosive outbursts shattered glass; their dogged occupation of buildings tied up some faculties for months at a time. But factionalism, fatigue, and its own organizational insufficiency soon weakened the Italian *movimento studentesco*, as they had in other countries.[17]

Beginning in 1969, when something had to be done to pacify some of the students some of the time, small changes were made. Access to all faculties was granted to the graduates of all the different kinds of secondary schools, replacing the streaming that had limited admission to graduates of the elite classical and scientific licei. The fixed national curriculum was made considerably more flexible when students were granted the right to devise individual programs of study. In practice, this entailed greater local determination of curriculum as students and faculties worked out requirements. The examination system was revised to allow students a better chance of passing within a given period, although faculty schedules now were even further crammed by time given to examinations. Too, "small laws" (*leggine*) gradually increased legal support and job security for teaching personnel below the chair holder, with stabilization (essentially tenure) given to about 15,000 *professori incaricati* who already had assumed many duties of the full professors.

Most important, the academic ancien régime's unresponsiveness during the increasingly turbulent 1960s led to a diminished respect for the professors by groups other than the students. Such an erosion of their fundamental legitimacy made possible a shift in the distribution of power. The political parties, trade unions, and other outside groups grew more willing to intervene and to form temporary, active coalitions. In the fall of 1973, by means of an executive decree that bypassed normal legislative channels, the government rammed through what may prove to be substantial changes.[18] The major provision was a projected increase in the number of full professors from 3,500 to 10,000 in a few years time. A second measure sought to weaken the politics of choosing professors for national personnel committees by substituting selection by lot for election by constituency. Other measures attempted to stabilize further the status of lower teaching personnel and to grant them more participation and representation in faculty bodies.

Meanwhile, beyond the purview of the established faculties, an interesting trend was accelerating. The Italian system has long provided an unpublicized option for local initiative: begin a university, university branch, or a faculty with local sponsorship and municipal financing, but without recognition by the national system; and then, before the first students have completed the work for a degree, have the new unit legally ratified, supported by national funds, and accredited to award the degree by lobbying the unit into the national system. This option recently has been exercised more and more, especially in the north, as local opinion, in the service of local need and ambition, has raced ahead of the system's willingness and capacity to respond. For example, embryonic subsystems seem to be forming around Milan and Turin, as small emerging units seek to collaborate for mutual advantage. Central Italy, long monopolized by the University of Rome, produced the new University of Chieti, which operates three campuses under a common budget. Such efforts are in the spirit of regionalization, a shift away from centralized government whose time may have come. It was promised in the Constitution of 1948 and even received some legislative action in 1970.[19] In short, increased activity at the local and regional levels may result first in a de facto and later in a de jure regionalization of the universities. The system has apparently grown too large to continue without some strengthened coordination at Levels 4 and 5 in the comparative scheme.

The nature of change in Italian higher education is heavily conditioned by the nature of the traditional structure that was reviewed in the first two sections of this chapter. The state monopoly has weakened greatly the leverage of market forces—for example, the competition among institutions for faculty and students. The guild controls of the professors within that monopoly have blunted bureaucratic intervention and isolated planners from the most powerful constituency, the professors themselves. Even the power of professionalism has been vitiated, as many of the scholarly and scientific disciplines have been fragmented and impeded by the conservative local academic clusters.

By default, the real leverage rests with uncontrolled numerical expansion and politics. The events following recently instituted reforms, the post-1968 small laws, suggest that when political considerations are so basic, reform becomes a matter of adjustment through political incrementalism, studied indirection, and planned bargaining.[20] The government cannot pay steady attention because of its overloaded agenda. When it does pay attention, it deals from the weak position of coalition government and mediocre bureaucracy. The overcrowded higher education sector strains with internal conflicts. The junior faculty and exasperated external groups are able to exercise growing influence in favor of reform, against the entrenched capacity of the traditional chair holders to dilute reforms forced upon them and to effect counterreforms; the need for increased coordination among the Balkanized domains of the chairs and the faculties conflicts with the idea that the way to open things up is to increase the number of operating units and risk an even more fragmented structure. Small victories are won now and again: easier rites of passage for students; greater job security and higher rank for lower personnel; an increase in professorships that may spread power at the senior level and in time produce de facto departments.

An effort is under way in Italy to change the political dimensions of a heavily politicized academic system. The general structural drift is toward establishing, where an entrenched power monopoly once stood, a political arena in which exchanges will be made, bargains struck, and tacit agreements reached by a larger number of groups that have an interest and stake in the structure of the system. The political alterations may then in turn provide an opening for such administrative changes as strengthened campus coordination that will help faculty federations become modern universities.

NOTES

1. Hastings Rashdall, *The Universities of Europe in the Middle Ages*, new ed. in 3 vol., ed. F. M. Powicke and A. B. Emden (Oxford: Oxford University Press, 1936) (1st ed., 1895), vol. 1 and 2; and *International Handbook of Universities: And Other Institutions of Higher Education*, 5th ed., ed. H. M. R. Keyes and S. J. Aitken (Paris: The International Association of Universities, 1971), pp. 550–73.

2. Rashdall, *Universities of Europe*, passim, especially Vol. 1, pp. 149–51; Charles Homer Haskins, *The Rise of Universities* (Ithaca, N.Y.: Cornell University Press, Great Seal Books, 1957); Alan B. Cobban, "Medieval Student Power," *Past and Present*, no. 53 (1971):28–66;

J. K. Hyde, "Commune, University, and Society in Early Medieval Bologna," in *Universities in Politics: Case Studies from the Late Middle Ages and Early Modern Period*, ed. John W. Baldwin and Richard A. Goldthwaite (Baltimore: Johns Hopkins Press, 1972), pp. 17–46.

3. Rashdall, *Universities of Europe*, vol. 1, p. 165.

4. Ibid., p. 218, and vol. 2, pp. 61–62; Cobban, "Medieval Student Power," pp. 36–37, 42–48.

5. Richard L. Kagan, personal communication. On the weakness of historical research on universities in the centuries after 1500 (the end point of Rashdall's coverage), and on developments in Spanish universities in the early modern period, see his *Students and Society in Early Modern Spain* (Baltimore: Johns Hopkins University Press, 1974).

6. Joseph Ben-David, *The Scientist's Role in Society: A Comparative Study* (Englewood Cliffs, N.J.: Prentice-Hall, 1971), Ch. 4, "The Emergence of the Scientific Role."

7. Matthew Arnold, *Schools and Universities on the Continent* (London: Macmillan, 1868), pp. 109–11; Edith E. Coulson James, *Bologna: Its History, Antiquities and Art* (London: Oxford University Press, 1909), pp. 159–60.

8. Denys Hay, "Introduction," in *The New Cambridge Modern History. Volume 1, The Renaissance: 1493–1520*, 1st paperback ed., planned by G. R. Potter, ed. with a new preface by Denys Hay (Cambridge: Cambridge University Press, 1975), p. 7.

9. On the evolution and structure of Italian government, see Robert C. Fried, *The Italian Prefects: A Study in Administrative Politics* (New Haven: Yale University Press, 1963); Dante Germino and Stefano Passigli, *The Government and Politics of Contemporary Italy* (New York: Harper and Row, 1968); Joseph LaPalombara, *Interest Groups in Italian Politics* (Princeton: Princeton University Press, 1964).

10. Burton R. Clark, *Academic Power in Italy: A Study of Bureaucracy and Oligarchy in a National University System* (forthcoming), Ch. 1, "University."

11. Ibid., Ch. 3, "Oligarchy," and Ch. 5, "Guild."

12. Ibid., Ch. 5, "Guild."

13. Luciano Cappelletti, "The Italian Bureaucracy: A Study of the *Carriera Dirrettiva* of the Italian Administration" (Ph.d. diss., University of California, Berkeley, 1966). Published in Italian, in revised form as *Burocrazia e Società* (Milan: Dott. A. Giuffrè Editore, 1968); Ezra N. Suleiman, *Politics, Power, and Bureaucracy in France: The Administrative Elite* (Princeton: Princeton University Press, 1974), pp. 75–79.

14. John Clarke Adams and Paolo Barile, *The Government of Republican Italy*, 2d. ed. (Boston: Houghton-Mifflin, 1966), p. 221; Germino and Passagli, *Contemporary Italy*, p. 163.

15. Clark, *Academic Power in Italy*, Ch. 4, "Reform."

16. For example, the so-called 'Brooks Report' on OECD on Italian science. Organisation for Economic Co-operation and Development, *Reviews of National Science Policies: Italy* (Paris: OECD, 1968).

17. Federico Mancini, "The Italian Student Movement," *American Association of University Professors Bulletin* 54, no. 4 (Winter 1968):427–32; Guido Martinotti, "Italy," in *Students, University and Society*, ed. Margaret Scotford Archer (London: Heinemann Educational Books, 1972), pp. 189–93; Gianni Statera, *Death of a Utopia: The Development and Decline of Student Movements in Europe* (New York: Oxford University Press, 1975).

18. Clark, *Academic Power in Italy*, Ch. 4, "Reform." This urgent measure was announced by the government on October 1 and became law 60 days later (Law 766, November 30, 1973).

19. On the limitations and possibilities of regionalization in Italy and France, see Sidney Tarrow, "Local Constraints on Regional Reform: A Comparison of Italy and France," *Comparative Politics* 7, no. 1 (October 1974):1–36.

20. The political and administrative constraints on planning in Italy as well as in France and Britain are discussed in Jack Hayward and Michael Watson, eds., *Planning, Politics and Public Policy* (Cambridge: Cambridge University Press, 1975).

4

FRANCE
John Van de Graaff
Dorotea Furth

The medieval roots of the system of higher education in France are as deep as Italy's; indeed "Paris was the archetype of northern [medieval] universities as Bologna was for those in Italy."[1] However, modern French higher education's centralized and yet diversified structure originated in measures taken during the French Revolution and the Napoleonic Empire; in fact, the rigid structures of Napoleonic heritage have weighed heavily on higher education to this day, despite the massive overhaul of the system undertaken since 1968.

Early in the French Revolution, the 22 universities in existence at the end of the ancien régime were suppressed. Only specialized professional schools were maintained—the precursors of the grand écoles, the elite and most prestigious segment of French higher education. Some of the grande écoles were founded during this period, among them the now venerable Ecole Polytechnique (1794) and the Ecole Normale Supérieure (1795).

Napoleon's reforms, instituted in 1808, created a single, unified organization called the Imperial University to oversee all public education in France, with 16 (later 23) regional administrative units called academies. Napoleon did not restore the banished universities but rather designated faculties as the basic units of higher education, parallel to the grandes écoles, and charged with the professional preparation of lawyers, doctors, and teachers. There were five faculties: theology, law, medicine, letters, and science. The theological faculties were later abolished, and in 1920 pharmacy was upgraded to faculty status, but otherwise the faculty divisions remained unchanged until they were abolished in 1968.

For most of the nineteenth century, the faculties were entirely separate from one another, administered directly by the Ministry of Public Instruction. Beginning in the 1880s, the government gave the faculties a certain autonomy by creating faculty councils and assemblies for their self-government, allowing them to select their own deans, and giving them their own budgets. In 1896, the universities were nominally reestablished as organizational units. Within each regional academy, the faculties (which were not always even located in the same town) were grouped into a university. Each university had a council consisting primarily of the faculty deans and other faculty representatives; it was chaired by the rector, who was head of the academy. But by that time the faculty interests were well entrenched, and such changes had little unifying effect.[2] Moreover, the faculties' mission remained extremely limited.

From about 1900 on, as national and regional needs for technologically trained manpower and applied research accelerated, additional institutions devoted to specialized tasks were established. Partly in response to the German example, these institutions developed ties to the universities and especially the faculties of science. In 1920, these units were given formal status within the universities. As institutes parallel to the faculties, they carried out tasks of research and specialized professional training which could not be fulfilled within the rigid framework of the faculties.[3] Certain of the university-linked institutes, such as the Higher National Engineering Schools (ENSI), were reckoned formally as grandes écoles.

Among more recent innovations was the establishment, in 1966, of the University Institutes of Technology (IUTs), which offer two-year technical training programs in such fields as electronics, computer programming, and management. Much in the mode of the grandes écoles, the IUTs provide intensive instruction and supervision, with continuous assessment. Though placed within the universities, the IUTs were made administratively independent of the faculties, as institutes under the framework of the 1920 decree.[4]

Scientific research became largely the province of a sector of institutions outside the faculties and the grandes écoles—institutions such as the Collège de France, the Ecole Pratique des Hautes Etudes (founded in 1868), and the National Center for Scientific Research (CNRS), founded in 1939. The CNRS not only established institutes in fields resisted by the faculties, but also stimulated more research within faculties through its loans of research personnel and the provision of services and equipment to the faculties.

As a whole, therefore, the traditional system of higher education and research was highly fragmented into diverse sectors with specialized functions. Research was primarily the responsibility of central research institutions, whereas training in the traditional professions was given in the faculties, and various administrative and technical cadres were recruited through the grandes écoles. Broadly defined, the grandes écoles include more than 250 institutions, of which some two dozen are renowned and highly elite. All of the grandes écoles serve primarily to recruit and train persons to assume a broad range of high positions in the public and private sectors, in government and in industry.[5] Some of the grandes écoles are privately supported and all are selective, admitting a fixed number of students through national competitive examinations (*concours*) or on the basis of other academic qualifications. Instruction in the grandes écoles is intensive and regimented, with the length and content of courses prescribed in detail. Attrition is negligible, assessment is continuous, and rank in class is often important in determining the positions entered after graduation. Although the teachers are not always intellectually eminent, instruction in the best grandes écoles is of a high scientific standard. However, students learn "the content of science but not the methods of science."[6] Despite the regimented character of their instruction the grandes écoles have for long attracted the most talented secondary graduates, thus usually drawing them away from potential careers in scholarship and research.

In contrast to the selectivity of the grandes écoles, the universities—with the exception of the faculties of medicine—are still open virtually without restriction to all holders of the baccalaureate, the degree awarded upon examination at the end of academic secondary education in the *lycées*. Even though severe attrition takes place, especially in the first two years, the universities' share of enrollment has continued to increase over the past decade. Policy makers had hoped that the availability of the IUT as an opportunity for short-cycle technical training within the university would draw students away from the traditional faculties in large numbers. Instead, students have continued to crowd into them, as figures in Table 1 make

Table 1
Enrollments in French Higher Education, 1964 and 1972

| | Enrolled Students | | | |
| | 1964 | | 1972 | |
	Number	Percent	Number	Percent
Preparatory classes in lycées[a]	25,720	5.7	32,787	3.7
Higher technical sections (in lycées)[a]	18,693	4.1	32,189	3.7
IUTs	—	—	35,951	4.1
Grandes écoles	60,000[b]	13.3	80,000[c]	9.1
Universities[d]	347,933	76.9	698,467	79.4
Total	452,346	100.0	879,394	100.0

[a] These figures include students in both public and private lycées; they are postbaccalaureate students and form an important part of postsecondary education.

[b] Estimated (public and private institutions).

[c] Estimated; includes 33,275 students enrolled in engineering schools under all ministries and under private auspieces.

[d] Includes foreign students.

Sources: For 1964: France, Ministère de l'Education Nationale, *Tableaux de l'Education Nationale. Edition 1966* (Paris: Service Central des Statistiques et de la Conjoncture [1966]), pp. 156, 18, 68, 245. For 1972: France, Ministère de l'Education Nationale, *Tableaux de l'Education Nationale. Edition 1974* (Paris: Statistiques et Sondages [1974]), pp. 331, 349, 363, 329, 369.

clear. The overloading of the system—and especially the overcrowded facilities in Paris and environs (with one-third of the total number of students)—precipitated the May 1968 upheavals, which led to the Orientation Act reviewed later in this chapter.

ADMINISTRATIVE CENTRALISM

The structure of French higher education has been profoundly influenced by the political and administrative system in which it is embedded, and especially by a strong centralization of authority.[7] Most government decisions, whether major or minor, are made in the ministries in Paris or even at cabinet level. At the same time, since lines of authority run vertically within bureaucratic sectors, there is strong administrative fragmentation.[8] Coordination of policies is possible, if at all, only at high levels. Both centralization and fragmentation are, paradoxically, reinforced by ambivalent attitudes toward authority among the French, who manifest "a fierce personal individualism suspicious of everyone,"[9] and a reluctance to enter face-to-face discussions aimed at easing the tensions of social and institutional life. In consequence, there is little grass-roots participation in politics. Rather, there is a proliferation of national associations through which the individual looks to the central government for protection of his acquired rights (*droits acquis*). Each group calls on the bureaucratic sector responsible for its realm of activity to preserve the interests of its members. Though individualism serves to limit the overall power of the state, the reluctance of individuals (and institutions) to cooperate at lower levels and the habit of resorting to higher levels of government for the settlement of controversies and the regulation of policies buttress centralization.

The particular feature of French secondary and higher education which most characteristically reflects administrative centralism is the system of national examinations and concours. By fostering fierce competition among students and rewarding their precise degree of achievement with entry into technical, bureaucratic, and political slots of specified prestige, the system reinforces individualism and maintains hierarchical authority. The most important national examination is the *baccalauréat,* which, as the capstone of academic secondary education in the lycées and colleges, has traditionally provided automatic admission to the university faculties. Various national concours (competitive examinations for a fixed number of places) govern access to the grandes écoles. An individual's performance in these concours, after two or more years of intensive postbaccalaureate preparation in the special classes of the lycées, may largely predetermine his career. Another immensely prestigious concours is the *agrégation.* Taken by students after four or more years at university, it originally provided access to secondary teaching in the lycées but now has become the usual qualification for a university career in the traditional humanistic and scientific fields.[10] The

French have traditionally favored the impartial, formally egalitarian mechanism of the concours for controlling access to the supposedly limited number of high-level positions over more informal, subjective, and potentially personalistic procedures.

In comprehensive fashion, the system of concours and grandes écoles fulfills the dual function of recruiting and training highly skilled technical and managerial cadres, as well as selecting the country's top administrative and political elite. The system has often been viewed, however, as inimical to the development of French science, for the content of the examinations emphasizes the mastery of prescribed, limited bodies of existing knowledge, usually abstract and theoretical in character, to the detriment of the habits of independent and empirical inquiry which are essential to productive scientific endeavor.[11] The concours foster individual achievement leading less to intellectual or scientific creativity than to technical and administrative authority, thus reinforcing the hierarchical, technocratic, and nonparticipative nature of French government and society. The system as a whole, with professional institutes—the grandes écoles—largely devoid of research facilities at the pinnacle of higher education, was unique among industrial nations. Although recent developments, particularly since 1968, have attenuated these conditions, the process of change has been difficult and slow.

TRADITIONAL STRUCTURE: PROFESSORIAL AUTONOMY AND MINISTERIAL AUTHORITY

In France, much as in Germany and Italy, the lowest unit (Level 1) of academic organization within the university system was the chair. Originally, the chair-holding professors (*professeurs titulaires de chaires*) were virtually the only teachers. From the last decades of the nineteenth century on, however, subsidiary categories of teaching staff were created, which by the 1960s included professors without chairs (*professeurs a titre personnel*), senior lectures (*maîtres de conférences*), assistant lecturers (*maîtres assistants*), and assistants. All senior staff, including the senior lecturers, had to hold a state doctorate, and all of them shared analogous formal rights and obligations, except that only professors had full rights of participation in faculty, university, and national decision-making bodies. Professors also received the highest salaries.[12] Among the two lowest categories, assistant lecturers enjoyed regular civil service status with tenure, whereas assistants were employed for limited terms. Both groups were authorized to teach only laboratory or recitation sessions under the supervision of professors or senior lecturers. For an aspiring academic, therefore, the attainment of a senior lectureship, with virtual professorial status, was a major career goal. As the essential qualification, the state doctorate played a role analogous to that of the German Habilitation.

Traditionally, French university staff were occupied mainly with teaching and examining functions, although their teaching load was light—three hours per week for professors and senior lecturers, and six hours for assistant lecturers. In contrast to the German Ordinarius, who within his institute reigned over substantial research funds and facilities provided directly by the state, the French professor seldom possessed research resources by virtue of occupying a chair. Rather, the faculties controlled the usually meagre allocations granted by the ministry. To establish substantial research enterprises French professors needed support from other outside sources, such as the CNRS. Structurally, the French professors' power was rarely linked to the control of research facilities like the German institutes; it depended almost exclusively on the influence they were able to exert over the careers of their students and disciples. Their main prerogative was a virtually unlimited freedom to use their time and organize their work as they pleased. With formal obligations of just three lectures per week and unrestricted outside professional activities, "the chairholding professor is his own master before God," in the words of Raymond Aron.

> "Neither the head of his department nor the dean is in a position to give orders or even mere directives to his colleagues. French professors are not bonded to the state, they are free in most respects to follow their own pleasures, to work much or little, to revise their courses or not. Administrative rigidity and anarchistic liberty within a framework of regulations: this combination, typically French, is also typically academic [universitaire]."[13]

Due to the centralized structure characteristic of the French system and above all to the concentration of talent, resources, and numbers in Paris, chairs in the Paris faculties carried higher salaries and far more prestige and influence than those in provincial universities. The Paris chair holders had larger staffs. They were also in a position to develop close links with other elite academic institutions, with research organizations, and with a variety of government agencies, above all the Ministry of National Education. Such patrons used their influence to consolidate their own positions and to further the careers of their followers—"clusters" of academics, including even chair holders in provincial faculties, who shared their approach and "were prepared to collaborate to advance research and instruction in a given area."[14]

At the level above the chair was the faculty (Level 2), the main structural unit of the higher education system since the Napoleonic reform of 1808. The faculty was governed almost exclusively by its professors. As a body, professors alone formed the faculty council and they also served on the faculty assembly together with the senior lecturers. (Though a small number of junior staff were also members of the assembly, they served in an advisory capacity only.) The council was much the more powerful of the two bodies. It allocated the funds granted by the ministry and, along with the central Consultative Committee of the Universities, ranked candidates for vacant chairs. On both matters the ministry technically had the final word but it exercised this authority only when the Consultative Committee disagreed with the faculty's choice, which happened rarely.[15] The assembly handled curricular matters and was also responsible for submitting a list of candidates for the faculty deanship to the ministry for its approval.

The dean, who was always a professor, served a three-year term which was normally renewed. Many deans stayed in office a decade or more and were therefore stronger, at least potentially, than their German counterparts. The deans of the Paris faculties were especially powerful, and they could be considered as an integral part of the centralized administrative system.

At Level 2, in addition to the faculties there were the institutes devoted to research and practical training which had developed since 1900. Although their personnel usually belonged to the faculties, the institutes functioned directly under the administrative authority of the ministry. The major institutions in this category were the ENSI and, since 1966, the IUTs. There were also disciplinary departments within the faculties.[16] A 1959 decree formally gave the faculties the option of creating such departments, although by 1968 only about 50 departments had been established in less than two dozen faculties, mainly science. Under the Orientation Act of 1968, many of the departments and institutes were converted into units of teaching and research (UERs).

The universities (Level 3) have led at most a skeletal existence. Even after they were formally reestablished in 1896, virtually all significant matters continued to be handled by the faculties, their deans, and the central government. The university's only institutional body—the university council—was extremely weak. This council included the dean and two elected professors from each faculty, one or two directors of associated institutes, and four lay persons nominated by the rector of the academy, who presided over its infrequent meetings. Though similar to its counterparts in Germany and Italy, this collegial council had even less power than they did, lacking above all an elected professorial rector as its chairman and the symbolic head of the university. The grandes écoles, generally smaller than the universities, were more tightly organized. The government usually appointed their directors, and lay persons often played an important role on their councils as links to public and private employers.

As governmental units at the subnational level, the academies, which were equivalent to state or regional administrative units, and their rectors can best be considered as belonging to Level 5. They had, however, only minimal autonomy and were accountable to the ministry. Any margin for maneuver depended greatly on the prestige of the rector, who as head of the academy was responsible for all state educational institutions within its boundaries. Although the rector was always a full professor, he acted as a government spokesman. Nominated by the minister of education, he was appointed by presidential decree (a procedure reserved for the highest state functionaries), after cabinet approval. The rector was the minister's direct representative in university affairs, and formal lines of communication and authority between ministry and faculties ran through him.

At Level 6, the central Ministry of National Education possessed extensive powers, exercised primarily by the Directorate of Higher Education whose head, together with the minister, had formal authority over all university matters. Structures of university governance, curricula, degree requirements, procedures for faculty appointments—all were determined at the national level, leaving little initiative to the individual faculties and universities. Strict budgetary regulations, including prior control of many expenditures, further enhanced the administrative and political influence of the central government. However, the coordination of policy for higher education as a whole remained difficult, for the faculties, the IUTs (from 1966), and the CNRS were all under distinct bureaucratic divisions of the education ministry, to say nothing of the grandes écoles which came under other ministries.

Under the prime minister, the General Planning Commissariat and its education commission, which consisted of administrative officials and outside experts, including a few from higher education, were responsible for broad planning for higher education. From the late 1950s on, the commission, which was independent of the education ministry, attempted to combine a manpower approach with projections of the student demand for various types of higher education.[17] However, since there was no way to guide the intake of students into the different faculties, the projections were of little value, and in some instances proved totally unrealistic.[18]

Although final authority at the national level lay with government officials, full professors exercised considerable influence on high-level decision making.[19] The professors had majority control of the two main advisory bodies for higher education—the Council of Higher Education and the Consultative Committee of the Universities. The council—or, more accurately, its permanent section of seventeen members—was responsible for advising the Directorate of Higher Education on general policy, particularly regarding the content of instruction. The Consultative Committee had a strong voice in the appointment and promotion of teaching staff of all ranks. Its numerous standing subcommittees in the various disciplines, consisting almost entirely of professors (two-thirds elected by their peers, one-third appointed by the government) placed all staff on national "lists of aptitude," usually according to possession of (or progress toward) a doctorate. Inclusion on the appropriate list was a necessary condition for formal appointment to a corresponding position in the university hierarchy. For professorial chairs, the subcommittees usually presented a list of candidates in order of preference, after which the faculty concerned proposed its list. The ministry thus had a choice in the infrequent cases when the proposals diverged. In that event, the proposals of the national subcommittee had more weight. As a body of experts above the particular interest of local faculty, the subcommittee would be most likely, in the French view, to come to an equitable and objective opinion.[20]

Like the national concours, this system tended to perpetuate rigidities in the disciplinary structure of the faculties; the senior professors who dominated the subcommittees valued research of a traditional sort most highly, discouraging innovative fields and approaches. The system's resistance to new disciplines and approaches has been notorious. Innovation has taken place almost exclusively outside the traditional faculties. The professors' main concern, regardless of the administrative level at which they exerted their power, was either simply to preserve their autonomy and acquired status or to expand their sphere of professional and disciplinary influence by promoting the careers of their disciples. In either case, their interests were narrow and they could easily forge alliances to resist change. Government officials, with their overriding concern for maintaining formal uniformity among universities, shunned broad reforms or formal recognition of major new disciplines, for to do so would have meant changing the curricula of all universities and secondary schools.

CENTRALLY ADMINISTERED STRUCTURAL CHANGE

The widespread student protests of May 1968 paralyzed the universities and dramatized the already long-evident incapacity of the Napoleonic structures to cope with such pressures as industrial and technological development and, above all, expanding enrollments.[21] The newly appointed education minister, Edgar Faure, drafted far-reaching legislation to reorganize the universities. After detailed consultations with interest groups and intensive negotiations within the bureaucracy and the cabinet, resulting in substantial dilutions and modifications, the Orientation Act for Higher Education was adopted by a unanimous parliamentary vote in November 1968. Faure's political experience and sensitivity, and the explicit support of President de Gaulle, were crucial to the outcome.[22]

In the view of Faure and his collaborators, the reform had three major aims: the promotion of interdisciplinary cooperation or pluridisciplinarity, the broadening of participation, and decentralization or the strengthening of university autonomy. The Orientation Act was implemented in stages. First, the 23 existing universities and their faculties were dissolved. Then, some 600 new teaching and research units (*unités d'enseignement et de recherche—* UERs) were created. Although usually smaller than the former faculties and in some cases roughly equivalent to the U.S. department, the UERs still represent Level 2 within the French system. And finally, the UERs were regrouped to form more than 60 new universities. The last two stages overlapped somewhat, especially in Paris, where the ministry negotiated numerous further divisions after the initial deadline for the formation of UERs, raising the national total to 674 by the end of 1969; by 1973 it reached 730.[23]

A principal aim of this reorganization, pluridisciplinarity—or the formation of universities that would foster interdisciplinary cooperation—was often ignored. A dozen of the smaller provincial universities, including seven established since 1962, emerged largely unchanged from the reorganization, although most of their letters and science faculties were subdivided into smaller UERs (following departmental divisions where they existed). The faculties of medicine and pharmacy maintained their institutional integrity nearly everywhere; most still call themselves faculties and are chaired by deans. Similarly, law faculties preserved an outward continuity, although many of the more liberal jurists and social scientists seceded to form their own UERs, and some letters faculties split in analogous fashion.[24] The greatest changes took place in Paris, as the central Sorbonne divided into more than 100 UERs, which after much prodding by the administration eventually formed seven universities, some made up to fragments of the former giant faculties. (Three maintain the name Sorbonne in their title: Panthéon-Sorbonne, Paris-Sorbonne, and New Sorbonne.) Six more universities were established on the outskirts of Paris, mostly as new foundations, making a total of 13 universities in the Paris region.

The Orientation Act dealt ambiguously with the complex issue of how to treat the various institutions of higher education outside the traditional faculties, from the grandes écoles to the IUTs.[25] Most of these institutions, unlike the faculties, had continued to function during May 1968. Thus there was strong sentiment for exempting all of them from the provisions of the act. An influential group within the government took this stand, including the prime minister and other ministers responsible for their own grandes écoles, which included some of the most renowned. Although the draft that Faure submitted to the Cabinet was applicable in principle to all of the grandes écoles, he had to retreat and a compromise was reached. The institutions under ministries other than education were excluded from the legislation; those within the education ministry's jurisdiction but independent of the universities could be individually brought under the act by decree; and finally, the university-attached schools and institutes (notably the ENSI and the IUTs) were largely to continue within the universities as UERs, although the applicability of the legislation to many of them was to be restricted. The ENSU, IUTs, and certain other units receive their budgetary allocations directly from the ministry and their directors are appointed by the ministry rather than elected.

The Orientation Act pursued two further goals: the expansion of participation and the strengthening of university autonomy. To promote greater participation the act provided guidelines for the composition, functions, and responsibilities of the various decision-making bodies to be set up at the level of both the universities and the UERs. The newly formed councils include representatives of all university groups—senior and junior teaching staff, research staff, students, and administrative and technical personnel—as well as representatives from outside the university. The provisions of the Orientation Act regarding the proportion of seats given to each group are fairly general. Teaching staff must have at least as many seats as the students (with at least 60 percent of those seats assigned to senior staff); outsiders are to make up one-sixth to one-third of the university councils. The act did not require UER councils to have outside members, although they are mandatory for many special-status UERs, such as the ENSI and the IUTs, to ensure liaison between these units and the professions for which they prepare. The actual distribution of seats in the university councils varies little; a typical council of 80 members would have 20 senior teaching staff, 12 junior staff, 4 researchers, 25 students, 5 administrative and technical personnel, and 14 laymen. But despite this broad formal representation, in practice attendance is low and the academic staff, particularly the senior members, usually dominate the proceedings. Students and outside lay persons tend to be especially uninterested, perhaps perceiving the councils' deliberations as irrelevant to their concerns.[26] Moreover, research affairs are reserved for a separate organ, the scientific council, consisting only of academics with a majority of senior members. Similarly, all deliberations concerning academic appointments, whether within the university or at the national level, are restricted to staff of rank at least equal to the position concerned.

To strengthen autonomy the new universities were given more control over their constituent units than they had had in the past. Although the UERs have some independence, especially in organizing their teaching, most of their councils' decisions must be approved by the university council, which is also responsible for the allocation of budgetary and personnel resources among the different UERs (except those with special status), as well as for general university policy.

The most important means for strengthening governance and management at the university level has been the introduction of a presidential system. The university president, who must usually be a professorial member of the university council, is elected by it for a period of five years, and cannot succeed himself. The president is assisted by a secretary general and an administrative staff, as well as by one or more vice presidents elected from among the academic staff, usually with the president's support. Most of the first cohort of presidents, elected in 1970 and 1971, were recruited from former faculty deans, who indeed were the president's most immediate counterparts in the traditional system. However, whereas the deans had presided over relatively homogeneous units and represented their peers, the presidents head universities that are heterogeneous collections of different disciplines, and therefore they must try to provide balanced leadership for the institution as a whole.

In general policy matters, the president and his staff, rather than the university council, have the initiative. Although the text of the Orientation Act is conspicuously vague on the division of authority between president and council, a legal opinion issued by the ministry to guide the universities in drafting their statutes maintained: "Any [statutory] provision tending to institute procedures for questions of confidence or motions of censure is illegal, and [the statutes] cannot provide, directly or indirectly, for any accountability of the president to the council."[27] Thus most universities are run by a *régime présidentiel* rather than the *régime d'assemblée* envisaged by certain authors of the 1968 Act.

In a sense, the strengthening of structures for academic administration has subordinated the goal of participation to the goal of university autonomy. Elected academic administrators at both university and UER levels have consolidated their influence. It is common, for example, for the university president to meet regularly with the UER directors to discuss policy matters. In the smaller provincial universities less affected by the Orientation Act, certain UER heads may serve as informal deans for sectors much resembling the former faculties. Such power on the part of academic administrators, and especially the presidents, certainly derives from the continued importance of the ministry in setting policy.[28] But administrative influence may also be reinforced by the more basic French tendency to avoid face-to-face discussions aimed at settling problems in pragmatic fashion and to appeal instead to higher authorities. Thus the representative councils often serve as arenas for ventilating grievances and debating ideological issues, but they shy away from making decisions on concrete matters, even when the central guidelines permit them to do so. Clearly, the fundamental elements of administrative style and behavior which have reinforced centralization in French academic life for nearly two centuries are not easily overcome.

At the level of the academy, the rector is now the "chancellor" of the universities in his jurisdiction. His role has been significantly reduced, although he retains supervisory authority over certain matters and he may, for "grave reasons," suspend decisions of the university council for three months pending a decision by the minister. Much more often, however, the rector helps facilitate links between lower-level administrators and the ministry. The Orientation Act provided for regional councils including academic members elected by the universities and a one-third membership of laymen. The decree formally establishing these councils (for 11 regions, each encompassing one to three academies) was issued in 1972. Although their members were elected, they have never met, due mainly to their uncertain role vis-à-vis new regional institutions of more general scope established later that year.

Paradoxically, at the national level, although most persons involved in drafting and implementing the Orientation Act favored decentralization, its implementation has reinforced ministerial control, at least in the short term. The text of the act is couched in general terms, leaving the ministry to prepare a long series of decrees, regulations, and circulars to interpret and apply it. At one point officials even had to issue "model statutes" to guide the UERs and the universities in drafting their statutes as mandated by the act, because of the alleged necessity "for the constituent assemblies to be able to proceed on the basis of texts juridically acceptable from the point of view of the central administration."[29]

In June 1974 the parts of the former Ministry of National Education responsible for higher education were split off to form the State Secretariat for the Universities—an independent ministry of higher education in all but name. So far this division in itself has not had any clear effect on policy. Although professorial influence at the center persists and may even be strengthened by the existence of a separate authority for higher education in the form of the State Secretariat, the character of academic power is changing somewhat, due to shifts in the nature of the national consultative organs. Only the Consultative Committee of the Universities has maintained its traditional influence on the appointment and career progress of academic staff. It has been marginally democratized through the creation of sections (and even subsections) for a greater number of disciplines and by the addition of a one-quarter share of elected junior staff to each section. Conservative professors still prevail, however, reinforced by the one-quarter portion still appointed by the government. Their criteria of assessment continue to be relatively narrow, stressing, for example, conventional research theses in traditional fields. Staff in new and applied or technological fields, as well as in more innovative institutions with a heavy teaching and supervisory load such as the IUTs, are still at a disadvantage under this system.

The two other major national organs are new. The professor-dominated Council of Higher Education was replaced by the National Council for Higher Education and Research (CNESER), which the authors of the Orientation Act intended as an extension of the elective, participatory principle to the national level. It includes 60 members elected by various intra-university groups and certain grandes écoles, and 30 appointed from a broad range of interest groups. The CNESER is a cumbersome organ, burdened both with minutiae—by law it must make recommendations on virtually all decisions to be taken by the ministry—and with a relatively high level of ideological controversy, since most members speak for groups with a definite political orientation.

In contrast, the second new body—the Conference of University Presidents—has become quite influential The Orientation Act did not make specific provision for such an organ but after a few informal meetings among the presidents the conference was formalized by decree in 1971. The ministry usually gives the greater weight to the recommendations of this conference than to those of the CNESER, thus reinforcing the predominance of academic administrators over the representative and participatory organs at the national level. Clearly the ministry feels better able to deal with the presidents, as managers responsible for the development of their universities, than with group spokesmen committed to representing the political stand of their constituents. The deliberations of the presidents are predominantly pragmatic, in contrast to the frequently politicized debates of the CNESER.[30]

The presidents are generally advocates of autonomy for the individual universities, and much will depend on the influence they can exert at higher levels. However, the presidents cannot necessarily count on staff and student support. In the 1971 controversy over whether to replace national academic diplomas with university diplomas (an option provided by the Orientation Act), the presidents advocated limiting national diplomas to law and medicine, leaving the individual universities to offer their own diplomas in other fields. Staff and student organizations of all political complexions argued in the CNESER for the retention of national diplomas, to ensure the continuance of uniform credentials and to minimize differences in academic status among universities and their graduates. Pressures were intense, and in the end the minister, decided to maintain the national diplomas.[31] The outcome demonstrates the continuing influence of traditionalism in academic circles of whatever political coloration. The presidents and ministry officials face much resistance when they attempt to cut the universities loose from their centralized heritage.

Another major barrier to innovation is financial. The budget for higher education as a whole has lagged behind inflation since 1970; until very recently, allocations for operating expenses were keyed to student enrollments, which expanded at a lower rate; and capital expenditure has dropped sharply.[32] These constraints have limited the universities' ability to exploit their newly granted freedoms and have thus compounded their inertia. Despite the university councils' broad authority to allocate budgetary resources and to shift vacant staff posts from one UER to another, they almost never do so; such measures would encroach on too many droits acquis. New programs initiated by individual universities—especially those leading to university diplomas—have been instituted without supplementary resources, which can only strengthen the traditional reliance on national diplomas and inhibit innovation.

The ministry has made substantial new allocations of funds only in areas that it wished actively to promote, usually by means of contractual grants. One of these areas is continuing education (*formation continue*)—a major undertaking designed to render the universities more responsive to the needs of the external world, that is, society and the economy. Following passage in July 1971 of an act promoting continuing education, the education ministry offered grants to the universities to assist them in establishing contacts with local employers and trade union branches leading to university-based training programs. All of the universities accepted grants, often at the urging of their presidents. The development of effective programs has proved extremely difficult, however. The act also required firms to set aside substantial sums for recurrent training, but distrust of the universities' alleged leftist and overly theoretical orientation has led many employers to channel the funds to training organizations under their own control. University staff, conversely, were reluctant to sacrifice their autonomy by designing courses to the specifications of private firms and meeting the practical needs of their employees.

Altogether the Orientation Act and subsequent measures have altered the structural landscape of French higher education in important ways. They have set in motion a subtle process of institutional differentiation and adaptation at both the UER and university levels. A plurality of UERs has replaced the former dual system of faculties and nonfaculty institutes and professional schools. For the most part the UERs are much smaller, more specialized, and more manageable entities than the faculties, and the possibilities for cooperation among them have increased. Among the universities, which vary significantly in size and mission, some are better suited than others to promote interdisciplinary programs or other kinds of innovations.[33] The compulsion for each of them merely to imitate the others is diminishing. Indeed, administrators at each level have an interest in promoting differentiation in order to render their institutions distinctive, and their leeway for doing so may grow if the current financial squeeze is eased.

Most importantly, this differentiation has tended to increase the professionally and technologically oriented component within the universities. Promulgated in early 1976, the controversial reform of the second cycle of studies (third and fourth years, leading to a *licence* or a masters) aimed primarily to accelerate this process. It would require the universities to revise their curricula extensively, cutting back on programs with meagre employment prospects and developing new programs in fields that offer better career opportunities. Committees composed of academics and lay persons from the relevant economic sectors were to assess the new curricula proposed by the universities prior to their final approval by the government. In protests more widespread than any since the events of May 1968, students and teachers, joined by the presidents' conference, objected vehemently to the utilitarian orientation of the reform, to the involvement of outsiders and to the failure to promise additional funds or resources for implementing the reform. Academics feared that many traditional fields of scholarship would face deterioration or extinction. In the end, the government agreed to reopen discussions on the implementation of the reform, and an uneasy calm gradually returned to the universities.[34]

Although the grandes écoles are not directly affected by these developments, the gap between them and the traditional sectors of the university may possibly be diminishing. The various professional schools—some ranked as lesser grandes écoles—which were formerly attached to the universities are now classified as UERs, and despite the special status which most of them have, they are still in a better position than previously to cooperate with the other units. The same provisions of the Orientation Act can be used to bring other grandes écoles into the universities as UERs, although this has been done in only a few cases so far.

Altogether, French higher education is moving slowly toward increased responsiveness to external societal and economic needs. It is above all in this sense that the greater pluridisciplinarity urged since 1968 is gradually being achieved. The goal of autonomy is faring still more ambiguously. Clearly, the government is not content to let the universities move at their own pace toward the reforms that it desires; indeed, governmental pressure provoked the protests of 1976. Among the majority of university presidents who endorsed the protests, a number were newly elected with support from the leftist National Union of Higher Education (SNESUP). This may indicate a shift by the presidents toward confrontation with the government and a defensive interpretation of university autonomy like that of most student and teacher associations. Most professors continue to favor unfettered scholarship in the traditional mode, while students want both unrestricted access to the universities and uniform national diplomas that guarantee employment. These traditional attitudes still constitute a significant barrier to change. Participation, the third of the main 1968 goals, has fared least well. The power of senior staff over academic careers and appointments, as well as research, remains virtually undiluted.[35] The university presidents may sometimes represent the interests of students and junior staff, but the latter are seldom effectively involved in the decision-making process.

Despite this continuing resistance to reform, developments since 1968 do provide unmistakable evidence that the French universities are not impervious to gradual, incremental change.[36] They are, at last, beginning to move away from their Napoleonic, nineteenth-century heritage.

NOTES

1. Gordon Leff, *Paris and Oxford Universities in the Thirteenth and Fourteenth Centuries: An Institutional and Intellectual History* (New York: Wiley, 1968), p. 15.

2. Roger Geiger, "Reform and Restraint in Higher Education: The French Experience, 1865–1914." Working Paper, Institution for Social and Policy Studies, Yale University, October 1975, pp. 53–57.

3. Jürgen Schriewer, *Die französischen Universitäten 1945–1968: Probleme Diskussionen-Reformen* (Bad Heilbrunn/Obb.: Verlag Julius Klinkhardt, 1972), pp. 84–88, provides an excellent brief discussion of this development. These institutes presaged the special-status units of teaching and research established under the 1968 Orientation Act.

4. See John H. Van de Graaff, "The Politics of Innovation in French Higher Education: The University Institutes of Technology," *Higher Education* 5 (May 1976):189–210.

5. John A. Armstrong, *The European Administrative Elite* (Princeton: Princeton University Press, 1973), pp. 194–99, provides a penetrating interpretation of the socialization function of the Ecole Nationale d'Administration, an elite grande école which trains many of the top civil servants. On the grandes écoles in the broad sense, see the Boulloche Report: *Les conditions de développement, de recrutement, de fonctionnement et de localisation des grandes écoles en*

France. Rapport du Groupe d'Etudes au Premier Ministre 26 Septembre 1963. (Paris: Documentation Française, 1964).

6. Robert Gilpin, *France in the Age of the Scientific State* (Princeton: Princeton University Press, 1968).

7. Ibid., 78–79; and Stanley Hoffmann, ed., *In Search of France* (Cambridge: Harvard University Press, 1963), especially Hoffmann's own essay, "Paradoxes of the French Political Community."

8. For a recent analysis, by Stanley Hoffmann among others, of the twin characteristics of centralization and fragmentation as they affect research in the social sciences, see OECD, *Social Sciences Policy: France* (Paris: Organisation for Economic Co-operation and Development, 1975), esp. pp. 184–206.

9. Gilpin, *Scientific State*, p. 79. On avoidance of face-to-face relations within local institutions, see Michel Crozier, *The Bureaucratic Phenomenon* (Chicago: University of Chicago Press, 1964), especially pp. 221–22.

10. This type of agrégation in letters and the sciences, which remains partly a qualification for elite positions in secondary education, should not be confused with the agrégation in law and medicine, which is a competition for senior university posts as *maîtres de conférences*. The doctorate (*doctorat d'Etat*, an advanced research degree roughly comparable to the German Habilitation) is an absolute prerequisite for permanent appointment to senior posts in all faculties. Law and medicine award a high number of doctorates and senior candidates must therefore pass the agrégation as an additional hurdle, whereas in letters and the sciences—especially the traditional fields—the secondary agrégation must often be passed before embarking on a doctorate.

11. For an exposition of this view, see Gilpin, *Scientific State*, pp. 101–105.

12. Georges Amestoy, *Les universités françaises*, special number of *Education et gestion* (1968), p. 332.

13. Raymond Aron, "Quelques problèmes des universités françaises," *European Journal of Sociology* 3 (1962):105.

14. Terry Nichols Clark, *Prophets and Patrons: The French University and the Emergence of the Social Sciences* (Cambridge, Mass.: Harvard University Press, 1973), p. 67.

15. Amestoy, *Universités françaises*, pp. 315–18. J. B. Piobetta, *Les institutions universitaires en France* (Paris: Presses universitaires de France), pp. 38–39.

16. Amestoy, *Universités françaises*, pp. 30–31.

17. Armin Hegelheimer, "Bildungsplanung im Rahmen der 'planification française'," *Bildung und Politik*, 3 (1967), pp. 11–12.

18. The Fourth Plan (in the early 1960s) projected that the proportion of university students in the faculties of science would rise to 42 percent by 1969; in fact it fell to 21 percent. The letters faculties, instead of declining to 26 percent as projected, enrolled 35 percent of all university students by 1969. Schriewer, *Französische Universitäten*, p. 461.

19. Amestoy, *Universités françaises*, pp. 359–75.

20. Ibid., p. 317; Piobetta, *Institutions*, p. 39.

21. The need for reforms had been increasingly recognized in the preceding decade and a number of innovations had been undertaken, especially in the curricular area, with mixed success; for these, see C. Grignon and J. C. Passeron, *Case Studies on Innovation in Higher Education: French Experience Before 1968* (Paris: Organisation for Economic Co-operation and Development, 1970). The most important discussion of reform proposals took place at a colloquium in Caen in 1966.

22. For the most complete account of the bureaucratic and legislative process leading to the act, see Jacques Fomerand, "Policy-Formulation and Change in Gaullist France: The 1968 Orientation Act of Higher Education" (Ph. D. diss., City University of New York, 1973).

23. For an account of the formation of the UERs, see Jacques de Chalendar, *Une loi pour l'université* (Paris: Desclée De Brouwer, 1970), pp. 173–80.

24. Michelle Patterson, "Conflict, Power and Structure: The Organization and Reform of the French University" (Ph.D. diss., Yale University, 1975), p. 210.

25. Chalendar, *Une loi*, pp. 83–88, and Fomerand, "Policy-Formulation," pp. 152–56, describe how the issue of the grandes écoles was dealt with.

26. Student membership in the councils of the UERs has been much lower than in the university councils, because of the application of the quorum: when fewer than 60 percent of the eligible students voted in a UER election, the students' share of seats in the UER council was reduced proportionately. Student participation was 52 percent in the first UER elections in 1969 (despite numerous calls for a boycott) but has decreased to about 25 percent since then. The student representatives in the university councils have been elected directly, by the members of the UER councils, and the quorum was not applied to them. However, an act of July 1975, although lowering the quorum to 50 percent, extended it to the university councils, much to the annoyance of student organizations.

27. Association d'étude pour l'expansion de l'enseignement supérieur, *De l'Université aux universités*. Cahiers des universités françaises, Vol. I (Paris: Armand Colin, 1971), p. 468.

28. One may expect many university presidents to assume essentially the role of "activist administrative entrepreneurs" which Tarrow has ascribed to mayors in France, who exploit a tight network of administrative relationships to get the central government to provide benefits for their communes. See Sidney Tarrow, "Local Constraints on Regional Reform: A Comparison of France and Italy," *Comparative Politics* 7 (October 1974):1–36.

29. For the model UER and university statutes (*statuts-typs*) drafted by the ministry, see Association d'étude pour l'expansion de l'enseignement supérieur, *De l'Université*, pp. 491–523; the quotation is from an introductory note on p. 491.

30. Cf. Patterson, "French University," pp. 194–203, 240–45, 248–50.

31. Ibid., pp. 224–28.

32. François Orivel, "Facts and Words: The Ambiguities of the French University System," paper presented at the Third International Conference on Higher Education, University of Lancaster, September 1–5, 1975.

33. For an interpretation stressing the obstacles to efficient cooperation created by the proliferation of UERs and universities since 1968, see OECD, *Social Sciences Policy*, pp. 196, 210.

34. For these events, see issues of *Le Monde*, especially April 15–17, 1976, and Roger L. Geiger, "The Second-Cycle Reform and the Predicament of the French University," *Paedagogica Europaea* 12, no. 1 (1977):pp. 9–22. However, even prior to the publication of the texts on the second-cycle reform (in January–February 1976), an increasing number of the regular UERs had been offering programs with a technological or professional orientation, preparing for such newly established diplomas as the masters in science and technology (*maîtrise de sciences et techniques*), offered in 30 specialties.

35. OECD, *Social Sciences Policy*, pp. 199–200.

36. Cf. Michel Crozier, *La société bloquée* (Paris: Editions du Seuil, 1970), pp. 145–63. The findings in this chapter are generally consistent with Jacques Fomerand's contention in "Policy Formulation and Change in Gaullist France: The Orientation Act of Higher Education," *Comparative Politics* 8 (October 1975):59–89, that the Orientation Act fits into a general pattern of piecemeal, incremental reform in French higher education during the past two decades, contrary to Crozier's "stalemate society" thesis. However, reforms prior to 1968 were for the most part less significant than Fomerand maintains, and change has substantially accelerated under the impact of the Faure Act.

5
SWEDEN
Dietrich Goldschmidt

Among the countries included in this study, Sweden is the smallest, with just over eight million inhabitants, and, next to Japan, the most homogeneous in ethnic, religious, and political terms. Historically, these characteristics have contributed to a marked continuity and coherence in educational policy, especially in recent years. Until the middle of the present century there were only two universities, Uppsala (founded in 1477) and Lund (1668). In the second half of the nineteenth century, other types of institutions of higher education were founded as a result of private and municipal initiative and were later taken over by the state and designated as universities. In Stockholm, for example, a college founded in 1877 was formally named a university in 1960; the college at Göteborg (1891) received this status in 1954. Umeå (1964) and Linköping (1965-70) are two recently created universities. At present there are six full-fledged universities (with three additional branch campuses), plus some fifteen more specialized institutions of higher education and professional training, of which only one is still private (the School of Economics of Stockholm).[1]

In the nineteenth century, the two Swedish universities were committed to the ideal of the liberation of the individual through pursuit of academic scholarship and research. Above all, individual professors were to be free to follow the path of knowledge wherever it led; students, too, were to be able to choose their topics of study. As there were few attempts by the state to restrict this freedom of research, teaching, and learning, the universities enjoyed an academic autonomy like that of the nineteenth-century German universities. However, unlike their German counterparts, the Swedish universities never asserted their autonomy as a matter of dogma. In Germany university-state relations were close but often tense, especially in the first half of the century, whereas in Sweden the universities were left to themselves, sharing in a broad consensus among politicians and professors about the values and goals of both polity and university. Sharp distinctions between government authority and the scholarly enterprise were unnecessary.

Until the 1950s, access to postsecondary education was governed by a traditionally differentiated system of secondary schools. A leaving certificate from the academic secondary school (the gymnasium) was required for access to higher study. In the early 1950s, some 5,000 students obtained this certificate each year, of which about 70 percent went on to higher education. As in such systems elsewhere, social status was the major determinant of access to the elite path. However, once students reached the plateau of entrance to higher education, there were no restrictions on their choice of fields, except in medicine, engineering, and certain other professional fields, in which a *numerus clausus* has existed for at least forty years. Expansion in the 1950s, although rapid enough (from 17,000 students in 1950 to 37,000 in 1960, for university-level higher education), barely foreshadowed the explosion of the 1960s, as undergraduate enrollment jumped to 118,000 in 1970 (about 30 percent in the restricted faculties). After that, however, enrollments fell off, to 108,000 in 1974.[2]

This shift from elite to mass higher education, which has occurred in all highly industrialized countries, received special impetus from a number of factors particular to Sweden. Industrialization reached Sweden relatively late; the economy remained dependent on agriculture and forestry through the end of the nineteenth century. Since then, the economic basis of society has been transformed; a people whose grandfathers were farmers now run a modern, industrialized welfare state. The proportion of the work force employed in agriculture decreased from some 20 to 25 percent in 1945 to 7 percent in 1975, The effects have been particularly far-reaching since Sweden was not set back economically by involvement in either world war. Human labor was extensively replaced by machines, causing structural changes in production, distribution, and the labor market as a whole, and in particular in the types of training and qualifications needed by the labor force. These changes in turn engendered sharp pressure for reforms to adapt vocational professional training to the new requirements.

A key factor in educational development has been Sweden's tradition of folk or popular organizations and social democracy, which has favored policies aimed at the eradication of social differences and the equalization of social opportunity. To attain equality of educational opportunity, efforts have been made since the mid-1930s to open all sectors of the system to the whole population. The Swedes have pursued this goal in evolutionary rather than revolutionary fashion. Educational reform has been achieved by pragmatic social engineering, in which experimentation, planning, implementation, and evaluation have been carried out rapidly but deliberately. This process of "rolling reform," as the Swedes themselves call it, has altered Swedish education step by step, so that the present educational system is fundamentally different from that existing prior to World War II.

Clear stages are difficult to discern, but by the 1950s—when in other countries there was only halting recognition of the need for reform—Sweden had already undertaken expansion and reform. Partly because of this early start, Swedish reforms never became as dramatic as those in, for example, France and the Federal Republic of Germany, although they have been more far-reaching than changes in other Western European countries.

The first target of the reformers was the differentiated lower secondary school. On the recommendations of a political commission which included spokesmen from various interest groups and representatives of the major parties, Parliament in 1950 unanimously endorsed the launching of a ten-year pilot program with the principle of comprehensive education throughout the period of compulsory schooling (until the age of sixteen) and authorized extensive experiments to implement the new policy.[3] By the early 1960s the way was clear for the universal adoption of the nine-year comprehensive school (*grundskola*), created by act of Parliament in 1962. The next step was extensive structural and curricular reform of upper secondary education, which was concluded in 1971. Since then, some 90 percent of the age group attend, from the tenth year on, a comprehensive *gymnasieskola,* which offers a range of vocational and academic programs or tracks (*linjer*), lasting two to four years.

Largely as a result of the reforms, the number of students starting upper secondary tracks that would qualify them for higher education rose from 7,000 in 1950 to 33,000 in 1970. (Since 1970 the number has decreased to 30,000[4], due partly to a reduction in the corresponding age cohort, and partly to economic conditions and to shifting pupil choices with the availability of more tracks at entry to the gymnasieskola.)

Swedish authorities had foreseen the need to expand tertiary education to accommodate increasing numbers. The process of policy research and of building political consensus, which had proved effective for the secondary level, was set in motion for higher education with the appointment of a commission of inquiry in 1955. Thus higher education reform began in Sweden more than a decade before student protests forced international recognition of the crisis of higher education in the late 1960s. Long before other nations, Sweden also anticipated the collision between expanding postsecondary enrollments resulting from social demand and the limited capacity of the economy to absorb trained manpower. Consequently, the primary motivation for the reforms undertaken in higher education since the 1950s has been to extend comprehensive structures from the secondary to the tertiary level and to plan enrollments according to employment needs and opportunities.

The political process of reform has been stamped by certain basic characteristics of Swedish democracy. Under the influence of the Social Democratic Labor Party (SAP), which has steadily grown in importance and has dominated the government from 1932 until 1976, the Swedes have sought to resolve even the most fundamental political and social controversies in pragmatic fashion, through extensive consultation, persuasion, and broad agreements at the national level; indeed, "compromise is traditionally considered *the* Swedish technique in politics."[5] Until the end of the 1960s, industrial relations were characterized by an almost total lack of strikes. Policy problems are often tackled initially by commissions, usually broadly representative of interest groups as well as the political parties, and their reports are formally submitted to a wide range of groups for written comments—the so-called *remiss* procedure. These elaborate consultations, which by law must take place on all major proposals by commissions or government agencies, often strongly affect the ultimate policy decisions. Within Parliament, further efforts at compromise usually take place. In such areas as schools and higher education, the bureaucracy, administered by a civil service with a high reputation for effectiveness and integrity, is responsible to the cabinet as a whole and is supervised by government-appointed boards which themselves include a wide range of interest-group representatives. In this complex system the political tone is set by the folk movements—which, with more than half the working population, traditionally include unions, and agricultural producers' and consumers' cooperatives—and by the SAP, which is closely allied with the trade unions. Yet the pressure for compromise and consensus is ever present, and most issues are resolved in a manner acceptable to the more conservative groups and parties. Not surprisingly, therefore, the non-socialist coalition government that came into office in 1976 has not deviated substantially from policies pursued by its Social Democratic predecessors. In most spheres of social and political life, Sweden can be termed a centralized consensus democracy, in which policies are decided by persuasion and broad agreement at the top.

TRADITIONAL STRUCTURES AND EARLY REFORMS

Until well into the 1950s, the internal organization of Swedish universities resembled the traditional German model, based on the autonomous authority of the individual professor as chair holder and, usually, director of an institute, which served as the basic unit of teaching and research. The government appointed the professor following a lengthy, elaborate, and public procedure, described below. Around 1950, the typical institute consisted of a single full professor as its head, one associate professor or *docent* and, in natural sciences, a small number of teaching and research assistants. The professor headed a small but strictly hierarchical unit; his power within the institute was absolute and rarely challenged; he had sole control over content and organization in his field of study at the university—a situation sometimes referred to as "professorial feudalism."

Since 1958 the staff structure has explicitly differentiated between staff with a primary commitment to research and graduate (doctoral) training (professors, associate professors, *docenter*, and research assistants), and staff whose only duty is instruction (lecturers), who are generally lower in prestige. This division corresponds to an increasing separation between basic, vocationally oriented programs and graduate studies. By the early 1970s, most institutes had expanded enormously while maintaining the hierarchical staff structure. At some places there might be up to three full professors, up to 20 associate professors, docenter, and lecturers, and 20 or more teaching assistants.[6] Only rarely do instructional staff receive formal tenure. In practice their positions were fairly secure during the expansion of the system but have become less so as enrollments decline; a considerable number of those without tenure have been dismissed.[7]

As in other Continental systems, the faculty formed the second level of organization. Originally there were the same four faculties as in Germany: philosophy (including natural sciences), theology, law, and medicine. As the system expanded, some faculties split and others were newly established; they now include humanities, social sciences, natural sciences and mathematics, technology, economics, medicine, dentistry, pharmacy, law, and theology. Each of the full-scale universities has three or more of these faculties, whereas the various specialized university-level institutions consist of a single faculty or professional field, such as technology, agriculture, business, social work, veterinary medicine, forestry, and teacher education.

Until 1964, the faculty as an administrative unit consisted of professors only and thus functioned as a collegial assembly of equals, each speaking for his discipline and his institute. From among their number the professors elected the faculty dean to serve a limited term as *primus inter pares*. The decision-making process was usually based on search for a consensus that would reconcile the various interests of the institutes federated within the faculty. The faculty was responsible for proposals for professorial appointments, examinations for the doctorate, designation of docenter (with scholarly qualifications beyond the doctorate—*docent kompetens*, analogous to the German Habilitation), and other academic matters. With the increasing regulation of basic studies and their separation from research, decision making and administration grew more difficult. In 1957, so-called education committees, consisting of the dean, three academic instructors, and three students (an assistant was added later), were formed at the faculty level. These committees were authorized to discuss "matters of curriculum planning, course outlines and textbooks and submit . . . proposals on these and other matters,"[8] to be approved by the faculty. They also became responsible for the training of researchers, in four-year doctoral programs. In retrospect, the establishment of these committees may be seen as an initial step toward coordination of university curricula, first at faculty level and later nationally.

At the university level, the highest decision-making organ was the senate (*konsistorium*), to which the deans and one additional professor from each faculty belonged. Like the faculty at Level 2, the senate was an essentially federative organ which strove for collegial, consensus-based decisions. It was the arena for deciding academic questions affecting the university as a whole. Parallel to the senate, a budget council (*drätselnämd*) handled financial affairs. Its membership—partly elected, partly ex officio—consisted solely of professors and administrative officials. The senate elected the rector, who had to be a professor of three years standing, for a four-year term. As chairman of the senate and as executive head of the university, the rector traditionally played a symbolic and ceremonial role. However, since World War II, as the universities have expanded the rector's power and influence have increased. He must assert his university's interests and serve as the faculties' channel of communication with the government, as well as mediating between them. In 1964 the budget council was dissolved and a rectoral office was created in each university, in which the rector and the chief administrative officer shared authority.[9] However, notwithstanding the rector's importance in negotiating for the university with the chancellor's office, his role diminished with the further centralization introduced from 1964 on.

The traditional Swedish system of higher education did not include administrative levels between the university and the national government. Until 1964, a national university chancellor was elected nationally by the professors and appointed by the "King in Council," that is, by the Swedish government. As a mediator between state and universities, the chancellor supervised the application of administrative regulations and the use of state funds. However, he was usually a professor and his main task, as a trusted emissary of the universities, was to represent their interests to the state. The chancellor thus played the role of a national-level rector.

Extensive centralization began during the 1950s under the leitmotiv of adapting postsecondary education to manpower requirements and providing growing numbers of students with effective professional training. A small commission on higher education was appointed in 1955, consisting of three professors, one politician, and one representative of the central authority for higher technical education. In its final report in 1963, it provided the basis for a law enacted by Parliament and an extensive set of governmental regulations promulgated in 1964 (*universitetsstadga*).

The main measure was the replacement of the hitherto dual authorities for the universities and the technical institutes by a single Office of the Chancellor of the Universities (Universitetskanslersämbetet, UKÄ). The only higher education institutions exempt from its authority were the teachers colleges, which remained under the counterpart authority for the schools, the National Board of Education (Skolöverstyrelsen, SÖ), and a few small professional schools which stayed under the corresponding government ministries. Henceforth, the chancellor was to be chosen by the government rather than elected by the universities. Since 1964 government and administration have become more and more centralized, with a distinction between the two levels at which educational policies are decided. First, the cabinet, supported by the minister of education and his officials, outlines the general policies leading to or based on fundamental legislation by Parliament; second, the two central bureaucracies, the Chancellor's Office and the Board of Education, handle administration and policy implementation. They work closely with the Ministry of Education; yet they are accountable only to the cabinet as a whole and exert considerable power of their own. Each office is overseen by governing boards that provide a direct channel of influence for nonacademic interest groups (mainly business and labor). The board of the Chancellor's Office consists of the chancellor as chairman and the only full-time member, the five directors of the faculty planning boards, and four members at large, including a student (since 1969), appointed by the government.[10]

The faculty planning boards were established in 1964 to carry out central planning for basic and advance training in each of the nine faculties, and their jurisdictions are as follows: humanities and theology; law and social sciences; medicine, dentistry, and pharmacy; mathematics and natural sciences; and technology. Each board has a part-time director and eight to twelve government-appointed members representing government, business associations, trade unions, professional organizations, and teachers and students in higher education. Spokesmen for higher education are in a minority on the planning boards; even the board directors are rarely from higher education. Because these directors are also members of the board of the Chancellor's Office, as are other nonacademic representatives, academic influence in higher education policy making at the national level has been significantly reduced. The group spokesmen help to link the Chancellor's Office and the planning boards to broad economic and political currents in Swedish public life. Consultations through the remiss procedure precede important policy decisions, and implementation generally requires acceptance by all groups, most notably trade unions, trade associations, and the National Labor Market Board. Furthermore, as a government appointee, the chancellor of the universities now represents the views of the government to the universities, rather than representing higher education to the government—as did the professor-as-chancellor during the decades before 1964.[11]

The institution of semi-independent administrative units with direct links to the key interest groups, such as the Chancellor's Office, reflects the attempt to give societal interests full consideration in the policy-making process. An organization such as the University Grants Committee in Britain is conceived very differently, as an organ of self-administration permitting the autonomous universities to represent their collective views to the government. None of the other countries discussed in this volume accords such weight to the representation of nonacademic interests in academic affairs as does Sweden.

The expansion and the reorientation of the duties of the Chancellor's Office during the 1960s marked a substantial transfer of political responsibility for university development to the national level, notwithstanding certain measures that were taken to strengthen administration at lower levels—for example, the establishment of the rectoral office within the university. Next to government and Parliament, the Chancellor's Office has decisive authority over university finances: since 1966 it has received budgetary requests directly from the faculties, rather than via the university authorities, "so that the financial needs and plans in different fields can be more effectively assessed and coordinated."[12] The national faculty planning boards submit advice on budgetary requests, and the final decision lies with the Ministry of Education and the government. Nevertheless, certain areas remain under academic control—for example, professorial appointments made by a somewhat shortened but still elaborate and largely public process, involving written evaluations and recommendations by three outside professors designated by the faculty, the faculty's recommendation, and recommendations by the Chancellor's Office, with few exceptions, the faculty's choice is appointed by the government. (Lower-level staff are proposed by the institute or the faculty and appointed by the university senate.)

The 1964 regulations also broadened the composition of the faculties. Previously, only full professors had been members; since 1964 the faculty has included all tenured research staff (full and associate professors) and the teaching lecturers with tenure, with the latter group in the majority in most cases. As a result of the inclusion of various groups with different status and divergent interests, as well as the removal of curriculum questions from their direct responsibility, the faculties have lost their character as collegial assemblies of equals and have become altogether less significant and influential.

RECENT STRUCTURAL REFORMS

Until the end of the 1960s, the government, in pursuit of the goal of reducing social distinctions and raising the general standard of living, sought to open access to higher education as wide as possible. Central authorities increased the capacity of higher education substantially. They also took successive steps to restrict the academic autonomy of the universities, thus strengthening the links between higher education and the needs of the labor market and the political system.

From 1968 on the government intensified its reform endeavors and gave them a new thrust. School leavers as well as the government recognized that the labor market would be incapable of absorbing ever-increasing numbers of higher education graduates at the levels to which they aspired. Therefore, policy makers not only continued the *numerus clausus* system, but also developed a system for regular review of institutional capacity and for central distribution of student places according to the available resources and the current condition of the labor market. In particular, the government sought to limit direct access from upper secondary school to higher education, while offering applicants of at least 25 years of age with five or more years of vocational experience (so-called 25–5 students) programs of continuing professional training or recurrent education. The traditional academic offerings of the universities and colleges are now being supplemented to meet the needs of such recurrent programs. Experimental programs have been undertaken in several fields, especially in the humanities.[13] And figures show a marked increase in the proportion of older students.[14]

The tertiary sector now includes institutions that are clearly of nonuniversity status, such as schools of art, navigation, library science, nursing, physical therapy, and other health-care professions. These institutions were previously under municipalities or a variety of central government authorities, but were outside the university chancellor's authority. Their expansion and their inclusion with the rest of higher education are intended to make them more responsive to economic needs. Everyone who has completed compulsory schooling is to have access to further vocational training. Higher education is to be organized according to the comprehensive principle already applied to lower levels of education; there is to be a coherent system of local institutional units of higher education (*högskolor*) grouped into a kind of comprehensive university, like the attempts being made by certain of the West German states. Within this system the individual institutions, and particularly the universities, are to have more autonomy than is permitted in secondary education.

This pragmatic reorganization moves away from the previous policy of response to social demand as the main determinant of the growth of higher education. The new policy strives for maximum adjustment to the need for vocational skills and to employment opportunities. Beyond this, it represents an attempted "redistribution of social values."[15] As far as possible postsecondary training is to be available to everyone and thus is to be stripped of its socially discriminatory and elitist character. New regulations governing admissions, together with the law of May 1975 and April 1977 are the latest step in this reform.

The implementation of these measures has only just begun; therefore this chapter can only summarize the most important structural trends, stemming from four important areas of reform since 1968.[16]

Curricular Reform

In 1968, Parliament adopted guidelines for curricular structure and phasing and student evaluation, as proposed by the Chancellor's Office—the so-called UKAS (*Universitetskanslerämbetets arbetsgrupp för fasta studiegangar m.m.*) guidelines, later PUKAS (UKAS and the first initial of the name of the then Minister of Education Olaf Palme).[17] They regulate and instill a vocational orientation in the so-called free faculties (humanities, theology, law, and, certain social and natural science fields) which had hitherto been untouched by such regimentation. At first there were guidelines for 17 such fields (now over 20). Although the imposition of this unified, school-like curricular system did not succeed in limiting student options to the degree originally planned, it was a clear instance of the growing powers of the national government over areas, such as curriculum, that were once the province of academics.

The education committees, which the 1964 reform had elevated to policy-making organs with independent authority over curricular matters side-by-side with the faculties, were supposed to be actively reforming the study guidelines. In fact, most of the committees seem to be fully occupied with the implementation of central directives and seeing to the practical organization of courses and examinations. They take little initiative in curricular improvements. Teaching staff have retained full authority over their class presentations and examinations, with no external supervision.

Broadening of Participation

Many students and teachers complained that the PUKAS guidelines had been imposed without adequate consultation with the colleges, and especially the institutes, which they directly affected. In response, the government proposed a number of so-called FNYS (*Försöksverksamhet med nya samarbetsformer*) models for the implementation of participation by all intra-university groups, authorizing a trial period to run to 1973, then extended to 1977.

The proposed modes applied primarily to the institutes, at the lowest level of organization. According to the 1974 university regulations, all decision-making authority remained with the professors as institute prefects. Councils consisting of the rest of the teaching staff plus two students had an advisory role, notably in curricular matters. The 1968 proposals permitted the transfer of authority to collegial organs in which senior staff and assistants together hold the same number of seats as the students, with a few representatives of the nonacademic staff. Altogether about one-third of the institutes participated in the experiment, most of them according to a single model, in which most decisions—especially curricular ones—were taken by an institute council (*institutionsstyrelse*). The legislation of 1975–77 followed this model but allotted one-third of the seats to representatives of outside professions. The council is chaired by the prefect, who retains sole authority for only a few policy areas, especially research. However, the importance of the institute council is limited. In nearly all policy areas the basic decisions are made at higher levels and the council does little more than distribute its budgetary allocation. The institutes are expected to cooperate with the education committees at faculty level and through these with the faculty planning boards of the Chanellor's Office in the practical application of the curricular guidelines at their local levels. However, the institutes rarely initiate actions beyond routine administrative implementation of the requirements. The professors have retained their prerogatives in decisions on research, and especially on the acquisition and development of supplementary resources for it.

At the next level, that of the faculty, the FNYS program applies only to the education committees and thus affects only the organization and content of the curriculum. The program permits further representation of assistants and nonacademic personnel on the education committees. The composition of the faculties themselves remains unaffected, and they continue to be exclusively responsible for such matters as the designation of docenter and appointments and research.

At the university level, the FNYS experiment applies only to the senate, providing for representation of students and nonacademic staff, the latter often through unions.

Extended participation in decision-making organs has had positive results, especially in the area of curriculum, but they should not be exaggerated. The expanded organs tend to have very limited authority or, in some cases, senior staff remain clearly dominant; either way the significance of participation is limited. The 1975 legislation analyzed below provides for expanding participation at the institute level as adopted in the FNYS experiments, a form which has proved practicable, and for maintaining participation at the other levels.

Planning of Access

The reforms in admissions procedures are indicative of the trend towards central regulation. The ad hoc Committee on Admission to Higher Education (Kompetenskommittén) was charged with preparing the reforms. Parliament approved its general proposals in 1972; detailed regulations implementing them are now in effect.[18] Admission to academic degree courses requires certain general qualifications, to be acquired either through the upper secondary school or by at least four to five years of vocational experience (and a minimum age of 25). Special qualifications may be needed for some fields. Medicine and certain other fields, most of which require laboratory facilities, still operate under a *numerus clausus*; a central admissions bureau in the Chancellor's Office regulates access on the basis of defined criteria, including school achievement, objective tests, and vocational experience. A comprehensive plan is to be prepared annually, setting maximum and minimum capacities by field and institution on the basis of available facilities and personnel. The plan will take into account both the demand for access and employment opportunities for graduates. The plan will be adopted as part of the government's budget process, after preparation by the new Office of Universities.

Counseling is provided to direct entering students away from over-crowded fields and into less crowded ones. Thus, admissions will be increasingly centrally administered even in the hitherto unrestricted fields of study. There has been little friction thus far, however, due to the lower numbers of entrants since 1968.

The U 68 Commission

The Education Commission of 1968—informally called U 68—was appointed by the education minister and charged with the development of a comprehensive plan for all institutions of postsecondary education, exclud-ing those dealing with research and research training.[19] Charged with giving special attention to questions of capacity, regional distribution, and organi-zation, the commission presented its main report in March 1973. After extensive public and parliamentary debates, legislation was enacted on May 21, 1975 which set a general frame for the future development of Swedish higher education or, more accurately, tertiary education.[20] A more detailed law of April 29, 1977 and further regulations took effect in the 1977–78 academic year. Five structural principles discussed in the following analysis are at the root of the recent reform measures:

1. All tertiary (postsecondary) institutions of education are organized as a single comprehensive structure, with the exception of agricultural schools.

2. To strengthen and extend central planning, a new National Board of Universities and Colleges (UHÄ) replaced the UKÄ. Courses of study, capacity, and resources are planned for the entire tertiary sector using the same procedure that had already been introduced for the universities on the basis of proposals by the Committee on Admission to Higher Education. All study programs—whether academic in a traditional sense or not—are to be planned not from the perspective of the scholarly disciplines, but rather with primary reference to professions. The UHÄ is to establish five planning committees responsible for training and research in the following profes-sional sectors: natural sciences and technology; law administration, econom-ics, and social work; medicine and health care; teaching; and cultural work and information.

3. To further decentralization, Sweden has been divided into six higher education regions, each containing one of the existing universities. Each region has created local higher education units. Each such unit embraces all state and local (municipal) institutions of postsecondary education in its area, including the universities. Only in the largest metropolitan areas has more than one such unit been established. Altogether the system comprises 26 local units.

4. Decentralization is intended to link both overall planning and the individual institutions as closely as possible with local economic and social

interests, and a significant part of the funds will continue to come from the municipalities. Such ties are to strengthen local and regional autonomy in higher education within the limits of overall policy set by the UHÄ. An administrative board is at the head of each region, with roughly a two-thirds membership from various public interests, including regional and local government, industry, commerce, and trade unions, and the remaining third from higher education. At the local level the proportions for the unit boards are reversed giving higher education two-thirds of the seats and other interests the rest. Group representatives participate in regional educational committees and local program committees for individual fields of study. In all boards and committees the higher education representatives are to be drawn in part from the students and the nonacademic staff.

5. Although stressing the need for links between teaching and research, the laws appear to continue the trend toward separating them. The laws reinforce the gap between discipline-oriented creative research and research training, on the one hand, and professionally oriented, school-like training for the great majority of students on the other. In practice, research can be carried out only in the universities, although a limited exchange of personnel between the universities as the central institutions in the regions and the others might counteract this concentration of research in the universities.

Many related reforms—the admission of students without traditional qualifications, the central planning of the study programs and their adaptation to the new student clientele, the separation between the faculty as a collegial body and the education committees, and the involvement of interest group representatives—are all the object of intense controversy within the universities and sometimes in the public arena.[21] Many scholars fear that the basic three-year course will develop into an entirely practical, unscientific sort of vocational training, at the expense of the educational goal of instilling a capacity for independent and critical thought. Academics also fear that the new system will not be able to train enough researchers.

From the perspective of the present study, this development is significant. Not only has the power of the professors been restricted over the years through participatory organs at institute and faculty level and through increasing state authority, but their authority over teaching, once virtually unlimited, has clearly been checked by the vertical separation between teaching and research.

CONCLUSION

To summarize the development of Swedish higher educational government over the past two and a half decades, the universities and colleges have lost more and more of their traditional autonomy as a result of reforms that began as the growth in student numbers accelerated. The national government assumed planning and administrative functions rather smoothly, for, in contrast to other Western European countries, the reformers were bolstered by consensus in the society on basic socioeconomic and educational policy and the need for systematic planning. Nonacademic laymen and representatives of outside interest groups now exert much influence in the planning and development of higher education.

Efforts to plan the development of education and professional training at a national level, and to coordinate it with the less manageable development of the labor market, have gone farther in Sweden than in the other countries covered in this volume. The recent legislation provides the clearest instance of this attempt to plan according to the labor market. The problem of linking education and the labor market is evident in a number of contradictions in Swedish policy for higher education. How can a total planning of student enrollments be reconciled with the social and educational goal of equality of opportunity? Should higher education be open to all? Universal access to universities and colleges conflicts with the needs of the labor market and the limited resources that can be made available for education. The Swedes seem to have resolved this conflict by expanding higher education into a comprehensive system of recurrent education and lifelong learning. On the one hand, there are restrictions on enrollments as a necessity of planning; on the other hand, access has been expanded, above all through the provision of further education for those who have already been employed. These are the two sides of a higher education reform that is more strongly oriented than in other nations toward the requirements of the labor market. The price is that, under the pressures of expansion and of occupation-oriented instruction, the concept of a close relationship between active research and teaching is being largely sacrificed.

These tendencies toward more vigorous state planning, administration, and supervision, with the risk of bureaucratizing education and professional training, have been accompanied by efforts to replace the traditional hierarchical structures of the university with democratic organs of governance at the lowest academic levels and—more recently—at local and regional levels. Thus the organizational answer to the political demand for democratization of the universities has been to extend participation rights of staff and students mainly at the lower levels of organization.

The acceptance and success of these attempts to expand participation will depend partly on whether there is a genuine decentralization of decision-making authority to the planned administrative regions and units.

Thus far the bureaucratic response to the expansion of higher education and to societal demands to make it more rational and efficient has fostered central planning and guidance, permitting effective state intervention. Even a semiofficial Swedish document admits dryly, with typical reserve: "Compared to the majority of university systems in Western Europe, the Swedish universities and professional colleges enjoy little autonomy in relation to the national government."[22]

NOTES

1. See National Board of Universities and Colleges (UHÄ), *Higher Education in Sweden, Some Facts and Figures* (Stockholm: UHÄ, 1977), p. 2.

2. The figures for graduate students were 14,600 in 1970 and 15,400 in 1974. Office of the Chancellor of the Swedish Universities, *Swedish Higher Education, Some Facts* (Stockholm: UKÄ, 1975), pp. 3, 14–15.

3. Rolland G. Paulston, *Educational Change in Sweden: Planning and Accepting the Comprehensive School Reforms* (New York: Teachers College Press, 1968), pp. 105–41.

4. U 68, *Higher Education: Proposals by the Swedish 1968 Educational Commission* (Stockholm: Allmänna förlaget, 1973), p. 16; and Swedish Educational Statistics 1970–74, Promemorior från SCB (Statistika centralbyrån; Central Office of Statistics), 1975:11. Stockholm, 1975.

5. Nils Stjernquist, "Sweden: Stability or Deadlock," in *Political Oppositions in Western Democracies*, ed. Robert A. Dahl (New Haven: Yale University Press, 1966), p. 139. (emphasis added)

6. The staff categories are as follows: professor—full professor (with tenure); biträdande professor—associate professor (some with tenure); docent—junior professor (after special examination similar to the German Habilitation—usually appointment up to six years); forskarassistent—research assistant (up to six years temporary appointment for Ph.D. holders); universitetslektor—senior lecturer for undergraduates (some with tenure); universitetsadjunkt—junior lecturers for undergraduates (only temporary appointment); and assistant. Personnel of first four categories are involved in research and graduate training; personnel of the next two categories are active almost exclusively in the teaching of undergraduates. The assistants do not teach on their own; they may be appointed to assist either in undergraduate training or in research. All personnel with tenure (all full professors, some associate professors, and some senior lecturers) can now participate in faculty decisions.

7. Rune Persson, "The Swedish Experience," paper presented to a conference on "*The Contemporary European University: Mass Higher Education and the Elitist Tradition*" (New York: Graduate Center, City University of New York, June 16–19, 1975), p. 4.

8. University Regulations (1956), Par. 43, quoted in Ludwig Fischer, *Die Produktion von Kopfarbeitern. Spätkapitalistische Bildungspolitik am Beispiel des schwedischen Hochschulwesens* (West Berlin: Verlag für das Studium der Arbeiterbewegung, 1974), p. 97.

9. Barbara B. Burn, *Higher Education in Nine Countries: A Comparative Study of Colleges and Universities Abroad* (New York: McGraw-Hill, 1971), p. 209.

10. The chancellor of UKÄ (now UHÄ) had been director general of the National Board of Education and undersecretary of state in the Ministry of Education before he was appointed to his position in 1969. As of 1975, the part-time directors of the five faculty planning boards, also appointed by the government, included one trade association representative, two trade union representatives, and two managers.

11. Troy Duster, *Aims and Control of the Universities: A Comparative Study of Academic Governance in Sweden and the United States* (Berkeley, Calif.: University of California, Center for Research and Development in Higher Education, 1972), pp. 65–66, 149.

12. Burn, *Higher Education*, p. 207.

13. A particularly important experiment of this kind is represented by the so-called decentralized university courses, which fit into programs of professional training and are offered by the universities in nonuniversity towns. Successful completion of a course brings a certain number of credit points toward eventual graduation. These courses are analogous in certain respects to programs offered by the University Without Walls in the United States. Cf. U 68, *Higher Education*, pp. 41–42.

14. From 1962–63 to 1971–72 the proportion of students over 24 years of age climbed from 14 percent to 30 percent. Swedish Institute, *Higher Education in Sweden* (Stockholm: January 1976), p. 1.

15. Bertil Östergren, "Planning for Change in Higher Education," mimeographed (Stockholm: Office of the Chancellor of the Swedish Universities, September 1975), p. 4.

16. To the extent that the following paragraphs go beyond summaries of the formal regulations and refer to actual practice, they are based on the report and evidence gathered by the German-Swedish Commission for the Investigation of Questions of Participation in School, Higher Education, and Research. See, for example, Bo Estmer, *Vem ska bestämma i skolan. Handbok i demokrati vid skolar och universitet* (Stockholm: Allmänna förlaget, 1973); Dietrich Goldschmidt, ed., *Demokratisierung und Mitwirkung in Schule und Hochschule. Kommissionsbericht* (Braunschweig: Westermann-Verlag, 1973); and "Participatory Democracy in Schools and Higher Education: Emerging Problems in the Federal Republic of Germany and Sweden," *Higher Education* 5 (May 1976:113–33. A more recent report is given by Dietrich Goldschmidt and Torsten Husen, "Der Übergang von der elitären zur Massenuniversität am Beispiel Schwedens," Neue Sammlung 17, no. 6 (1977):502–37. (Includes international bibliography)

17. Bengt Hansson and Erik Janson, eds., *UKAS—en utmaning. En Debattbok om universitetreformen* (Stockholm: Wahlström och Wikstrand, 1968); Marina Stenius Aschan, ed., *UKAS och samhället* (Stockholm: Aldus, 1968).

18. Kompetenskommittén, *Om behörighet och antagning till högskolan* (Stockholm: SOU Statens offentliga utredhingar; government publication 1974, no. 71).

19. The chairman of the commission was the state secretary for education in the Ministry of Education and Culture; other members were the chancellor of the universities and the general directors of the National Board of Education (SKÖ) and the National Labor Market Board. Representatives of the political parties, of the school and higher education systems, and of the employers' associations and trade unions also participated in the deliberations. For the main report see U 68, *Högskolan*, SOU 1973, No. 3 (Stockholm: Allmänna förlaget, 1973). An English summary is available in U 68, *Higher Education*, see especially pp. 7, 73, 74. A vigorous pedagogical criticism of the organizational scheme of U 68 is presented in C. Arnold Anderson, "Sweden Re-examines Higher Education: A Critique of the U 68 Report," *Comparative Education*, 10 (October 1974), pp. 167–80.

20. Regeringsproposition, *Reformering av högskoleutbildningen* (Stockholm, 1975, Regeringens proposition no. 9); Utbildningsdepartementet, "Högskolelag och andra författningar för högskolan," mimeographed (Stockholm: Ds U 1975, no. 19, December 1975); Swedish Ministry of Education and Cultural Affairs, "The Reform of Higher Education 1975," mimeographed; Bertil Ostergren, "Swedish Higher Education to be Broadened: Reform to Start in 1977," in The Swedish Institute, ed., *Current Sweden* (Stockholm, September 1975, no. 92), pp. 1–9; Bertil Ostergren, "Planning for Change in Higher Education. A Description of Interim Reports of a Swedish Study," mimeographed (Stockholm: Office of the Chancellor of the Swedish Universities, September 1975). Premfors, Rune, and Östergren, Bertil. "Systems of Higher Education: Sweden," mimeographed Stockholm: Universitet, July, 1977; to be published by International Council for Educational Development, New York); Regeringens proposition 1976/77:59: Om utbildning och forskning inom högskolan m.m. Stockholm; Ruin, Olof, "External Control and Internal Participation. Trends in the Politics and Policies of Swedish Higher Education," mimeographed (Stockholm: University of Stockholm. Department for the Study of Higher Education and Research Policy, May, 1977).

21. Vgl. Gunnar Brandell, *Skolreform och universitetskris* (Stockholm, 1969); Torsten Husén, *Universiteten och forskningen. En studie av forskningens och forskarutbildningens villkor; i multiversitetens samhålle* (Stockholm: Natur och Jultur, 1975); idem, *"Swedish University Research at the Crossroads,"* in: Minerva 14 (Winter 1976/77)4:419–46 (shortened translation of Husén 1975); Torgny T. Segerstedt, *Hotet mot den högre utbildningen* (Stockholm: Askild och Kârnekull, 1974).

22. Swedish Institute, *Higher Education in Sweden*, p. 3.

6
GREAT BRITAIN
John Van de Graaff

University government in Great Britain, as so much else in British society, is the complex product of an extended process of historical development.[1] The British university ideal and the structures of academic government owe much to the venerable tradition of Oxford and Cambridge, sometimes reinforced by the heritage associated with the five Scottish institutions founded in the fifteenth and sixteenth centuries. Yet the contemporary forms of the British university rarely go back more than a century. Indeed, apart from "Oxbridge" and the old Scottish foundations, no British university had been established before the nineteenth century, and half the present number received university status after World War II. The result is a paradoxical combination of strong adherence to tradition, both in ritual and symbol and in day-to-day practice, and of considerable de facto flexibility and adaptability.

Oxford was in existence as a university by the end of the twelfth century, and Cambridge was founded shortly thereafter, following a temporary cessation of lectures at Oxford in 1209. In the course of the fourteenth century, with royal support, they consolidated their position as national institutions monopolizing higher learning in England. At the outset their structure followed the same faculty divisions as on the Continent, but gradually the residential colleges came to predominate. With the ascendency of collegiate organization there occurred a corresponding shift in mission, from professional training to moral education—the inculcation of aristocratic, gentlemanly virtues within the framework of the established church and through a close relationship between teachers and taught. This was a mission analogous to that of the arts or philosophical faculties on the Continent, as institutions of general education, but those faculties remained preparatory and subordinate to the professional faculties at least until the eighteenth century, while in Oxbridge the professional faculties atrophied.

By the eighteenth century, Oxford and Cambridge were in a state of advanced decay. They served few outside the Anglican upper class, excluding members of all nonestablished faiths; the education they provided was of dubious standard, largely nonvocational in character and nearly completely divorced from British intellectual and scientific life. The fellows of the richly endowed colleges, who controlled their affairs, rarely taught and were often not even residents. The tradition of academic self-government, which to this day remains a crucial element in the powerful spell still exerted by Oxbridge over the rest of British university life, lay virtually dormant for many decades.[2]

The institutions founded during the nineteenth century for the most part attempted to fill the gap left unfilled by Oxbridge and to provide opportunities for higher education open to members of nonestablished religions. These university colleges, which later became the civic universities, were provincial institutions, drawing most of their students from their own regions.[3] Most were founded by local notables and, to a certain extent, responded to the requirements of industrial development by offering relatively specialized courses suited to the pursuit of middle-class careers. None of these institutions had authority to grant degrees to their students, who therefore had to sit the external examinations of the University of London, chartered in 1836 purely as an examining and degree-granting body. The new colleges therefore tended to teach the London curricula.

At the end of the nineteenth century, aside from the venerable Scottish universities, there were six full-fledged universities in Great Britain. The University of London was still no more than an examining body for the dozen or so university colleges and other institutions in London and the provinces, although it was then being reorganized to assume a teaching role in London as well, on the basis of an Act of Parliament passed in 1898. All of the other five universities were federations of colleges, in one form or another: Oxford and Cambridge, Durham (founded in 1832), Wales (1893), and Victoria (1880, centered on Manchester). The latter two institutions, each of which linked three colleges in different cities, exemplified a federal structure that many viewed as an appropriate way to upgrade the status of the remaining provincial university colleges, freeing them from the academic apron strings of London examinations while ensuring standards and avoiding too great a fragmentation. When Birmingham was chartered as a unitary university by Act of Parliament in 1900 and soon thereafter Liverpool petitioned to break loose from the Victoria federation and receive similar status, the issue of federal versus unitary structures became acute. To consider Liverpool's petition, the prime minister appointed an ad hoc committee of the Privy Council (the vestigial government body that to this day must formally recommend to the Queen the granting of a royal charter). The committee recommended the dissolution of Victoria University, thereby establishing the unitary institution as a pattern for the future. Altogether six university colleges were chartered as independent, unitary universities in the decade between 1900 and 1909.[4] Standards in these institutions were to be maintained by outside professors as external examiners, chosen so that they would have the last word and "could not be overruled by the in situ professor."[5]

Between the wars only one provincial college was elevated to university status (Reading in 1926). However, the central government steadily increased its financial support for the universities. Beginning in 1889, it appointed a series of ad hoc committees to provide grants to selected institutions, and in 1919 it established a permanent body, the University Grants Committee (UGC) which, then as now, included a majority of academic members. The UGC was placed under the Treasury, not (as is commonly supposed) to ensure greater university autonomy than would be likely under an administration also responsible for the rest of education, but because the Treasury's authority covered the entire United Kingdom whereas the (then) board of education was responsible only for England and Wales.[6] Although intended as more than a mere channel for the distribution of Treasury funds, the UGC aimed at the outset only to stimulate the universities to plan their own development more comprehensively than they would otherwise have done. In 1925, for example, it urged that each university attempt to formulate a "definite policy, in the light of which the many problems of its future development ... can be considered and decided." Among the factors to be weighed were "the general needs of the nation and the interests of university education as a whole." In 1946 the national Committee of Vice-Chancellors and Principals (CVCP) noted that the universities "will be glad to have a greater measure of guidance from the Government than until quite recent days they have been accustomed to receive." Soon afterward, the government expanded the UGC's terms of reference to include assisting in "the preparation and execution of such plans for the development of the universities as may from time to time be required in order to ensure that they are fully adequate to national needs."[7]

As World War II ended, the UGC's contribution to the universities' overall income had risen to about one-half, from the one-third that it had provided in 1920, and by 1967 the proportion was to reach nearly three-quarters of the total.[8] On its list of receiving institutions in 1946 were 16 universities, including one in Wales and four in Scotland. By 1962 six more university colleges in the provinces had been chartered as independent universities. Sussex University (chartered in 1961) initiated a series of eight entirely new foundations within six years, and between 1964 and 1967 ten technological institutions were raised to university status, most of which had been designated as colleges of advanced technology (CATs) in 1957. Two universities were formed by the fission of long-standing partnerships (Newcastle left Durham, and Dundee split from St. Andrews in Scotland). Thus there are now 42 full-fledged universities in Great Britain, including the federal University of Wales (now with five units) and eight in Scotland.[9] In the fall of 1973, there were 245,000 full-time students at these universities.[10]

In conventional parlance, the universities are termed the "autonomous sector" of higher education, due to their legal autonomy granted by royal charters. There also exists a large and diverse nonuniversity sector of higher education (called the "public sector" in Britain), for which overall policy is set by the central government but which is mainly under the day-to-day control of local (municipal or country) authorities. This nonuniversity sector has evolved rapidly since 1965, when the government declared its so-called binary policy with the aim of ending the process of promotion from nonuniversity to university status which the CATs then were just completing. Since the boundary between the two sectors of higher education was henceforth to remain sealed, the nonuniversity institutions would supposedly lack any further motivation to neglect their distinctive technological and vocational functions in the pursuit of university status. To serve as a capstone for that sector, 30 polytechnics were formed in 1969-70 from the amalgamation of more than 60 of the leading technical colleges, with the intent of concentrating nonuniversity-degree-level work in them.

Currently, nonuniversity higher education consists of two main segments: the polytechnics, which now enroll nearly half of their students for university-level degrees; and a larger number of technical and other colleges with varying proportions of students in degree-level and other advanced courses.[11] Most of the teachers colleges, which until very recently represented a substantial nonuniversity segment, are currently amalgamating with polytechnics or technical colleges.

The difficulty of characterizing the nonuniversity sector is compounded by the fact that—except for the fast-disappearing teachers colleges—it is formally considered part of further education, a vast sector that includes some 700 colleges offering varying mixtures of degree-level, advanced-level, and secondary-level work, plus several thousand evening institutes. By 1970, the number of students (both part-time and full-time) at all levels in the colleges of further education had exceeded two million.[12] Among these were 88,000 full-time students in advanced and degree-level programs. Nonuniversity higher education as a whole (including the 116,000 students then still enrolled in teachers colleges) represented just over half of the total full-time enrollment in all of higher education, a proportion that was still growing at that time.[13]

In this brief review of the historical development of British higher education, certain points are of particular significance for this study of academic government. First, British universities have traditionally been open to lay influence, to an extent surpassed only in U.S. institutions. The nineteenth-century foundations initially made little provision for participation by teaching staff, which was consonant with the relative dormancy of academic self-government in Oxbridge. Lay persons held large majorities on the governing bodies, court and council, of the new institutions and were extremely influential. Today, although lay influence has significantly diminished, lay' persons are still in a majority on the governing bodies and occasionally play a decisive role.

As lay influence declined, that of academics grew, in part through informal involvement in day-to-day affairs and in part through the influence of the many Oxbridge products who became professors at the new institutions. (As late as 1961–62, 31 percent of all university teachers were still from Oxford and Cambridge. Academics who both studied and began teaching there had very high prospects of reaching a professorship if they moved to another university.)[14] With the tradition of their own universities in mind, these scholars sought academic self-government, and by 1900 a structural pattern had been set which, although deviating from the collegiate structures at Oxbridge, was to permit steadily increasing academic control in the civic universities during the twentieth century. This pattern was first found in embryo at University College, London, which established an academic senate in 1832. However, the real landmark was the formation of an essentially modern mixture of lay and academic government at Owens College, Manchester, in 1870, which quickly became the norm.[15]

This two-tier structure—to be analyzed more fully in the following section—had, as the first tier of government, a large and inactive court and a smaller executive council, each with large lay majorities but some academic members. Court and council bore formal responsibility for all institutional affairs. The main role of the council, most of whose members were locally recruited, was to seek financial support, which came from a variety of chiefly private and even local sources at the outset. At the second tier of government was an academic senate consisting of the principal (later vice-chancellor) and the professors in charge of the various subjects, which soon were organized largely as departments. From the turn of the century on, the senates "began to acquire both formal rights and, more important, extensive customary rights of decision-making."[16] Often the appointment of a strong vice-chancellor or principal facilitated this shift of power, just as the strong American university presidents of the turn of the century effectively reduced the authority of lay boards of trustees and prepared the way for increased faculty powers.

Another manifestation of Oxbridge influence is the persistence of the British concept of the university as a community with moral education as its chief task. The ideal institution, like the Oxbridge college, is small-scale and residential, "affording close contact of teachers with taught in a shared domestic life."[17] Although nowadays, residence is more the exception than the rule, in 1966–67 more than one-third of all British students lived in colleges or other university accommodations.[18] The department is usually quite small, at least by Continental standards, and the overall student-teacher ratio has traditionally been kept at about eight to one. The graduates of each university form an organized body—a community, however diffuse, that persists and can potentially influence the development of the institution.

Because of the importance still accorded to moral education, vocational training tends to play only a secondary part in the British universities' view of their mission, although courses of a vocational and technological nature have had a place in the universities since the latter part of the nineteenth century.[19] In 1930, Abraham Flexner, impassioned advocate of the research university on German lines, was able to cite critically numerous vocationally oriented diplomas and certificate courses, such as brewing in Birmingham and automobile engineering in Bristol.[20] Yet as the universities outgrew their provincial origins, they tended to shed such lower-level courses, which could be equally well taught in the growing technical colleges. The main path to parity of esteem with Oxbridge did not lead to emphasis on professional instruction; although higher-level technology held its place within the universities, their preeminent mission remained the education of gentlemen. By and large, the universities' relations with industry have never been particularly close, even in the nineteenth-century days of lay enthusiasm for the new civic institutions. At no point have the universities contributed significantly to Britain's economic development, and this undoubtedly was a factor in the mid-1960s decision to establish the binary policy and to emphasize separate provision for professional and industrial courses in the polytechnics. The government felt that the need for such courses could probably never be fully met by the universities, due to their distinctive nonvocational tradition.

A further legacy of Oxbridge is the national character of the university system. Notwithstanding the provincial origins of the civic universities, most major steps affecting the development of the system have been taken or decided at the center. For example, the first real alternative to Oxbridge was established in London (University College), and the chartering of new universities has always been a matter for government decision. The establishment and growing strength of the UGC is also evidence of the accelerating trend toward central policy making. Clearly, however, although British universities form a genuinely national system, they have not been under state auspices to the extent that the Continental universities are.

Overall, the historical evolution of British universities, to use a phrase of Robert Berdahl's, provides numerous variations "on a typical British theme, namely the operation of forces to bring about substantial changes without causing any break in the outer fabric."[21] Academic institutions have changed gradually, with practice seldom being constrained by the letter of constitutional or statutory provisions. Pragmatic interplay between the "dignified" and the "efficient" aspects of government, as Walter Bagehot distinguished them, is as evident in the universities as in politics per se.[22] Just as the monarch and the House of Lords lend legitimacy to the actual conduct of British government through Parliament and the cabinet, so the monarch, on the advice of the Privy Council, charters universities, symbolically conferring autonomous power on the lay court and council which today they largely yield to the vice-chancellor and the academic senate as the efficient aspects of university government. In both the political and the academic realms, the dignified part of government acts as a check on the powers of the efficient part. Such a system, more than most political institutions in other countries, greatly depends on a tightly woven fabric of trust and understanding among those who bear policy-making responsibility.

LEVELS OF CONTROL

The lowest level of British university structure[23] is almost universally the department, which embraces a teaching subject or discipline in a manner analogous to the U.S. case. Based on Scottish precedent and German influence, this organization by subject developed in the new foundations of the nineteenth century. As in Germany, authority for the subject was normally entrusted to a chair-holding professor, who almost always became the head of department as more formal organization crystallized. From the outset, assistants were recruited and, increasing steadily in number, they outnumbered the professors by two or three to one by the early 1900s.[24]

Since World War II the nonprofessorial staff structure has become standardized. It now includes readers, senior lecturers, and lecturers. In 1973, professors represented 12 percent of all staff paid wholly from university funds; readers and senior lecturers, 22 percent; and lecturers, 63 percent.[25] Readers, although now paid on the same scale as senior lecturers, still tend to be appointed on the basis of their research accomplishments and enjoy somewhat more prestige than senior lecturers, who are generally promoted internally on the basis of their teaching ability; both are appointed permanently. Beginning lecturers normally serve a three-year probationary period and then receive permanent appointments.

Within the department the professorial head retains formal supremacy, although a certain proportion of headships are held by nonprofessors. Moreover, most professors serve in departments with at least one other professor. Thus, at a given time, as many as half the total number of professors may not be department heads.[26] Traditionally, the hierarchy of authority within the department has been less strict than in Germany or Italy,[27] and formal provisions for some democratization of decision making are now common. Most frequently these take the form of departmental boards including all staff and sometimes student representatives. Some boards have only advisory authority and limited scope.

As on the Continent, at the next level there is the faculty, which groups related departments. The pattern of division into faculties is comparable to that in Europe, although with somewhat greater variation from university to university. Organizationally, the decision-making body is the faculty board, which normally includes all professors, as well as the nonprofessorial heads of departments and sometimes all readers and senior lecturers. This group of ex officio members is normally augmented by representatives of the other staff, up to an equal number. Thus the board may become very large, with up to 50 or 100 members at the larger universities.

The dean of the faculty, as its executive and chairman of the faculty board, is elected by the board. Usually a professor, the dean serves a two- to three-year term in most faculties and may be supported by one or more subdeans who are often from the nonprofessorial staff. In some professional faculties, especially medicine, the dean is full-time and has permanent tenure.

Organization at the university level is complex, more so than the traditional Continental institutions, with features somewhat resembling U.S. structures. There are four main organs. The first two, court and council, form the top organizational tier. The senate forms the second tier. The vice-chancellor, as the chief academic and administrative officer of the university, links the two tiers.

In many charters, court formally retains supreme authority within the university, although its function is still largely ceremonial. It now ranges in size from 50 or so to more than 600 (as at Sheffield); the average is perhaps 250. The members include local notables and municipal officials, representatives of associations and groups of all kinds, and—from the university—representatives of graduates, staff, and (increasingly) students. Court meets annually in most cases. Its most important potential role is as a link to local informed public opinion.

The council is more important than court in the government of the university. Ordinarily much smaller than court, it has an average of 30 members. Lay members, from a similar range of groups as on court, are still in the majority on councils. However, academic membership is on the rise, from roughly 20 percent on the councils of the unreformed civic universities to the 40 percent and more granted in the charters of some of the newest universities. The council meets six to ten times a year, usually once a month in term time. Its primary domain of responsibility is finance and the planning and maintenance of the physical plant; in addition, it formally confirms staff appointments. The council does most of its work through committees, of which the most important is usually the planning committee, often formed jointly with senate. The university is linked with the outside through the lay membership of the council and its committees (as well as the vice-chancellor). Council members are likely to be useful locally—for example, in negotiating for acceptance of the university's site and construction priorities by local authorities. Sometimes laymen serve as impartial mediators on intra-university matters, as when they "chair working parties charged with the allocation of resources in an atmosphere of competition."[28]

At the university level, except for the vice-chancellor, the senate is the only governing organ that deals directly with the faculties and the departments. It bears virtually complete authority for formulating university academic policy; in this sense it is a fairly close equivalent of the German or Italian academic senate. It generally consists of all professors in the university plus nonprofessorial department heads and certain other ex officio members, as well as elected representatives of the nonprofessorial staff. Like the faculty boards, the senate can be unwieldy, ranging in size from about 50 to more than 200. The trend is toward limiting ex officio seats to a very small number, with a broader range of elected representatives, thereby increasing senate's representational character and reducing its size. Senate meets with roughly the same frequency as council and also does nearly all of its business through committees. There is often an executive or steering committee, chaired by the vice-chancellor and including the deans and various other members elected by senate, which prepares and expedites the senate's deliberations.

Perhaps the most fascinating aspect of British university government is the position of the vice-chancellor, who is denoted by charter as the "chief academic and administrative officer" but is otherwise endowed with virtually no formal powers.[29] The academic side of the vice-chancellor's role is important; although for some years there has been a tendency to recruit more often from the lay world, more than three-quarters of vice-chancellors in office in the mid-1960s came from the ranks of academics, and on the whole they behave more as academics and less as administrators than do American university presidents. The vice-chancellor is appointed by the council, often on the nomination of a council committee including senate members (or a joint senate-council committee); he must in any case have the support of both council and senate. He usually takes office in his fifties or (increasingly) his forties and serves an indefinite term, typically until retirement in his mid-sixties.[30] This length of tenure helps to make the vice-chancellor "normally the most important single figure in any university."[31]

The vice-chancellor derives his influence and authority, not from statutory provisions, but from a number of sources. First, as chairman of senate and usually of its committees, the vice-chancellor serves "very much [as] an executive chairman proposing decisions rather than someone to arbitrate between debators."[32] As chief administrator, he is at the focal point of communication within the university and, in particular, he represents the main link between senate and council. On council, he is chief spokesman for the academic viewpoint; yet at the same time he can rely on the lay members' support, since they play the main formal part in his appointment and therefore tend to regard him as their man. The very existence of council serves to bolster the vice-chancellor's meager formal powers, for he can often hold up a measure that he opposes simply by suggesting that he would find it difficult to recommend to council. However, when matters do reach committees or the full council, the academic side normally has the vice-chancellor's support and thus prevails, even in the rare cases when there is lay opposition.[33] Although less dominant than it used to be, the vice-chancellor's role in finance and the budgetary process is central; he is normally the key member of the finance committee of council. He is also responsible for the university's relations with outside institutions and groups, most notably the UGC and the CVCP.

Within the complexities of structure at the university level, the distribution of responsibility for matters of curriculum, appointments, and budget must be briefly sketched. Curriculum and examinations are largely departmental matters, although to maintain degree standards there is in each subject an external examiner, always from another university, who has the final word on examinations. Basic aspects of curriculum, such as course and degree structures, are subject to approval by faculty and senate. Normally the faculty board gives the department's proposals more searching scrutiny than does the senate, for the bulk of the board members are usually from related fields.

Professorial appointments are normally proposed by a committee of council, with an academic majority, whereas the appointment of nonprofessorial staff is more typically handled by a senate committee, on which the department head will have a powerful voice, and with council playing at most a confirmatory role.

The budgetary process falls into two parts.[34] First, the departments make proposals in preparation for the submission made by the university to the UGC every five years. These proposals are reviewed at faculty level and are then examined by the responsible university officers, often including a senate committee; final approval is given, usually routinely, by council and its finance committee. Once the size of the UGC's grant is known, the reverse process takes place, with the disposable funds apportioned by council between nonacademic and academic purposes, and the academic portion then divided by senate between general services and the departments as the lowest level units. The role of those members of the university with the greatest administrative responsibility—the professorial department heads, the deans, and above all the vice-chancellor and other senior officials—tends to be even greater in financial matters than in academic affairs generally.

Lord Ashby has provided a vivid interpretation of this policy-making process:

> Academic business . . . flows from below upwards. It originates in departments or faculty boards; it ascends as recommendations to the senate. The senate may hold it up or refer it back; only rarely would the senate change it. . . . Finally (there may be several other steps) it comes to the governing body, the council, as a recommendation to be approved. The council, like the senate, may hold it up or refer it back; it would be a grave breach of convention for the council to change it.[35]

Ashby sees such an upward flow of academic business as the most desirable "technique for working almost any form of [university] constitution."[36] It may indeed by an accurate description of the decision-making process in British universities much of the time, but it has its negative side. Indeed, one administrator criticized the "haphazard distribution" of his senate's policy-making attention in terms that put Ashby's in quite a different light: ". . . in its progress up the ladder, from department to faculty board to senate to council, a proposal becomes a rubber stamp without at any point being an effective decision—and so responsibility is lost between the rungs of the ladder."[37]

A more precise assessment of the relative power of the different levels would be that—on academic matters at least—decisions are made usually in departments and sometimes in senate, with the faculty serving "essentially [as] an intermediary body."[38] Although the power of senate over lower levels is limited, the potential influence of the vice-chancellor must always be reckoned with. Therefore, organization at the university level in Britain must be classified as somewhat more hierarchical than the traditional Continental systems. Altogether the triad of senate, council, and vice-chancellor possesses a distinct capacity for aggregating, coordinating, and unifying policies for the university as a whole. Indeed, substantial measures such as the founding of new departments, must be handled primarily at that level, often by a long-term planning committee.

Insofar as traditional Continental systems—especially those of Germany and Italy—permit any concentration of power above the institute or the individual professor but within the university, it is primarily at the faculty level. The universitywide academic senates are weak or even virtually nonexistent, as in France. However, on the Continent, the state provides at least as great a force for uniformity and coordination as does the relatively strong university level in Britain, so that in practice the differences may not be very great. Nevertheless, academic involvement in policy making is certainly higher in Britain, for the large senates typically include all professors and a substantial number of nonprofessorial staff, and the influence of the vice-chancellor as chief academic officer promotes a certain degree of unity and coherence. More than "any other individual within the university," he bears "an unmistakable responsibility to speak for and think about the university as a whole."[39] In much of his work, the vice-chancellor relies on support from a number of relatively senior and experienced academics, including the deans. The fragmentation among departments, as small hierarchical units at the lowest level, is thereby to some extent overcome at the university level by informal reduction of the large oligarchy of professorial "barons" to a small one operating in league with the vice-chancellor on senate, council, and their committees.[40]

Before turning to the national level, attention can be given briefly to the two federal universities at Level 4—Wales and London—left over from the period around 1900, when it appeared that federal rather than unitary universities might become the dominant pattern in Britain.[41] The constituent units of Wales have virtually complete autonomy and are so widely scattered that they hardly comprise even an informal system. London, with some 44 units and 31,500 full-time students in 1968, is more significant from the perspective of this book. Its role as an examining body for institutions in Britain and overseas is diminishing, although it still had nearly 34,000 external students in 1968. London's court (equivalent to council elsewhere) amounts to a counterpart (for London) of the UGC, distributing funds among the units. Moreover, the university has established "a very extensive system of service and specialist support for its autonomous units" of a sort that may well be needed elsewhere as more cities and metropolitan regions acquire greater numbers of university-status institutions.[42]

A regional level of university government does not exist in Britain.[43] Nationally, power is shared by the Department of Education and Science (DES, formerly the Ministry of Education) and the UGC, although the autonomous Research Councils (under the DES) allocate the bulk of support for research in universities and other institutions. The UGC, which was transferred from the Treasury to the DES in 1964, traditionally serves as a buffer between government and the universities, helping to maintain the latter's autonomy. It consists of some 20 members, of whom three-quarters are from universities and the rest from other sectors of education and from industry, in roughly equal portions. Members serve overlapping terms of five years, sometimes renewed, and are appointed by the government, after consultation with the chairman but often without the prior knowledge of the current members. All are part-time, except for the full-time chairman, and serve in their personal capacities, not as delegates of the group or institution from which they come. Significantly, service on the UGC is probably the single most common path to a vice-chancellorship.

The UGC's main function is to distribute central government funds for recurrent and capital expenditures to the universities. Beyond that, it provides advice and guidance to universities and government alike on all aspects of policy. Thus it has served as the key instrument, although a subtle one, for university planning in Great Britain since its formal establishment in 1919. In the late 1950s, for example, the UGC played a crucial role in foreseeing the rise of students numbers that was likely to come in the 1960s, in getting the government to raise its projections, and in laying the groundwork for the new foundations of the 1960s.[44] Customarily, the UGC makes its grants by quinquennium. Thus every five years, usually in conjunction with visitations by the UGC, the universities must go through the process of assessing their budgetary needs and deciding how much to ask for. On the basis of the universities' proposals, the UGC presents a detailed submission to the DES and receives its five-year allocation as a lump sum. The UGC then apportions this among the universities, ostensibly as it sees fit, although since relations between the UGC and the DES are confidential, it is difficult to know to what extent the latter may express its preferences, and the Treasury, as provider of the funds, may also play a role.

The universities receive their grants as lump sums. In principle they have been free to use grant funds as they wish. However, for some time the UGC has offered funds earmarked for particular fields that it wished to support. In distributing the quinquennial grant for 1967-72, the UGC issued for the first time a "Memorandum of General Guidance,"[45] together with specific letters to each university informing them (for example) which of their proposed projects had been taken into account in making the grant. The universities will want to be on firmer ground than ever if they deviate from the UGC's expectations. In Lord Annan's opinion, the UGC is in the process of "becoming a ministerial sub-department, though without direct ministerial control. . . . The trend of the times is transforming it into a watchdog trained to bark at what were once its masters."[46]

The UGC is responsible only for the universities; nonuniversity higher education is under a complex blend of central and local government control. The government's current policy for that sector and, more than ever, for higher education as a whole, is so recent that it will be dealt with in the final section.

Certain major interest groups, above all the CVCP, and secondarily the Association of University Teachers (AUT), and the National Union of Students (NUS), increasingly vie for influence with the UGC and the government.[47] Until recently, however, the immense prestige of the UGC as a neutral advocate of the universities' views rendered advocacy by other groups relatively ineffective. The bulk of the universities' relationships with the government still run through the UGC, and government-UGC contacts are confidential, so that groups find it difficult to intervene. Links between the UGC and the vice-chancellors are close, doubtless facilitated by the fact that the academic members of the UGC belong to the elite of their universities. Moreover, as already noted, former UGC members often become vice-chancellors.

STRUCTURAL EVOLUTION AND POLICY TRANSFORMATION

The past decade has witnessed an acceleration of the kinds of intra-university structural changes noted in the preceding section—above all in the direction of broader participation in academic government. Despite the large cumulative effect of these changes, they have occurred gradually and pragmatically, in characteristically British fashion, with the letter of statutory instruments lagging behind actual developments.

Greater internal democratization of academic authority has been common in both the old and the new universities and represents, in a sense, an extension of the shift from lay to academic control noted above. Although the charters of the early twentieth century reserved academic participation in government almost exclusively to professors, even when they were already outnumbered by other staff,[48] democratization of government proceeded gradually as nonprofessorial staff were included first on committees and then on the parent organs. Nationally, the AUT, whose membership included an increasing majority of nonprofessorial staff, exerted the main pressure for such participation, beginning just after the First World War. Today nonprofessorial representation, although limited overall, tends to be strongest at the faculty level, where the number of nonprofessorial staff often approaches half of the total membership. At university level, many of the new charters deprive professors of their ex officio seats on senate, to make it a smaller and presumably more efficient body. Within most departments, provisions for collective decision making now exist, often spurred by senate recommendations. Arrangements vary greatly, however; "a-constitutional and hierarchical departments" persist.[49] Reducing hierarchical authority within the universities is a complex task, and changes at one level must be complemented by changes at another. In particular, the voice of nonprofessorial staff members at university and faculty level appears to be most effective when they also have a say within their departments.

Demands by students for participation are much more recent than those of the nonprofessorial staff, and they intensified sharply after the mid-1960s. Most universities met the pressure by granting student membership on committees, whether specially established staff-student bodies or regular committees of senate or council. Such moderate concessions, which had already served as the initial response to nonprofessorial demands for participation over many years, usually satisfied a majority of the students, isolating the radical leaders and thus often defusing the agitation. By now, most councils and many senates have student members. In notable contrast to Germany, nonprofessorial staff did not provide much support for the students, precisely because their own position relative to the professors had substantially improved over time. Altogether, as one observer noted, "manifestations of student protest in Britain have been short in duration, limited in scope and size, and restrained in action," relating this partly to the difficulty British protesters had in linking "wider political problems to the more local questions of university development. . . . It is characteristic of the British situation that the possibility of establishing such global-local relationships has been limited."[50] In light of the evolutionary and pragmatic character of British political culture, this is not surprising.

So far, a distinct although modest rise in the power of nonprofessorial staff and students has been achieved, at substantial cost to the power of professors. The position of laymen and administrators is less clear. As the majority group on council, laymen collectively have clearly lost power. Yet there is as much scope for influence on the part of individual laymen as ever, and perhaps more, for the growing complexity of the nonacademic side of university affairs inevitably entails more frequent needs for expert outside advice.[51] For the same reasons, the influence of specialized, full-time university administrators is probably growing. They have always played a more important part in British universities than on the Continent, where many administrative tasks were assumed by civil servants directly responsible to their governments. Yet skepticism regarding the role of administrators is widespread, and there appears to be little inclination to expand their function to anything like the U.S. pattern. Generally the traditional system of government by vice-chancellors supported by amateur professorial oligarchies persists, although these elites must take ever-increasing account of the desires of other groups within the university.

Although the new universities were in large part intended as sources of innovation, their governing structures are hardly novel. They conform to the evolutionary pattern just outlined and have made little independent contribution to it. "On the whole," noted the UGC as early as 1964, "we should have welcomed in the statutes of the new universities some greater changes in the system of university government."[52] The most interesting changes in the new universities are below the university level. The new structures appear in some cases to have established effective nuclei of authority at Level 2—a significant departure from the traditional constellation of weak faculties and strong departments. Schools or boards of studies have replaced faculties and departments, to foster interdisciplinary teaching across traditional lines. In theory, such schools assume some or all of the authority that traditionally rested with the department and its head, further tempering the traditional subordination of junior staff to a professor. However, such changes have often had only a limited effect. Where schools are large, department-like particularisms tend to develop within them, either informally or formally, as in Lancaster, where "the Boards of Studies are as much federations of sovereign Departments as are traditional Faculties."[53] Where the units are relatively small, they differ little from large departments.

The major innovation in this period was the Open University, which began its first courses in 1971 with 25,000 students. Structurally it is truly a national-level institution, under the direct authority of the DES rather than the UGC.[54] Thus its rate of expansion depends entirely on the budgetary allocation provided by the DES and the Treasury. Although the Open University admits all applicants largely on a first-come, first-served basis, it confers degrees that are fully up to British standard, guaranteed partly by the familiar device of the external examiner.

In 1962 the Privy Council, which must approve royal charters, prepared a model charter to guide the numerous bodies then in the process of drafting charters for new foundations.[55] The model was a vague and cautious document that retained much that was conventional and traditional. It did, however, provide for up to one-third of senate to consist of elected nonprofessorial staff (a substantial proportion at that time). The model charter was the closest the British have come to anything remotely resembling the comprehensive legislation on university structure that has been enacted in France, Sweden, and Germany. In 1966 the Privy Council, evidently on DES advice, took a stand on student involvement. Although not going as far as the NUS would have liked, the Privy Council gave its blessing to joint staff-student committees of the sort that were to become common over the next three years.[56]

At the national level, the government has taken a series of policy decisions for higher education as a whole which are affecting its development in an abrupt manner. These decisions have established a clear "parity of governmental esteem" for the nonuniversity sector, headed by the polytechnics, thereby diminishing the universities' preeminence within higher education and rendering their traditional status as the autonomous sector effectively obsolete.

The quantitative growth of student enrollments which took place in the 1960s has been associated with the Robbins Committee, which reported in 1963, and its guiding principle "that courses of higher education should be available for all those who are qualified by ability and attainment to pursue them and who wish to do so."[57] That principle was immediately accepted by the Conservative government of the day and succeeding governments have held to it. Yet the UGC and the education ministry had foreseen that expansion and had been preparing for it since the end of the 1950s; the Robbins Committee's main function was to legitimize it.

Otherwise, "the real significance of the Robbins Report is that it has been systematically repudiated since 1964, by Conservative as well as Labour Governments."[58] Robbins recommended a ministry for science and the universities, separate from a ministry for education, to ensure their independence; instead, the government created the all-embracing Department of Education and Science, and placed the UGC under it. Later, the universities' financial accounts were opened to the Public Accounts Committee of Parliament and the Comptroller and Auditor General. Although the CATs were promoted to full university status as planned, no further CATs were designated for promotion in the coming decade as Robbins proposed; rather, the DES created 30 polytechnics to head the nonuniversity sector and barred them from ever attaining university status. Although the Robbins Committee recommended the establishment of a validating body to monitor the conversion of the future CATs into universities, the DES created such a body, the Council for National Academic Awards (CNAA), for the far-reaching purpose of validating degree courses to be given independently by the polytechnics.[59] Rather than absorbing the teachers colleges into the universities, as Robbins proposed, the DES decided to merge them with the polytechnics, or other university institutions, to form the basis for two-year liberal arts courses leading to a newly created Diploma of Higher Education (Dip.H.E.). The 1974 Houghton Report awarded the teaching staff in polytechnics salary scales virtually equivalent to those in universities.[60] Altogether, the DES "has deliberately shrunk [the universities'] position within the system,"[61] while consolidating and substantially strengthening the nonuniversity sector; some teachers colleges have been closed. Moreover, after inflation destroyed the UGC's grant to the universities for the 1972-77 quinquennium, the entire system of quinquennial block grants has been abandoned, with no prospect of its restoration.

The polytechnics have been controversial ever since the first ones were formally designated in 1968. They were intended to strengthen and concentrate the further education tradition by providing both degree-level and diploma-level programs, largely with a vocational orientation, to full-time and part-time day and evening students. Critics charge, however, that the polytechnics are in fact neglecting their lower-level courses and part-time students, thereby diminishing opportunities for older and working-class students, in just the sort of "academic drift" or quest for higher academic status the bar to their promotion as universities was intended to prevent.[62] By the fall of 1975, although growing steadily in most areas, the polytechnics were having trouble recruiting students in some of their degree courses, mainly in science and technology, thereby adding to the surplus of unfilled places already existing in those fields in the universities.[63]

Such duplication of provision can only add to growing doubts about the government's policy for higher education. The driving force for the various measures—incremental in themselves but adding up to sweeping changes in overall structure—appears to have come largely from civil servants within the DES.[64]

As the full import of its measures has become apparent, the DES has been increasingly criticized for excessive secrecy and lack of consultation. A group of OECD examiners, though praising the DES for the quality of its planning techniques, sharply critized its limited consultation with interested groups and its reluctance to make public the data on which its policies were based. The examiners linked these tendencies, at least by implication, to the powerful role of the permanent civil servants within the DES, stressing "the momentum of thought and action within a Department composed of career officials who have long known one another, who have the same training and prospects, and who work within a common tradition and point of view."[65]

This is the negative side of the British reliance on policy making through close informal interaction among cohesive communities of elites. Such a process depends greatly on a high degree of trust and mutual understanding among the persons involved.[66] The UGC and the key vice-chancellors could easily protect the interests of the universities as long as such institutions were in favor with the Treasury and the DES. But as the universities have recently fallen from grace, their defenders are weakened; the UGC is left to dole out an ever-decreasing share of the total allocation for higher education and has no higher authority to appeal to. It now seems clear that the government has the power to alter the underpinnings of higher education in Britain—conventions and informal understandings—without warning.

NOTES

1. As used in this chapter, the terms Great Britain and British refer to England, Wales, and Scotland, although often predominantly referring to England.

2. For an overview of the history of university government, see Graeme C. Moodie and Rowland Eustace, *Power and Authority in British Universities* (Montreal: McGill—Queen's University Press, 1974), pp. 25–44, and Rowland Eustace, "The Origins of Self-Government of

University Staffs," paper prepared for the Annual Conference of the British Sociological Association, 1970.

3. A. H. Halsey and Martin Trow, *The British Academics* (London: Faber and Faber, 1971), p. 40; in 1908 between 73 and 87 percent of the students at four civic universities came from within 30 miles; even at University College, London, 66 percent did so.

4. These events are recounted in detail by Eric Ashby and Mary Anderson, *Portrait of Haldane at Work on Education* (London: Macmillan, 1974), pp. 60–74.

5. Ibid., p. 64. London University can be considered as a special case of the external examiner system, and it continued to serve as an examining institution for higher education institutions in Britain and (increasingly) overseas.

6. Ibid., pp. 150–52.

7. The various passages are cited in Robert O. Berdahl, *British Universities and the State* (Berkeley: University of California Press, 1959), pp. 60, 61, 76.

8. Halsey and Trow, *British Academics,* p. 63.

9. Northern Ireland possesses the Queen's University of Belfast and the new University of Ulster. The UGC's grants list included a small number of other institutions without full university status.

10. University Grants Committee, *Annual Survey: Academic Year 1973–74* (London: H.M.S.O., 1975), p. 6.

11. It is difficult to define the lower boundary of nonuniversity higher education precisely, because technical colleges enroll greatly varying proportions of students in courses preparing for degrees or for other advanced level diplomas and certificates (mainly Higher National Diplomas and Certificates); technical colleges which are considered as part of higher education enroll a substantial proportion of students in such advanced courses, which are broadly defined as higher than the Advanced Level of the General Certificate of Education (GCE A-Level), qualifying for university. For a description of the various types of advanced work, see Leonard M. Cantor and I. Francis Roberts, *Further Education in England and Wales* (London: Routledge & Kegan Paul, 1969), pp. 46–55.

12. Further education below higher education includes students enrolled for courses at a level roughly equivalent to secondary education (GCE A-Level), preparing for such qualifications as Ordinary National Diplomas and Certificates; for a description of the various types, see Cantor and Roberts, *Further Education,* pp. 55–73. The boundary between nonuniversity higher education and the rest of further education is fuzzy in the extreme, and the problem of compiling statistics is immensely complicated because many colleges offer degree, advanced, and nonadvanced courses side by side, for full-time (including sandwich) students, and day and evening part-time students as well.

13. Cf. John Pratt and Tyrrell Burgess, *Polytechnics: A Report* (London: Pitman Publishing, 1974), p. 55. The relative development of the two main sectors is currently somewhat distorted by the amalgamation of the teachers colleges into the rest of nonuniversity higher education, which is associated with a sharp cutback in the number of student teachers in training and the closing of some teachers colleges. But in the longer term it is certain that nonuniversity enrollments will grow faster than those in universities.

14. The figures are from the survey commissioned by the Robbins Committee and are cited in Halsey and Trow, *British Academics,* pp. 224–26. In a 1968 mail survey (with a response rate of 68 percent), reported in Harold Perkin, *Key Profession: The History of the Association of University Teachers* (London: Routledge & Kegan Paul, 1969), pp. 238 and 260, 29.5 percent of the respondents recruited to university teaching since 1960 had attended Oxford or Cambridge—a lower proportion than older cohorts, but still strikingly high.

15. Moodie and Eustace, *British Universities,* pp. 29–30.

16. Ibid., p. 31.

17. Halsey and Trow, *British Academics,* p. 67.

18. University Grants Committee, *University Development 1962–1967* (London: H.M.S.O., 1968), p. 202.

19. Eric Ashby, *Technology and the Academics: An Essay on Universities and the Scientific Revolution* (London: Macmillan, 1963), pp. 55–64.

20. Altogether, Flexner did give the British universities relatively high marks on the German standard, observing that the former had "not run wild, as have our American institutions" and that degree-level work was "fairly" well protected from "excrescences" of technical training such as those cited in the text; Abraham Flexner, *Universities: American, English, German* (New York: Teachers College Press, 1967), pp. 229–332.

21. Berdahl, *British Universities,* pp. 132–33; the responsibility for this particular use of the phrase belongs to the author of this chapter.

22. Walter Bagehot, *The English Constitution* (New York: Doubleday, n.d.).

23. The author has relied heavily on Moodie and Eustace, *British Universities,* in the following discussion of levels of control, especially for internal university government. Other useful recent works on university organization are Hugh Livingstone, *The University: An Organizational Analysis* (Glasgow: Blackie, 1974), from a sociological perspective; and J. Fielden, G. Lockwood, and R. A. Nind, *Planning and Management in Universities: A Study of British Universities* (London: Chatto & Windus, 1973), intended as a practical handbook on university administration.

24. See the illustrative figures provided in Moodie and Eustace, *British Universities,* pp. 38–39.

25. University Grants Committee, *Annual Survey 1973–74,* p. 6.

26. According to figures from the Robbins Report cited by Halsey and Trow, *British Academics,* pp. 375–76, in 1961–62 80 percent of professors were department heads (a figure that has certainly decreased sharply since) and 26 percent of departments were headed by nonprofessors (a figure that may have declined, as the top men in professorless departments were given professorships).

27. An early postwar report by British academics visiting German universities provides some comparative insight into relative degrees of hierarchy; they were negatively impressed by "the domination exercised by a small number of senior professors," who "too often hold fast to these authoritarian controls." It may be concluded that British dons were (or at least viewed themselves as) considerably less authoritarian than their German colleagues. See "The Universities in the British Zone of Germany," Report of the Delegation of the Association of University Teachers, *University Review* 19 (May 1947):210, 212.

28. Fielden *et al., Planning,* p. 67.

29. This and the following paragraph are especially indebted to Moodie and Eustace, *British Universities,* pp. 126–53, passim. The "administrative" aspect of the vice-chancellor's role was added to charters after World War II.

30. The federal and collegiate universities (London, Wales, Oxford, Cambridge) all have rotating vice-chancellors. Fielden et al., *Planning* (p. 52) observes that the twenty or more years which a vice-chancellor appointed in his forties may expect to spend in office (assuming he does not resign) may be too long a period, but they see no alternative to unlimited tenure if the vice-chancellor is to have sufficient power to exercise leadership. However, a recent report on the structure of the University of Kent recommended a limited ten-year term for the vice-chancellor *(Times Higher Education Supplement,* April 30, 1976).

31. Moodie and Eustace, *British Universities,* p. 129.

32. Moodie and Eustace, *Power and Authority,* pp. 132–33; the quotation is cited there from Jack Straw, *Students Today* (Young Fabian Pamphlet No. 17, 1968), p. 24.

33. One of the very few cases of exaggerated lay influence—and certainly the most notorious—was dramatized by events at the University of Warwick in 1970; see E. P. Thompson, ed., *Warwick University Ltd.: Industry, Management and the Universities* (Baltimore: Penguin, 1970), as well as the more dispassionate analysis in Moodie and Eustace, *British Universities,* pp. 234–41.

34. Moodie and Eustace, *British Universities,* pp. 173, 176.

35. Eric Ashby and Mary Anderson, *Universities: British, Indian, African* (Cambridge, Mass.: Harvard University Press, 1966), p. 303.

36. Ashby, *Technology,* p. 108.

37. From an internal memo by a university registrar, cited by Moodie and Eustace, *British Universities,* p. 77.

38. Moodie and Eustace, *British Universities*, p. 67.

39. Ibid., p. 146.

40. Halsey and Trow, *British Academics*, p. 111, note that expansion without reform of governing structures "has had the unintended consequences of producing both a professorial oligarchy and Senates so unwieldy as to give rise on the one hand to smaller circles of power within the Senate and fragmentation of power to 'barons' who run departments." In their survey of academic staff, 77 percent of the respondents agreed with the statement: "A serious disadvantage of Redbrick universities is that all too often they are run by a professorial oligarchy" (p. 377).

41. Oxford and Cambridge, of course, are also federally structured in the sense that they consist of constituent colleges. However, they are certainly more unitary and less dispersed than either Wales or London.

42. Moodie and Eustace, *British Universities*, pp. 49–50.

43. The government's White Paper on devolution of control to Wales and Scotland, published in November 1975, envisages their universities as continuing under the central UGC. There have been proposals for regional councils within England (for example by the Council of Local Education Authorities in September 1975, for further education only), but they appear to have little prospect of realization.

44. Harold Perkin, "University Planning in Britain in the 1960's," *Higher Education* 1 (February 1972):111–19.

45. The text of the memorandum is in University Grants Committee, *University Development*, pp. 220–26.

46. Noel Annan, "The Reform of Higher Education," *Political Quarterly* 38 (July–September 1967), p. 243.

47. The NUS and the AUT play an adversary role; the latter, for example, was recognized by the government as a full-fledged partner in salary negotiations for university staff only in 1970. In 1976, spurred by the enforced austerity of recent years, the AUT membership voted to join the national Trades Union Congress.

48. This followed the pattern established by Bryce's statutes for Manchester in 1870, when the teaching body still consisted mainly of professors. But by the early 1900s, as the charters of the first civic universities were drawn up, professors were already in a minority of less than one in three, as Moodie and Eustace point out (*British Universities*, pp. 38–39). The original oligarchical pattern persisted long after its intention was obsolete.

49. Bruce R. Williams, "University Values and University Organization," *Minerva* 10 (April 1972), p. 274.

50. Colin Crouch, "Britain," in *Students, University and Society: A Comparative Sociological Review*, ed. Margaret Scotford Archer (London: Heinemann, 1972), p. 197.

51. Cf. Fielden et al., *Planning*, pp. 53–54, 67–69. "If the earlier power and authority of the Council as a body has diminished, or is now shared with the Senate, the role of individual lay members is probably increasing in importance. . . . The contribution they can now make need not be restricted exclusively to membership of the Council or its committees" (p. 67).

52. This paragraph is based on H. J. Perkin, *New Universities in the United Kingdom* (Paris: Organisation for Economic Co-operation and Development, 1969), pp. 139–50. The UGC is cited on p. 142.

53. Perkin, *New Universities*, p. 147.

54. For a detailed account of the politics of founding the Open University and its governmental structure, see Walter Perry, *The Open University: History and Evaluation of a Dynamic Institution* (San Francisco: Jossey-Bass, 1977), pp. 1–30, 212–42.

55. Eustace, "Origins of Self-Government," pp. 30–31 (note 2).

56. Eric Ashby and Mary Anderson, *The Rise of The Student Estate in Britain* (London: Macmillan, 1970), pp. 109–10; the occasion was the approval of charters for the upgraded CATs.

57. *Higher Education.* Report of the Committee appointed by the Prime Minister under the chairmanship of Lord Robbins, 1961–63 (London: HMSO, 1963), p. 8.

58. Brian MacArthur, *Beyond 1980: The Evolution of British Higher Education* (New York: International Council for Educational Development, 1975), p. 8.

59. For a general account of the CNAA, see Michael Lane, *Design for Degrees: New Degree Courses under the CNAA—1964–1974* (London: Macmillan, 1975). A unique recent foundation, independent of any government sponsorship, is the University College of Buckingham, with Max Beloff as principal. However, its innovative two-year B.A. courses have had difficulty in getting CNAA validation.

60. *Report of the Committee of Inquiry into the Pay of Non-University Teachers* (London: HMSO, 1974).

61. MacArthur, *Beyond 1980,* p. 10.

62. Pratt and Burgess, *Polytechnics,* are the best-known proponents of this critique; their volume includes the basic documents setting forth the government's policy for the polytechnics. A recent study largely confirming their analysis is Lex Donaldson, *Policy and the Polytechnics: Pluralistic Drift in Higher Education* (Farnborough: Saxon House, 1975).

63. *Times Higher Education Supplement,* November 14, 1975.

64. Anthony Crosland, who took over the DES soon after the Labour government came to power in 1964, has revealingly confessed that at the time of his April 1965 speech proclaiming the binary policy—the absolute division between university and nonuniversity sectors—he did not yet fully understand its ramifications, but yielded to the desire of his civil servants "to get the policy on the record as soon as possible." Maurice Kogan, Edward Boyle, and Anthony Crosland, *The Politics of Education* (Harmondsworth: Penguin, 1971), pp. 193–94.

65. OECD, *Reviews of National Policies For Education: Educational Development Strategy in England and Wales* (Paris: Organisation for Economic Co-operation and Development, 1975), p. 29. For a more specific and bitter critique, see J. R. Lukes, "Power and Policy at the DES: A Case Study," *Universities Quarterly* 29 (Spring 1975):133–65. The OECD Report provoked Parliament to establish a select committee to look into the structure and procedures of the DES.

66. Hugh Heclo and Aaron Wildavsky, *The Private Government of Public Money: Community and Policy inside British Politics* (Berkeley: University of California Press, 1974). The concepts of community and trust are among the keystones of their analysis.

7

UNITED STATES
Burton R. Clark

Higher education in the United States developed under conditions vastly different from those of the Continent and Britain. Beginning with Harvard (1636), William and Mary (1693), and Yale (1701), the early institutions were established in a sparsely populated colonial territory devoid of old cities, medieval heritage, and substantial resources. They were tiny colleges, not universities, originating a form known today as the liberal arts college. Their form came from England, where clusters of colleges composed Oxford and Cambridge, but the distinctive American pattern was to become the single college operating in isolation. The colleges were started by religious groups—Congregationalists, Presbyterians, Baptists—as chartered corporations, a form also borrowed from the home country, and were placed under the control of laymen, managers who were drawn from outside academic life and from outside governmental authority but from within the founding group.[1] The control device thereby established was the board of trustees, a form that was later used even in public institutions, where the trustees were to represent "the public interest." The trustees hired a president and a few tutors to compose a small faculty. Organization therefore came about from the top down, with the parental external group establishing a superior body—the board of trustees—that, having all powers, then delegated authority as it pleased to the president and the faculty. Composed of local notables, the controlling board was physically as well as psychologically close to the college, able and usually willing to shape the decisions of those they hired and to check their behavior for deviation. This pattern of sponsorship by local religious interests and institutional control by laymen was the converse of the original European forms of organization, where faculty (and sometimes students) banded together in guilds, attempted to govern themselves through collegial principles, and maneuvered as best they could against the somewhat removed officials of state and church who claimed wide authority.

Nine colleges were established in the colonial period, before the Revolutionary War.[2] Although some of them were related to state governments in their early history, they were even then importantly independent in comparison to Continental institutions that were under government ministries of education and to later American public institutions that were directly financed by the individual states. The great impetus in the founding of such colleges came during the first half of the nineteenth century. As the population moved westward, small communities and religious groups spawned colleges in a chaotic fashion across the landscape, particularly in the western reaches of the eastern and southern states and in the new territories that now make up the Midwest and the Border States. During this period the small college, isolated in the countryside or in a small town, became institutionalized as the American model of voluntary support of higher education. Any group or sect could try its hand. Good intentions and high hopes, however, easily outran the resources available to many founding groups, and thus the growing cohort of scattered small colleges experienced a high death rate as well as a high birth rate. Of the more than 500 colleges chartered by the individual states between 1800 and 1860, only about one-fourth survived.[3] But in this Darwinian struggle, the form was gradually strengthened. It took 150 to 200 years, between 1650 and 1800–50, to develop effectively the control mechanism of a private board that managed the endowment, property, and affairs of an institution possessing the legal status of a charitable trust.[4] As commerce and industry produced considerable private wealth in the last half of the nineteenth century, the colleges were able to turn more fully to support from individuals and families in the form of both permanent endowment gifts and annual contributions—support that, together with tuition fees paid by students, provided a private financial base. Businessmen also replaced ministers on many of the boards of trustees, attenuating the influence of churches at the same time that the colleges were shedding any lingering connections with state officials. By 1900, the crowd of small private colleges had grown to nearly nine hundred, located in all parts of the country, with heaviest concentration in New England, the Middle Atlantic States, and the Midwest, and the lightest on the West Coast, where the drive for public higher education was strong from the beginning.

The university came late to the United States, long after Bologna and Paris and Oxford had experienced centuries of development, decline, and renewal. The first university to be established as such, Johns Hopkins, dates only from 1876. Other institutions were slowly evolving from college to university throughout the nineteenth century, with Yale developing graduate work in the 1850s and awarding the first American Ph.D. in 1861, and Harvard establishing a graduate department in the 1870s.[5] Other private colleges—Princeton, Columbia, Brown, and Cornell—soon followed, making up a sector of prestigious private universities that, joined by Chicago and Stanford in the 1890s, was well in place by the turn of the century. During this period, presidential leadership came into its own, beginning with the reign of Charles W. Eliot at Harvard (1869–1909) and including the entrepreneurship of Daniel Coit Gilman at Johns Hopkins, William Rainey Harper at Chicago, and David S. Jordan at Stanford.[6] These were models of the captain of erudition, the swashbuckling leader who vigorously solicited money, recruited faculty, assembled an administrative staff, and proclaimed the greatness of his own institution. The competitive dynamism of the U.S. "system," already endemic among the colleges, took a leap forward when the autonomous universities, influenced by the German emphasis on research, set out to become great research universities.

At the same time, a sector of public universities was also emerging. The first universities supported by the governments of the individual states dated from before 1800, but it was after the Civil War and toward the end of the century that they developed full form and strength, in part due to the resources provided the states by the federal government through the famous land-grant legislation of the Morrill Act. Developing major strength first in the Midwest and later in California, the state universities spoke of serving the sons and daughters of the average man, the farmer and the mechanic, assuming populist overtones that contrasted with the elitist qualities of the private universities concentrated in the eastern part of the country.[7] They were precursors of the modern open-door philosophy. Linked to popular support, they admitted high school graduates on a relatively unselective basis and oriented the undergraduate part of the institution to consumer demands and manpower needs of the home state. Like the comprehensive secondary school, they emphasized comprehensive purpose and tended to promise something for everyone. They entered freely into such areas as agriculture, forestry, engineering, and, later, home economics for the girls whose jobs would be in the home.

But, like their private counterparts, the American public universities married the German model of specialized research and advanced training to the older English-American model of liberal education by augmenting undergraduate colleges with graduate and professional schools. The higher tier had selective enrollment, provided advanced training, and, particularly in the graduate school, centered on research. The graduate school became the home of the research scholar, and its standards reflected the interests of prestigious cosmopolitan members of the faculty. The state universities thus developed a hybrid character, linking a wide range of vocational fields to the natural sciences, social sciences, and the humanities, with a structure that had to face in fundamentally different directions. Thus, the University of Michigan, for example, might obtain its support from the state legislature primarily on the basis of what it did for the students of the state at the undergraduate level, but it developed national and international standing on the basis of attractive conditions at the graduate level for research-minded faculty and students. And here, even more than in the private universities, a separate administrative staff was assembled for the purposes of development and coordination, headed by a president whose powers were delegated by a board of trustees.[8]

Along with the private college, the private university, and the state university, other types of institutions emerged. Before 1900, a separate set of public colleges for teacher training had developed. First known as normal schools, and closely associated with the school structures of the individual states, they gave a few years of training to prospective elementary school teachers. In the early decades of the twentieth century, these schools changed their names to teachers colleges as they gained the right to give the bachelor's degree and undertook the preparation of teachers and administrators for secondary schools. Between the two world wars, many began to evolve beyond teacher training into their current form of public comprehensive colleges whose undergraduate scope is virtually as wide as that of the university, with fewer of the esoteric scholarly specialties but more of the occupational ones. These state colleges, many of which acquired the title of state college university, or simply state university, have grown rapidly since World War II, operating with a low-to-moderate degree of selectivity at a time when the established public universities have become more selective.

Still other sectors developed, among them the public and private engineering (or technological) colleges and universities, headed in a prestige hierarchy by the Massachusetts Institute of Technology (MIT, founded in 1861) and the California Institute of Technology (Cal Tech, 1891). Because the right to sponsor institutions has been so dispersed, among private as well as public hands, many kinds of miscellaneous postsecondary institutions have emerged, creating a bewildering array of proprietary, nonprofit, and specialized schools and colleges. By 1960, official statistics counted about 300 assorted theological schools, art schools, and detached professional schools that were giving courses toward a bachelor's or higher degree. In addition, as a purely twentieth-century phenomenon, a genuine "short-cycle" unit emerged in the form of the junior college, which slowly developed a niche in the educational structure. Limiting itself to the first two years beyond the secondary school, the junior college has provided both terminal programs of one- and two-years' duration and courses that parallel the regular first two collegiate years and allow transfer to four-year bachelor's programs at other colleges. Two-year colleges have been under private auspices as well as public control, but the public sector became the main site of their development as the community college concept took hold. With the first several public institutions appearing before 1910, the junior college movement developed momentum in the 1920s and the 1930s, particularly in California, establishing an organizational base for rapid proliferation and expansion in the era of mass higher education following World War II. Swelling to a thousand institutions by the early 1970s, this sector became preeminently the open-door part of U.S. higher education, a filter that allowed other sectors to become more selective while the system as a whole became less selective.

The private sector, which has been gradually giving way numerically to the public sector and now has only one student in four, remains enormously varied when seen in cross-national perspective. The private university has had at least three important subtypes: the research-centered university, highest in prestige and national in orientation—for example, Chicago, Columbia, and Yale; the secular urban-service university, lower in prestige and more local in orientation—for example, Boston University, New York University, George Washington University, and the University of Cincinnati; and the Catholic municipal university, usually standing well down the prestige hierarchy and oriented both to locality and Catholicism—for example, the University of Portland, University of Dayton, Seton Hall University, and St. John's University. The private college has shown equally great variation in quality and commitment among its 800 members: the secular elite liberal arts college, able to compete with the top universities— for example, Swarthmore, Reed, and Amherst; the middle-rank institution that usually maintains a modest religious connection—for example, St. Olaf, Baldwin-Wallace, and Westminster; and the rear-guard places struggling to gain or retain marginal accreditation and sometimes still completely dominated by a denominational board or an autocratic president—for example, Oral Roberts, Rio Grande, and Bob Jones. The institutions found at the tail end of the academic procession, inferior to the best high schools, are "colleges only by grace of semantic generosity."[9]

Similarly in each type of public institution—university, state college, community college—dispersed public control has produced a great range in the mixture of purpose, program, and academic quality. The University of Mississippi qualitatively differs from Berkeley; Western Kentucky University differs extensively from Brooklyn College or San Francisco State University; and suburban Foothill Community College (Los Altos, California) is an academic showpiece differing radically from Chicago Loop College and Los Angeles City College—downtown community colleges that, within a huge scale of operations (more than 20,000 students), have large numbers of poor students from minority backgrounds, and dozens of one- and two-year terminal programs along with academic courses that permit transfer to four-year institutions.

The development of so much variance among and within the major sectors had led long before World War II to an unparalleled national diversity. This primary characteristic of U.S. higher education has interacted with a second: marked competition among institutions in the search for financial resources, personnel, and clientele. Not only did the privately controlled institutions compete with one another but also with the public campuses. That such competition became a habit is indicated by the way public institutions took to rivaling one another, explicitly and sharply, even within the same state system: for example, Michigan State University versus the University of Michigan, the University of California at Los Angeles

(UCLA) versus Berkeley in California, Southern Illinois University versus the University of Illinois.

A third characteristic of the system, especially remarkable when viewed in cross-national perspective, is the huge size of some major parts as well as the whole. After a quarter-century of rapid development of mass higher education following World War II, official statistics in 1970 showed more than 2,500 institutions and 8 million students. By the mid-1970s, New York State had moved rapidly into an immense state system of 64 institutions and 325,000 students; New York City operated a separate system of its own, with 11 institutions and 250,000 students. The total scale of operations for the entire state of New York was second only to the huge public system in California where the university has 9 campuses (122,000 enrollment), the state colleges numbered 19 (291,000 enrollment), and the community colleges numbered 103 (757,000 enrollment), with total enrollment for the state in excess of 1,372,000.[10]

Because of such enormous scale and extensive diversity, it is difficult to identify and describe modal patterns of control, especially in terms appropriate for cross-national comparison. To establish a first approximation, the observations here are limited to the university, and there primarily to the public sector, and proceed up the levels of organization common to the chapters of this volume.

LEVELS OF ORGANIZATION

At the lowest level of organization in the American university, the standard unit is the department. The reasons for the development of the department rather than the one-person chair have not been documented historically.[11] It appears that the style of top-down organization, with its similarity to business structure and bureaucratic delegation of power to impersonal offices, probably accounts in large measure for the department form. The guild forms of older countries, which locate so much power at the bottom in the person of the master, the chair-holding professor, never obtained in the early colleges of the United States. In any event, by 1825 the department was in being at Harvard and by 1900 it was firmly in place throughout the nation's universities and colleges as the basic way to accommodate specialization and divide the ever larger structures.[12]

In comparison with the chair and its often related institute, the department distributes power more widely: first, among a group of full professors; then, in reduced portion, to associate and assistant professors. The chairmanship of the department is an impersonal position in the sense that it commonly rotates on three-year terms among the senior figures rather than remaining the fixed possession of one person. On some issues the incumbent must consult with other full professors and perhaps tenured associate professors; on others, the chairman must take up the matter with the entire teaching staff. In such meetings, majority vote has been the common device for decision making. Thus, the department has been first of all a collegial body, one that is relatively unitary around common interest in a discipline, and mildly hierarchical in the vertical arrangement of the ranks of full professor, associate professor, and assistant professor (and sometimes instructor).

But the department is also a bureaucratic unit, the chairman being the lowest arm of general academic management. He is responsible to one or more deans and one or more campus officials (president, academic vice-president, provost). To a much greater degree than the chair professor, the chairman is accountable "up" an organizational hierarchy as well as "down" to colleagues of equal or near-equal status. Often appointed by the administration after consultation with department members, the chairman serves at the pleasure of the central campus officials. Therefore, at the level where the personal rulership of the professor is strong in chair systems, bureaucratic and collegial authority are heavily intertwined in the U.S. department system. On occasion the department can be highly particularistic, through personal dominance of a towering figure in its midst or through logrolling politics in the voting of a collective body. But the forces of particularism and personalism are damped by the lateral control within a collegial body and the department's vertical links to higher officials. Because there is dual authority, the collegial body and the bureaucratic staff also tend to watch one another, thus providing some check on the arbitrary exercise of power within the department. The tensions of the system fall most heavily on the chairman, as the person in the middle, straddling the line between faculty and administration and assuming responsibility on an ambiguous foundation of authority.

The next level up in the American university structure is the college, or the school, for example, the College of Arts and Sciences or the School of Medicine, Law, or Business.[13] The College of Arts and Sciences commonly contains the basic disciplines, thus embracing all the departments of the humanities, the social sciences, and the natural sciences. This central college also commonly has hegemony over undergraduate and graduate education—that is, everything other than the professional schools, which in the American scheme now exist almost entirely at an advanced, graduate level, in contrast to the European system where the study of medicine and other professional fields begins immediately after the secondary level and is organized in faculties. The basic college, or closely related unit, commonly has a dean for the undergraduate realm and another for the graduate. At most universities the staff of the departments teach at both levels and hence fall within both of these two major administrative jurisdictions. The college deans are usually appointed by top officials of the university and, more than the department chairmen, operate as true members of the central administration. The deans of the professional schools, though somewhat more autonomous, are still appointed rather than elected for the most part and have the status of administrative officers. Each deanship is an administrative office staffed with assistant deans and other supporting personnel, a base of administrative power independent of faculty bodies and above the constituent departments.

The college or school also has one or more collective bodies—for example the Faculty of Arts and Sciences, the Faculty of the Undergraduate College, and the Faculty of the Graduate School—which meet occasionally, hear reports from their own committees and the deans, and decide by collective voting. There is thus a dual structure within which the administrative officials and the professorial bodies must work out ways of separating and joining jurisdictions. Typically, the administration controls the budget, the teaching staff supervises the curriculum, and both are involved in student conduct. There are many dual-membership committees, and there are professors who develop administrative capacities and relations of mutual trust with certain administrators, thus serving as a bridging oligarchy. Notably, on most campuses, the broad academic collective bodies have little say in the crucial area of personnel. The hiring, promoting, and firing of teaching staff falls between the individual department, which does the basic personnel work and usually has primary influence in junior appointments, and the higher administrative officials and committees of professors appointed by the administration, who approve all appointments and exercise this power of approval (and funding of requisite positions) with great care in the case of expensive tenured personnel.

The complex intersecting of administrators and academics at this level of organization may be characterized as a bureaucraticized federation of collegial groups. As in the chair-based systems, where the counterpart unit is the faculty, the U.S. college or school is a relatively flat structure, since it contains a number of formally equal collegial bodies in the form of departments that may total 50 or more in the central college (Arts and Sciences) on large campuses. But it has also an administrative office that is hierarchically superior to the departments and is clearly a part of a large administrative framework. Bureaucratic authority is here much stronger than in the traditional systems of the Continent. It systematically intrudes upon the power of the clusters and it encourages the application of common standards. The diffusion of overlapping power among faculty and administrative units also makes it difficult to exercise particularistic judgments.

At the third level of the university campus as a whole, the American structure has for some decades exhibited a complex blending of the authority of trustees, administrators, and professors. The laymen who serve on the board of trustees (or regents) that is formally at the apex of control are supposed to guide the long-term development of the institution in the name of broad interests of the larger society. In public universities, they are largely appointed by the governor of the state, with only a few states providing for popular election. Terms of appointment vary greatly among the states and the institutions themselves, ranging from such short terms as two to three years to very long ones of 14 and 16 years. The state governors, in uneven fashion, select trustees who are congenial to their own political point of view, or are wealthy, or have the capacity to understand the management of large organizations, or are spokespersons for groups that need representation in order to balance the board. In comparison with faculties and students, trustees are politically conservative; but recent surveys (for example, Hartnett, 1970) suggest that they are not now so much concentrated in business and law as once seemed the case.[14] In private universities, they are generally elected by the existing trustees, occasionally by alumni, and hence have the character of self-perpetuating boards. Like such boards in other sectors of society, the members are part-time, meeting perhaps once a month, or as infrequently as three or four times a year, although some among them (the chairman and members of an executive committee) will meet more often and give much time to the institution. The trustees, as their most important function, appoint the administrative head, the president or chancellor, and officially delegate much to him, while retaining residual powers and ultimate legal control.

Of course, what is delegated has been determined broadly by the historical evolution of respective powers of the board and the administration. The long-run drift has been from close trustee supervision to management by professional administration. Beginning with the reign of the strong institution-building presidents, formal administration increasingly came into its own at the campus level of organization.[15] Here, unlike the Continental systems and chair-based systems around the world, there has developed a large class of administrators who are neither of the faculty and controlled by it nor of a state ministry of education and directed by it. As experts in such specialties as student admission, record-keeping, personnel policy, physical plant management, library operations, budgeting, public relations, alumni affairs, and university planning, they compose an administrative structure within which they work for and at the pleasure of the president, the vice presidents, the treasurer, and the business office. Their specialized roles and training dispose them to points of view different from those of trustees, faculty, and students.[16] They are generally grouped together in a large administration building that physically reinforces mutual contact and interest.

At the same time, the academicians have some collective and representational bodies, such as an academic senate or a board of permanent officers, that operate across the campus and major segments of it. But the faculty grasp tends to have a narrower scope than that of the administration and trustees; the professional-school bodies are usually split off from those of the central liberal arts faculty of the undergraduate college and the graduate school. All-university committees that embrace all the schools and colleges are commonly appointed by, and report to, the chief administrative officer.

The American structure at this level thus differs considerably from the other countries considered in this volume in the combination of the presence of laymen as trustees, responsible for general policy and holding ultimate responsibility and power, and the operation of a major administrative corps answerable to the trustees and holding delegated authority, jurisdiction, and responsibility. As at the levels beneath it, the all-campus structure is relatively flat and considerably federative, since the many departments, colleges, and schools retain impressive powers and degrees of influence in many sectors of decision making, particularly personnel and curriculum. But the structure also shows a clear hierarchy, with central administrators and trustees set above. As a result, day-to-day activity entails an intermingling of the forms of authority natural to the separate rule of professors, bureaucrats, and trustees. Stripped to stark simplicity, the control structure of the American university is a federation of collegial groups that is bureaucratically ordered and supervised by laymen. Systematic, predictable, and dependable connections are not hard to find, but they take unusual shapes in blending two or three forms of authority or in establishing a division of labor among contradictory forms, and hence are not well conceptualized if they are lumped together as a "bureaucracy" or a "community" or even an "organized anarchy." [17]

Beyond the single campus, at wider administrative levels, the patterns of control become more divergent. The private university largely drops from view, since it is not formally a part of large webs of organization; its own trustees are the highest point of control. Outside supervision of the conduct of private institutions has indeed been light, taking largely the form of periodic evaluations by regional voluntary associations for general institutional accreditation and by professional associations for specific professional and scientific programs (discussed below), which pose little threat to institutions other than those of very low quality. The basic fact that the private institutions, in nearly all states, have not been part of a superstructure remains a primary cause of the unusual leeway and necessity for institutions to compete with one another.

In the public sector, since World War II a set of arrangements has emerged at essentially the fourth level of the comparative schema. There are coordinating structures for sets of universities within multicampus state universities such as the University of California, which at one time was virtually synonymous with the Berkeley campus but has become a nine-campus system of institutions placed formally on a par with Berkeley, not under it. (In addition, sets of state colleges and community colleges also became, as nonuniversity sectors, more strongly organized as multicampus state systems.) [18] The controlling board of trustees moved up from the single-campus to the statewide level and a statewide university administration was created on top of the growing campus administration. The central administrative staff rapidly became an imposing force, allocating resources, and controlling decisions of field officers (campus administrators) by establishing uniform categories and checking for compliance. Central multicampus administration has less need to answer downward to the teaching staff than does campus administration, and stronger need to answer upward to the trustees. The administration and faculty of a campus are now finding common cause in the welfare of their own unit within the system, against the universitywide administrators who have a responsibility for the whole and a view from the top that is shared only with the trustees. With this elaboration of administrative superstructure, control has moved even farther away from the dominant modes of chair systems, where the collegial control of professors has tended to dominate all levels up to that of state or national ministry of education. In the first level above the campus, professors have only minor roles: in general, the higher the level, the lower the participation of professors.

Because education in the United States was long ago made the responsibility of state rather than national government, Level 5 in the comparative scheme is a key level in the U.S. structure. It has been to the state executive branch (the governor, budget and finance officers, and sometimes the department of education) and to the state legislature that the trustees and chief administrative officers of the universities and university systems must turn for support, a situation that has persisted despite the great increase in federal grants of the postwar period. Higher education in the United States assumes a place as a segment of public administration in the form of a large set of subgovernments within the separate states. The degree of integration into state government has varied considerably among the states, given their different traditions, politics, and administrative structures. In some states, the government has exercised specific approval of narrow items in university budgets—faculty travel or the purchase of typewriters; in others, there is constitutional autonomy and lump-sum allocation that set higher education apart from all other governmental activities.

Also at this level, but apart from the regular offices of government, recent years have seen the rapid growth of superboards established for the purpose of coordinating all units of higher education importantly supported by the state, thus bringing state colleges, community colleges, and universities together in one loose administrative framework. In attempting to map this organizational territory, recent research has pointed to four types of situations that vary in degree of central control and in proportion of members drawn from the public compared to members drawn from the institutions. The first type, no state coordinating board at all, was found in as many as 17 states as late as 1959 but in only two states a decade later. The second type, a board voluntarily organized by member organizations, also decreased in the same period from seven states to two. The third type, a formal coordinating board, spread from 10 to 27 states; and the fourth and most rigorous type, a "consolidated governing board," increased from 16 to 19 in number.[19] Thus, the shift was clearly to the third type, which is essentially a formally mandated superboard placed over the existing boards of trustees that top the institutional sectors at the fourth level of organization. And within that type, a big shift has taken place from boards that largely have institutional representatives and hold only nominal coordinating influence to boards that have either a public majority and *advisory* powers (11 states), or a public majority and *regulatory* powers (14 states).[20] In these high councils, professors have virtually no role: "Faculty representation at the level of the 'superboard' is likely to be minimal or nonexistent."[21] Groups of professors may make occasional presentations, but they must turn to the officialdom of their own professional associations and, increasingly, to their own unions to influence state-level control.

Another aspect of the state and regional level of academic organization is the special role of nongovernmental associations in accreditation, the awarding of legitimacy to institutions and to the degrees they confer. The six voluntary associations that judge whole instituions are regional: for example, the North Central Association of Colleges and Secondary Schools and the New England Association of Colleges and Secondary Schools.[22] Supported by annual fees paid by the member institutions of the region, each association has its own headquarters and small administrative staff. The associations draw on professors from within their own area, and sometimes from the outside, to compose the ad hoc committees that visit, evaluate, and report on various institutions on, commonly, a five-year cycle. Their operation permits a mild degree of professorial supervision. And the occasion of the accreditation visit calls always for the administration and faculty to assess their institution's weaknesses and strengths in a report prepared for the visitors. But, as suggested earlier for private colleges, the accrediting association is an important pressure only on institutions that hover around a low threshold of quality—or, occasionally, an experimental college whose new ways deeply offend established academic canons.[23] Notably, these associations do not attempt to administer institutional equality: in no important way do they serve as a private counterpart to the European ministry of education that, as in Italy and France, attempts to equate the work at various institutions within the framework of state-certified national degrees. Nor are they equivalent to the English system of external examiners with its institutionalized commitment to the uniform maintenance of high standards. The associations arose in the U.S. context of dispersed control as a device for ensuring some minimal competence. They do not attempt to stop established institutions from doing largely as they please. They recognize that there is considerable inequality among institutions and they do little to discourage diversity and institutional competition in a market of detached units.

As for Level 6, until recently American higher education was without any formal national organization. There was no ministry of education, no structure that reached from Washington, D.C., to embrace universities, nor any standing committees, councils, or commissions to play an important voluntary coordinating role. As late as the 1950s, the national Office of Education gathered statistics and administered a few categorical aid programs such as vocational education for the public schools, but it dared not disturb state superintendents of public instruction, much less presidents of universities. Leaving aside special wartime efforts centered on scientific research, the nearest thing to systematic federal intervention was the GI Bill, which gave financial support to veterans of World War II and later wars, administered by the Veterans Administration. In the 1950s, the National Science Foundation and the National Institutes of Health began to influence scientific research and teaching in the universities, in patterns of voluntary rather than mandatory linkage. Gradually, however, professional schools of medicine and scientific departments at some universities have become heavily dependent on national funds, essentially evolving into federal-grant units within the universities, state and private.[24] The Office of Education also became a major enterprise in the 1960s, administering major grants for higher education as well as for elementary and secondary schools.

Federal funds have come to universities and colleges in several forms. One form is student-centered funding, whereby the government makes grants and loans to individuals who in turn can "purchase" their education anywhere they want, including private institutions. This form plays heavily on the market features of U.S. higher education, relying on consumer choice as the invisible hand that will guide the development of a system. A second form is institution-centered, whereby funds flow directly from the government to the institution. As in national systems in other countries, such funds vary from categorical allotment for specific programs to lump sums for general institutional support. A third form is discipline-centered, whereby research and sometimes teaching funds flow to specific departments and professors as research grants or awards for improvement of teaching and training.

An increasing amount of indirect manipulation by various bureaus and central councils of the national government has resulted from national funding. The early 1970s saw the emergence of direct influence when the Department of Health, Education, and Welfare together with the Department of Labor decided on the withdrawal of all federal funds from institutions as a sanction against those who failed to present an effective plan of affirmative action for the employment of women and minorities. Other such direct interventions are under consideration: for example, in the name of national medical manpower policy, medical schools may be required to set targets and quotas for training certain types of doctors as a condition for the continuation of federal funding.

Yet, American universities do not think of themselves as part of a nationally administered system. In comparative perspective, they are not. The basic institutionalized lines of influence that are found at the national level in Italy, France, and even Britain remain strongest in the United States at the level of the 50 states. Although the federal lines are growing in importance, they remain uneven and secondary. Moreover, some federal policies are designed to enhance control of the individual states. A national law enacted in 1972 required all states to have some type of planning group ("1202 Commissions," named after the number of the law) for all public higher education, thus backing superboard influence at the state level.

In formal organization, the United States has at best a quasi system of largely indirect influences at the broadest level of control and coordination. Compared to the situation that existed before World War II, there is now much more of a system; but compared to what obtains nationally in most countries today, there is not much of a system. The private sector, headed by such universities as Chicago, Columbia, Harvard, Princeton, Stanford, and Yale, remains independent and strong. And the public sector is still essentially composed of the 50 states within which individual public universities and colleges control personnel selection and compete with one another, as well as with the private places, for students and faculty. Therefore, among the major advanced systems of the world, the U.S. system remains the most unorganized and approximates a market of freely interacting competitive units.[25] It remains the most influenced by the unorganized decision making that can be seen as social-choice, at the opposite end of the continuum from unitary bureaucracy.[26] The historic trend is clearly toward administered order, with some coordination provided by voluntary associations of administrators and professors headquartered in Washington, D.C., as well as by the increasing influence of a number of federal agencies.[27] But market conditions remain the basic element. The national level of control exhibits little structure and fragmented influence over a congeries of universities that vary greatly in purpose and ethos as well as in size and resources. Fragmentation remains strong relative to the forces of system building.

To summarize the nature of academic control across the whole of the six levels in the United States, the national center possesses relatively little formal authority; the middle levels (state, multicampus, and university) are strongly organized, with trustee and administrative authority predominating over faculty prerogatives; and the lower levels (college and department) retain impressive decision-making powers over personnel and curriculum— areas in which professors care most about exercising collegial rule. The various levels and the several major forms of authority constitute a set of countervailing forces. In organization and authority, the system is not only inordinately large and complex but also fundamentally disorderly.

The interests of students remain only weakly voiced at any level in formal councils, despite the great attention paid in the 1960s to student protest and student participation in governance. It remains true in the United States that students vote mainly with their feet, exercising considerable choice of place to attend as well as field of study. In such a system, consumer demand plays a large role compared to manpower planning. The consumers have had leverage that the planners do not; they not only can choose what unit to enter but also can make the "exit" decision, moving from one institution to another.[28] Because there is so much initial choice and later exiting and transferring, the viability of many individual colleges and universities depends on either adaptive response to clientele or the establishment of a claim of unique performance. Since distinctiveness lays claim to clients in a way that sameness does not, many institutions have thus attempted to develop a special character instead of passively accepting a uniform role.[29]

CHANGE

When the distribution of authority in the American system is compared with that of Continental systems, it is seen that powers usually elsewhere found at the top are located at the middle levels in U.S. institutions. In other systems provincial and national ministries of education have been in charge of the administrative services involved in making appointments, paying salaries, running the physical plant, and supporting students. Until recently little administration was considered necessary immediately above the domains of the professors. In any case, their strong guild organization did not permit it. As a consequence, weak administrative structure at the university level became characteristic. But in the United States the historic tradition of institutional autonomy demanded that the university itself handle overhead services. The required government and administration became fixed in trustee and administrative authority that was separate from and above the domains of the professors. As administration became located on campus, the emerging class of university officials developed a vested interest in keeping it there, fighting against a shift that would move jurisdiction to the staff of state bureaus.

The forces for change in the 1960s and early 1970s affected this complicated control structure in a number of ways. Growth has led to an increase in unit size at all levels, deepening the need for coordination both within and between the units, and thereby favoring the development of more and larger administrative groups. Campuswide administration (Level 3) has grown measurably and has become increasingly professionalized, tending toward the use of scientific management techniques to improve central assessment and effective intervention. Administrative systems have also grown larger and stronger at the level of state government (Level 5); and new kinds of administrative systems have developed at a level between the university and the state in the form of multicampus university systems (Level 4). A major trend is thus that of the ascendance of administration at these three levels. So important have administrators become that they overwhelmingly make up the membership of commissions—private or public, national or state—that advise on educational policy, in contrast to European commissions that contain prestigious professors. The growth of federal intervention, itself important, remains a minor phenomenon compared to that of the growth of administrative strength at the university-to-statehouse levels of the U.S. system. Within these levels, the tilt has been definitely upward, toward a centralization of authority and administration.

These three levels have come under greater public scrutiny and political pressure in recent years. The student discontent of the 1960s caused a wide range of specific publics to watch university affairs more closely, a rise in concern that was also propelled by escalating costs, growing interest in access, and the greater visibility of a larger enterprise. Even without the organized student actions, increased interest would have brought more political attention in its wake. But hostile public reaction to radical tactics on campus ensured intervention by external political groups at the levels that are primarily controlled by system administrators, boards of trustees, and state officials. A second major outcome of growth therefore has been an increasing entanglement of administration with the politics of the general political arena.

However, these administrative levels are but the top of a gigantic academic iceberg whose drift is by no means determined solely by administration at supra-university levels and external political forces. The work of teaching and research is still done in the department and in such auxiliary units as the research institute and interdisciplinary programs. Policy directly relevant to the basic work is decided largely at the second level of college and school. At these levels, collegial control remains strong, challenged mainly by bureaucratic authority of the campus administration. The understructure is thick and tough and resistant to externally imposed change. And political groups, to their constant frustration, are usually unable to penetrate to these levels. The governor of a state, as in California, may fume about the little time that the faculty devotes to teaching in the state university, but the faculty goes on finding ways to save time for research, often shielded by campus administrators interested in attracting and holding faculty talent.

Put broadly, the growth in knowledge and in the demand for experts that has been characteristic of recent decades has reinforced the strength of the disciplines inside the organizational mass of the systems that have been made ever larger. Increased specialization in scientific and other academic fields, as well as in the upper reaches of the general labor force, strengthens the influence of those whose authority is rooted in expertise.[30] Administrators in the 1970s are less, rather than more, qualified to pass judgment in the many specialized academic sectors and hence must depend heavily on judgment by professorial peers. In the face of the elaboration of administrative superstructure, the levels of department and college remain grounded in various forms of personal and collegial rulership. Thus, there has been a strengthening of the disciplines that crosscut institutions and that comprise a national system of higher education along lines of occupational specialty. Because of this increased strength of the diverse clusters of experts, organizational structure is pressed toward greater differentiation and decentralized decision making.

In a national system of institutions that is so large and internally diverse, however, major segments may move in quite different directions. In the segments where faculty influence has been weak, the growth in organizational scale has exacerbated faculty feelings of powerlessness. And instructors in those segments, preeminently the community colleges and the state colleges, concentrate so much on teaching that they do not receive the rewards of research. With these conditions, the 1970–75 recession in U.S. higher education, raising employment and job security to crucial issues, has sparked a major leap forward in faculty unionization. Union hierarchies are now added to the organizational web of higher education, replacing the disciplinary associations in first importance for many academics, while professors who do research, have national visibility, and can bargain for themselves will have less need for union protection. Seniority status through union membership may even replace tenure in those places where trustees and administrators wish to diminish tenure guarantees and have the power to do so.

Despite these trends, the market conditions under which institutions have traditionally operated still prevail. Private colleges and universities still make their way by individually raising funds, recruiting faculty, and attracting students. Public institutions, although they are within administered systems and are more accountable to higher bodies, still have to face the competition generated by more than 2,500 institutions operating under dispersed control. Strengthened state coordination has not eliminated the market. The growing power of administrative staffs during the 1960s was congruent with enhanced, even flamboyant, competition in the affluent higher education economy of those years: The *nouveau riche* among the state systems—Texas, Florida, and Arizona—eagerly sought to buy and stock faculty talent on newly built or greatly expanded campuses; developing campuses in the New York state system such as Stony Brook and Buffalo tried to lure professors from Michigan and UCLA, Princeton and Chicago. The financial turndown of the early 1970s has reduced the competitive zeal, but the basic structure and established custom of the national system continue to promote a level of competition different in kind from that in the other countries examined in this volume.

With such complex and contradictory trends in academic government, no simple picture can be drawn that typifies the whole country. Some observers have predicted homogenization under greater control by the state.[31] But any trend in that direction is slight when seen in a cross-national perspective, and it may actually be to the contrary, toward greater diversity. The combination of huge size and decentralization seems to be bringing about an increased number of modal patterns for the distribution of power. An enlarged division of labor in matters of academic control also makes possible the simultaneous growth of divergent forms of authority. In the American set of universities the professional authority of faculty has increased at the lower levels, the bureaucratic authority of administrators has increased at the middle levels, and the public authority of trustees and other laymen has increased at state and national levels.

Thus, the organizational evolution of the American university system, and American higher education as a whole, is simultaneously unilinear and multilinear.[32] The unilinear evolution is toward ever larger systems, offering more power to high public officials and senior administrators and calling for the attention of planners. The multilinear movement is toward greater diversity within systems, a looseness within which various professorial (professional) interests are vested in group control over slices of the educational domain. Academic control in the United States is part of the broader modern problem of how general policy makers, administrators, and professional experts will all be able to express and combine their legitimate interests in systems of ever-growing complexity.

NOTES

1. Richard Hofstadter and Walter P. Metzger, *The Development of Academic Freedom in the United States* (New York: Columbia University Press, 1955), Part I, "The Age of the College"; Frederick Rudolph, *The American College and University* (New York: Knopf, 1962); John S. Whitehead, *The Separation of College and State: Columbia, Dartmouth, Harvard, and Yale, 1776–1876* (New Haven: Yale University Press, 1973).

2. Hofstadter and Metzger, *Academic Freedom*, Chapter 3; Whitehead, *Separation*, Ch. 1; Donald G. Tewksbury, *The Founding of American Colleges and Universities Before the Civil War, With Particular Reference to the Religious Influences Bearing upon the College Movement* (New York: Teachers College, Columbia University, 1932).

3. An estimate made on the basis of Tewksbury's data. Tewksbury, *Founding of American Colleges*, p. 28. For a useful reinterpretation of the classic Tewksbury study, see Natalie A. Naylor, "The Ante-Bellum College Movement: A Reappraisal of Tewksbury's Founding of American Colleges and Universities," *History of Education Quarterly* (Fall 1973):261–74.

4. Peter Dobkin Hall, "The Trusteeship of Charitable Endowments," Yale Higher Education Program, Institution for Social and Policy Studies, Working Paper (forthcoming).

5. Hofstadter and Metzger, *Academic Freedom*, Part 2, "The Age of the University"; Richard J. Storr, *The Beginnings of Graduate Education in America* (Chicago: University of Chicago Press, 1953).

6. Laurence R. Veysey, *The Emergence of the American University* (Chicago: University of Chicago Press, 1965), Ch. 5, "The Pattern of the New University."

7. Rudolph, *American College*, Ch. 13; Merle Curti, *The Growth of American Thought* (New York: Harper & Row, 1943), pp. 456–57.

8. Veysey, *American University*, Ch. 5.

9. David Riesman, *Constraint and Variety in American Education* (Lincoln, Neb.: University of Nebraska Press, 1956), p. 49.

10. American Council on Education, *A Fact Book* (Washington, D.C.: 1974); State University of New York, *Facts and Figures of the State University* (Albany, N.Y.: 1974); Eugene C. Lee and Frank M. Bowen, *The Multi-Campus University* (New York: McGraw-Hill, 1971).

11. E. D. Duryea, "Evolution of University Organization," in *The University as an Organization*, ed. James A. Perkins. A Report for The Carnegie Commission on Higher Education (New York: McGraw-Hill, 1973), pp. 24–25.

12. Ibid., p. 24.

13. A high degree of institutional autonomy in the U.S. system has led to great variation and confusion in the nomenclature of organizational units, especially at this level of organization. American readers will need to forgive the overly neat and uniform picture here portrayed in an effort to point to cross-national similarities and differences. Those in other countries who are unfamiliar with the U.S. structure should realize that such specific names as College of Arts and Sciences are not uniformly applied within individual states, let alone the nation. Specific

labels aside, this chapter is characterizing, in comparative frame, the level of organization that falls between the department and the university as a whole campus.

14. On American trustees, see Thorstein Veblen, *The Higher Learning in America* (Stanford, Calif.: Academic Reprints, 1954); Hubert Park Beck, *Men Who Control Our Universities* (New York: King's Crown Press, 1947); Morton A. Rauh, *The Trusteeship of Colleges and Universities* (New York: McGraw-Hill, 1969); Rodney T. Hartnett, "College and University Trustees: Their Backgrounds, Roles, and Educational Attitudes," in *The State of the University: Authority and Change*, eds. Carlos E. Kruytbosch and Sheldon L. Messinger (Beverly Hills, Calif.: Sage Publications, 1970), pp. 47–71.

15. On the early rise of complex administration in the U.S. university, beginning before the turn of the century, see Veysey, *American University*, "The Rise of Administration," pp. 302–17.

16. On the increasing separation of a large administrative group and the development of a separate administrative ideology in the modern American multiversity, see Terry F. Lunsford, "Authority and Ideology in the Administered University," in *State of the University*, ed. Kruytbosch and Messinger, pp. 87–107.

17. See John D. Millett, *The Academic Community* (New York: McGraw-Hill, 1963); Herbert Stroup, *Bureaucracy in Higher Education* (New York: The Free Press, 1966); and Michael D. Cohen and James G. March, *Leadership and Ambiguity: The American College President* (New York: McGraw-Hill, 1974).

18. For relevant data and description, see Eugene C. Lee and Frank M. Bowen, *The Multicampus University: A Study of Academic Governance*. A Report Prepared for The Carnegie Commission on Higher Education (New York: McGraw-Hill, 1971).

19. See Robert O. Berdahl, *Statewide Coordination of Higher Education* (Washington, D.C.: American Council on Education, 1971), p. 35.

20. Joseph W. Garbarino, *Faculty Bargaining: Change and Conflict* (New York: McGraw-Hill, 1975), pp. 8–9.

21. Ibid., p. 11.

22. William K. Shelden, *Accreditation: A Struggle Over Standards in Higher Education* (New York: Harper, 1960).

23. For example, Parsons College in Iowa, which in 1967 lost its accreditation from the North Central Association of Colleges and Secondary Schools. See James D. Koerner, *The Parsons College Bubble: A Tale of Higher Education in America* (New York: Basic Books, 1970), especially Ch. 7, "Adventures in Accreditation."

24. On "the federal-grant university," see Clark Kerr, *The Uses of the University* (Cambridge, Mass.: Harvard University Press, 1964). On the increase in federal influence, see Homer D. Babbidge, Jr., and Robert M. Rosenzweig, *The Federal Interest in Higher Education* (New York: McGraw-Hill, 1962); Harold Orlans, *The Effects of Federal Programs on Higher Education* (Washington, D.C.: The Brookings Institution, 1962); Logan Wilson, ed., *Emerging Patterns in American Higher Education* (Washington, D.C.: American Council on Education, 1965).

25. Joseph Ben-David, *American Higher Education: Directions Old and New*. An essay sponsored by the Carnegie Commission on Higher Education (New York: McGraw-Hill, 1972).

26. See the Introduction to this volume for a review of four types of decision-making contexts (bureaucratic, federative, coalitional, and social-choice) set forth by Warren for analysis of interorganizational relations. Roland T. Warren, "The Interorganizational Field as a Focus for Investigation," *Administrative Science Quarterly* 12 (December 1967):396–419.

27. Harland G. Bloland, *Higher Education Associations in a Decentralized Education System* (Berkeley: Center for Research and Development in Higher Education, University of California, 1969); and Harland G. Bloland and Sue M. Bloland, *American Learned Societies in Transition* (New York: McGraw-Hill, 1974), Ch. 2, "The Traditional Function and Character of American Learned Societies."

28. On the use and conditions of efficacy of the market decision of "exit," versus the political decision of "voice," see Albert O. Hirschman, *Exit, Voice and Loyalty* (Cambridge, Mass.: Harvard University Press, 1972).

29. Burton R. Clark, *The Distinctive College: Antioch, Reed, and Swarthmore* (Chicago: Aldine, 1970); and Burton R. Clark, Paul Heist, T. R. McConnell, Martin A. Trow, and George Yonge, *Students and Colleges: Interaction and Change* (Berkeley: Center for Research and Development in Higher Education, University of California, Berkeley, 1972), Ch. 4, "Channels of Entry."

30. See Talcott Parsons, "Professions," in *International Encyclopedia of the Social Sciences*, Vol. 12 (New York: Macmillan and The Free Press, 1968), pp. 536–47; Christopher Jencks and David Riesman, *The Academic Revolution* (Garden City, N.Y.: Doubleday, 1968).

31. For example, the first "Newman Report." Frank Newman, et al., *Report on Higher Education* (Washington, D.C.: U.S. Department of Health, Education, and Welfare, 1971); Harold Hodgkinson, *Institutions in Transition: A Profile of Change in Higher Education* (New York: McGraw-Hill, 1971), p. xv.

32. On these twin evolutions among sets of organizations generally, see Herbert Kaufman, *The Limits of Organizational Change* (University, Ala.: The University of Alabama Press, 1971), pp. 110–13.

8
JAPAN
Donald F. Wheeler

The postwar system of higher education in Japan reflects largely unchanged the status hierarchy of universities already in place in prewar times.[1] In this hierarchy, several prestigious universities served as models for, and exerted strong influence on, other institutions of higher education in such matters as curriculum, educational policy, and patterns of administration. They have also dominated the major higher education interest groups that articulate the position of the universities vis-à-vis the Ministry of Education and academic and professional associations. Finally, they have attracted the ablest students who have later been placed in the most influential positions in society.

Indicators of the position of an institution in the hierarchy of Japanese universities include difficulty of the entrance examination, number of applicants for admission, ratio of entrants to applicants, job recruitment and promotion records of graduates, size of budget, opinion surveys on university prestige, and so forth. These matters and the effectiveness of various high schools in getting their graduates accepted into college are researched by commercial publishers who provide the information to potential university applicants and their parents. Some companies also produce practice entrance examinations.

DEVELOPMENT OF THE UNIVERSITY SYSTEM

Tokyo Imperial University, the prestigious model for so many other universities in Japan, was established by the national governent in 1866 as the first of seven Imperial Universities that were to "provide instruction in the arts and sciences and to inquire into the mysteries of learning in accordance with the needs of the state."[2] The two most prominent private universities today were also founded early. The Tokyo Semmon Gakko, predecessor of Waseda (1882), was founded by Okuma Shigenobu after he left the government; its purpose was to train progressive leaders. Keio (1871) was founded by Fukuzawa Yukichi to provide modern enlightenment and practical learning.

By 1935, Japanese higher education consisted of a national and a private sector, each containing two different types of institutions: universities and Special Schools or colleges (*Semmon Gakko*). National institutions were higher in prestige than were private institutions, and universities were higher than colleges. The prestige hierarchy among these institutions was, and to some extent continues to be, supported by the deliberate government policy of selective distribution of the most important resources for the development of the system: financial support, legal recognition, and easy access by graduates to the civil service.[3] For example, before World War II Tokyo Imperial University (which later became Tokyo University or *Todai*) was the leader in the elite club of Imperial Universities. It received the largest appropriations and its graduates could enter many branches of the higher civil service without an examination. In contrast, private institutions were denied legal recognition as universities until 1918, and received almost no government monies; moreover, their graduates were required to pass a battery of examinations for civil service posts.

From the point of view of the government, there was a definite division of labor between different types of institutions. The Imperial Universities, particularly Tokyo Imperial, were charged with the task of basic and applied research, including the introduction and diffusion of Western learning. They also had the task of educating the highest echelon of professionals and public officials. The national-level Special Schools trained middle-echelon technicians, professionals, and public officials. National institutions were established to serve the needs of the national government and were administered by the Ministry of Education. A few local government universities were established by municipalities and prefectures to fulfill particular needs of their localities.

The private sector was left with the task of responding to nongovernmental needs: the increasing demand for the opportunity for higher education and the manpower needs of industry and business. The private institutions originated as Special Schools. They were legally treated as juridical persons under the authority of their own boards of trustees. Because the private colleges were dependent on student tuition for their survival, the curriculum was heavy on the side of the social sciences and humanities, fields that could accommodate many students in large lecture halls. Private colleges also increased their enrollments by establishing several courses of study requiring different levels of preparation. The best private Special Schools gradually added new and more advanced courses of study, and were eventually given status as universities, becoming the leading private universities.

After World War II the U.S. occupation reforms replaced multitrack secondary education with a single-track system that made broader access to higher education possible. The Imperial Universities were downgraded and many Special Schools were upgraded to the status of universities. Graduates from any high school were allowed to take the entrance examination for any university. Although these reforms opened up access to higher education and flattened the prestige hierarchy of universities somewhat, the prewar government policy of preferential resource allocation to certain elite institutions has continued and the prestige rankings of universities have remained basically unchanged. Postwar expansion of student enrollments took place largely in the private sector. (See Table 2.)

Table 2
Japanese Higher Education Institutions, National and Private, (1935 and 1970) (in percent)

	1935		1970	
	Students	Institutions	Students	Institutions
National universities				
Research universities[a]	11	2	6	1
Other national institutions[b]	25	38	14	7
Total national	36	40	20	8
Private and local Universities				
Large[c]	23	10	40	12
Other private and local[d]	41	50	40	80
Total private and local	64	60	80	92
Total	100	100	100	100
	(N = 189,511)	(N = 263)	(N = 1,714,054)	(N = 921)

[a] In 1935, these included the Imperial Universities. In 1970, these included the former Imperial University, Tokyo Institute of Technology, Tokyo University of Education, Hitotsubashi University, and Hiroshima University.

[b] In 1935, these institutions included 12 national universities with one or two faculties, Special Schools, normal schools, and teacher training institutes. In 1970, these included universities, technical colleges and junior colleges.

[c] In 1935, these were the only local and private universities. In 1970, these universities enrolled 8,000 or more students.

[d] In 1935, these were Special Schools. In 1970, these included universities, technical colleges, and junior colleges.

Sources: Tokyo Educational Research Institute, *Zenkoku Gakko Soran, 1971* (National review of schools, 1971) (Tokyo: Tokyo Kyoiku Kenkyujo, 1972); Ministry of Education, *Educational Statistics in Japan, August 1971* (Tokyo: Ministry of Education, 1971); Ministry of Education, *Nihon Teikoku Mombusho Dai 63 Nenpo* (The 63rd Annual of the Japanese Imperial Ministry of Education), vols. 1 and 2 (Tokyo: Mombusho Tokeikyoku, Chosaka, 1935–36).

TYPES OF INSTITUTIONS

Higher education in Japan today consists of the following types of institutions differing in prestige, relationship to the state (national, local government, or privately administered), and function (emphasis on research, education, or training).

National Institutions

The leading national research universities are multifaculty institutions including most disciplines and professions. They are largely composed of undergraduates working for the B.A. or B.S. degrees, but offer graduate education in each faculty leading to the M.A. and Ph.D. degrees, accompanied by strong research programs. The chair system is exclusive to these universities and to the medical faculties of other national universities.

Highest in prestige is the University of Tokyo, followed by Kyoto University. Considerably below these are the other former Imperial Universities (Tohoku, Kyushu, Hokkaido, Osaka, and Nagoya). The prestige ranking corresponds to the order in which they were founded. Several other important national universities located mainly in Tokyo, such as Tokyo University of Education (now becoming Tsukuba University), Tokyo Institute of Technology, and Hitotsubashi University, and Hiroshima University are also leading research universities.

The remaining national universities have from one to several faculties and some graduate programs leading to the M.A. degree. All were formerly Special Schools upgraded to universities in the postwar system. Multifaculty universities are generally the result of the amalgamation of several former Special Schools. There is at least one of these national universities in each of Japan's 47 prefectures and more than one in the most populous prefectures, such as Tokyo and Osaka. Ranking below these universities are the short-cycle technical colleges and junior colleges.

Private and Local Government Institutions

The most prestigious private and local government universities have more than 8,000 students and were all granted university status before World War II. At the top in prestige are Waseda and Keio, followed by Chuo, Doshisha, Hosei, Jochi, Meiji, Rikkyo, and others. Each university is likely to have some prestigious undergraduate faculties and a few graduate departments offering the Ph.D. Although their commitment to research is much less than that of the leading national research universities, the best of these institutions are equivalent in prestige to some of the research universities. There are a few small prestigious private universities such as International Christian University and the big three private women's institutions: Japan Women's University, Tokyo Woman's Christian College, and Tsuda College. Universities administered by prefectures and cities have been able to maintain rather high standards and prestige because of local government support.

The smaller private universities and junior colleges are less prestigious institutions. Some are the successors of Special Schools; others are newly created postwar institutions with meager resources. The two-year junior colleges admit mainly women and are at the bottom of the prestige hierarchy.

Factors Affecting Prestige

From the above, it is clear that several factors are highly correlated with prestige: founding body, time of founding, centrality of research or training function, number of faculties and graduate faculties, number of prestigious faculties, and size. The most prestigious university is likely to be national, founded early, research-oriented, comprehensive with a large number of renowned faculties and graduate faculties, and large in terms of student enrollment and number of faculty members. The University of Tokyo (*Todai*) best fits the description and occupies a commanding position in Japanese higher education not matched by any other single university in the countries treated in this book.

The steep prestige hierarchy of institutions of higher education strongly influences, and is reinforced by, patterns of student admissions and career recruitment. To oversimplify the matter, the best students go to the most prestigious universities and receive the best career opportunities.[4] The prestige ranking of a university is maintained through its ability to place graduates in the most prominent companies and government bureaus.

The basic device for allocating students of differing ability to universities of differing reputation is competition via the university entrance examination.[5] Powerful pressures are exerted on most Japanese young people from an early age to go to the best university they are capable of entering. Parents see this as the path to security and upward mobility. Secondary schools push their students because their reputation depends on their success rates in entrance examinations. A national university is preferable because of low tuition, but the places available are limited (only 20 percent of entrants to higher education attend national universities).

Entrance examinations are administered by the individual faculties of universities and are open to all secondary school graduates. Students usually take the exams of several of the highest ranking faculties of universities they think they could enter. They judge their probability of success on the basis of commercially administered practice exams and advice from secondary school counselors. Most students who fail try again after a year of individual study or examination-preparation school.

The basic mechanism for allocating talented graduates to key employment positions is the corporate practice of hiring a set quota of graduates from a selected group of high-prestige universities each year for top and middle management positions in the future. These universities maintain their reputations by supplying larger numbers of graduates than other institutions to the best corporations. The corporations can still be highly selective concerning whom they hire from within these universities. The prestigious universities are also favored in the higher civil service, not through quotas, since anyone can take the qualifying examination, but through the rapid promotion of their graduates after entering.

This system, based on the delicately balanced relationship among the prestige hierarchy of universities, selection of students, and employment of graduates, is widely regarded as fair (based on achievement and high motivation rather than favoritism), efficient (there is a manageable method for selecting a few from the many), and effective (the net is cast wide and highly talented persons are found). However, the high priority placed on written entrance examinations is criticized because of the emphasis on rote learning and because life chances depend too much on the results of one examination and too little on subsequent performance. The university entrance examination system thus supports the patterns of student admissions and career recruitment which, in turn, reinforce the hierarchy of universities.

LEVELS OF ORGANIZATION

Although decision making differs considerably among the four kinds of institutions identified earlier—leading national research universities, other national universities and colleges, high-prestige private and local government universities, and lower prestige private universities and colleges—a brief analysis of the process at various levels or organization will emphasize features that are common to many universities. Because the leading research national universities exemplify some of these features, they will be the primary example.

The smallest unit of organization in the leading national research universities is the chair.[6] Headed by the chair holder, who is a full professor (*kyōju*), the chair includes an associate professor (*jokyōju*) and one to three assistants. Since the chair consists of several members and not simply the full professor, it is often referred to as a "sofa" rather than a chair.[7] The chair is fundamentally a unit for research activities and for the organization and teaching of a given body of knowledge on both undergraduate and graduate levels. It is also the basic administrative unit for calculating the budget for teaching and research (excluding salaries). There are three kinds of chairs with differing but fixed stipends: the ordinary chair, the experimental chair, and the clinical chair. Four times the ordinary chair budget is available for the experimental chair and more than that for the clinical chair. Chair holders are not usually heads of research institutes in their universities (as they are in Germany), but they may have research institute chairs in addition to their university chairs.

The degree of control the chair holder has over decision making related to his chair differs greatly by university faculty and in individual cases. The chair holder tends to be more powerful in fields where the chair budget is high and outside research funds are available, as in the natural sciences and medicine. In some cases, the chair holder plays a dominant role in the selection of the other personnel for his chair, including his heir apparent. The chair holder may also determine the research topics of the other personnel of the chair and graduate students. Typically, however, the members of the chair accommodate each other.

In many cases the locus of decision making on Level 1 is in the department (*gakka*) rather than the chair. For almost all Japanese universities—national, local, and private—the department is the basic unit of organization. The allocation of research funds formally tied to the chairs and personnel decisions generally take place at the departmental level. Junior faculty members usually carry more weight in such departments than in the chair-system national universities.

The faculty (Level 2) is a federation of chairs in a few national universities (as formerly in Germany and France and still in Italy), and a federation of departments in most universities. An autonomous, self-contained educational and administrative unit, the faculty has power to establish its own educational program within broad limits set by the Ministry of Education. The faculty is administered by a dean (elected by the faculty members for a two-year term) and the faculty council (*Kyojukai*), assisted by an administrative staff of Ministry of Education employees in the case of the national universities. The dean receives no extra salary and usually continues to teach although with a reduced course load. The dean has little independent power since decisions are arrived at through group consensus. Policy decisions are made by the faculty council with professors, associate professors, and in some cases, lecturers (*kōshi*) and assistants (*joshu*) participating. Faculty committees, such as those handling academic affairs, student affairs, and admissions, often do spadework for the faculty council relying on the clerical assistance of civil servants from the Ministry of Education.

On Level 3 are the president, the university senate (in national and other public universities) or the board of trustees (in private universities), and the administrative staff. The president is elected by the faculty members typically for a first term of four years with the possibility of reelection once. Most universities and certainly the most prestigious ones invariably elect one of their own faculty members as president. The less prestigious national universities often select as president an eminent professor from a prestigious university who is approaching the usual mandatory retirement age of 60.

The university senate of the University of Tokyo illustrates the typical composition of senates. It includes deans (10) and two additional elected faculty representatives from each faculty (30 in all), directors of research institutes (14), the director of the administrative staff (*jimukyokucho*) who is ex officio, and the president of the university as chairman. Members of the senate are assigned as chairmen of university committees such as those on academic affairs, student affairs, and the library.

The director of the administrative staff is appointed by and responsible to the Ministry of Education, although the university president often plays a part in his selection. He serves under the president, but he is also the direct representative of the ministry in many matters. Within the ministry this position carries little prestige or political power. Members of the administrative staff are rarely experts in the substance of the educational matters they deal with. However, in private universities the professionalization of administrative staff and their initiative in policy matters have increased greatly in recent years. Their skills have been greatly needed in the face of financial problems and student disputes.

The senate (national universities) has impressive formal powers, but these are largely delegated to an informal and much more manageable body called the dean's meeting (*Gakubucho Kaigi*), which typically gathers once a week in contrast to the senate's monthly meetings. The main criterion of a good president is his ability to achieve consensus among the deans. There are virtually no legitimate means for making important overall decisions without a consensus of the deans. The opposition of a dean or even his absence from a meeting can prevent or postpone decisions for a long period.

The boards of trustees of private universities are structurally equivalent to university senates in national universities and serve similar functions. They are composed mainly of alumni, friends of the university, and often faculty members. The top university administrators are typically members of the board. There is little support in Japan for the concept that those who represent outside interests or the public interest should be on the governing boards of either private or national universities. It is assumed that outsiders could never comprehend the unique complexities of a particular university. Behind this rationale is the realistic prognosis that outsiders would make the achievement of consensus much more difficult. In the case of private universities, however, the concept of insider includes representatives of the interest of the founder or establishing group, such as a religious body.

The standing committee of the board of trustees (*jōmu rijikai*) of private universities corresponds to the dean's meeting in national universities in that it works out a consensus for the trustees' approval. It differs from the dean's meeting in that the leading members are loyal aides of the president, helping to formulate and implement his policies. Although members of the standing committee are faculty members and are largely untrained for administration, they and the president act as full-time administrators. Committeemen are likely to have (and to need) more power than the president and senate members at national universities, since they directly bear the highest responsibility for administration and finance. Private universities cannot fall back on the ministry to carry them through a crisis.

There are some multicampus universities (Level 4) in Japan, but the pattern of control does not significantly differ from that of other faculties within universities—that is, they operate as semiautonomous units and represent their interests through participation in the university senate (national) or board of trustees (private). There are two prominent examples. The University of Tokyo has facilities spread throughout Japan; its Faculty of General Studies, where all undergraduates spend their initial two years, is ten miles from the main campus where the facilities for upper classmen, graduate students, and most of the research institutes are located. It is represented on the university senate. Japan's largest private university, Nihon (80,000 students), has several campuses with representatives on the board of trustees. In this case, however, there is a high degree of financial independence for each campus.

Before World War II, the control of the Ministry of Education (Level 6) over higher education was direct and pervasive. Only the Imperial Universities were favored with autonomy and academic freedom. This was with the expectation that open inquiry would in the long run lead to a greater contribution to the state. Faculty members of Imperial Universities could choose their deans and presidents. Their faculty councils had independent authority. Other national institutions of higher education were not granted autonomy or academic freedom. Although private universities had independent boards of trustees and status as juridical persons, they were also subject to periodic state inspections. Direct interference in the internal affairs of all types of institutions of higher education occurred regularly during World War II.

The U.S. occupation forces successfully diminished the power of the Ministry of Education and decentralized control of higher education.[8] These reforms were enthusiastically supported by the universities, the progressive political parties, news media, and public opinion. A strong allergy to state interference in the internal affairs of universities had developed as a result of the state's abuses of the university during the war.

The occupation reforms were translated into national policy through Article 23 of the Constitution of 1947 which states, "Academic freedom is guaranteed," and also through the Fundamental Law of Education (1947) and the Basic School Education Law (1947). Other laws gave guidelines for the establishment of the new university system. Because of the strong opposition of the university community and the public to interference, the Ministry of Education was not able to pass any law regulating the internal governance of the university until 1969. As the 1964 White Paper on Education states:

> [In the postwar period] universities began to function without having clarified the relationships between university administrative organs, its teaching members, and the other employees or the regulations for smooth cooperation. Such important questions as the extent of the powers of the faculty conference, its size and its relation to the deans and the president; the relations between the autonomy of the university and the political freedom of individual teachers; the connection between the supervisory rights of a university as an educational institution and the self-governing activities of the students, etc. were optimistically left for the future to solve.[9]

This helps to account for the haphazard, nonbureaucratic manner in which decision making in universities evolved in the postwar period. The Ministry of Education often attempted to exert its influence in an ad hoc manner. The boundary lines of authority were unclear, and it was in the interest of the universities to keep them unclear since any clarification would very likely mean a diminution of their autonomy. For many reasons, including the lack of legal authorization and the opposition of the university community and the public, the Ministry of Education has exercised its powers with considerable restraint. In most cases reasonable compromises have been worked out between the Ministry of Education and university officials.

As a result of U.S. occupation reforms of higher education, the government no longer gives accreditation nor supervises the standards of established academic institutions. To regulate standards, the universities established the University Accreditation Association. However, the Association has not succeeded in enforcing adequate standards for initial accreditation, nor has it reviewed the many cases where accredited institutions have significantly relaxed their standards.[10]

Though substantially reduced since the war, the powers of the Ministry of Education are hardly negligible, particularly as they apply to the national universities and colleges for which it has direct responsibility. The ministry determines national policies toward higher education; through its organ, the University Chartering Council, it establishes and abolishes institutions; it establishes new chairs, faculties, and institutes; with the approval of the Ministry of France, it determines the budget for higher education and individual institutions as well as salaries and student fees; it approves university recommendations of staff promotions and appointments of faculty members, deans, and presidents; and it sets standards for degrees. The Ministry of Education also has some control over course offerings through setting degree requirements, although not over the content of the courses.

The Ministry of Education has exercised its authority in a variety of ways. Under the strong influence of the ruling Liberal Democratic Party (in power except for a few short lapses throughout the postwar period) the ministry has set policies for higher education. It has commissioned its own appointed internal consultative organ, the Central Council for Education (CCE) to study aspects of higher education and make recommendations. The CCE has strongly reflected the views of Japan's financial circles and because of this and because the ministry exercises firm control over its agenda, procedures, and reports, most scholars—particularly those of a liberal bent—have refused to serve on it. The Japan Teacher's Union, the National Universities Association, various private university associations, the Japan Academy of Science, and various on-campus political groups of students and professors have firmly opposed the general policies of the CCE. Thus CCE policies have been implemented only slightly. The leading national research universities usually control their everyday internal affairs with considerable autonomy (sometimes by default), and can more adequately respond to the carrot-and-stick approach of the ministry than can the other national universities. Private universities can avoid the stick but because of their weak financial situation are often vulnerable to the carrot.

The power of the Ministry of Education to establish new institutions has been amply used. The University Chartering Council (the Private University Chartering Council, in the case of private universities) must screen all applications. In the process, the chartering council influences decisions on the number and kinds of faculties, the disciplines that will be included in each faculty, and even the names given to the faculties. For example, several years ago the council refused to approve a Human Sciences Faculty at Wako University.

During most of the postwar period, the University Chartering Council has had lax quality standards, sometimes approving new universities that did not meet minimum standards. One scholar argues that, in order to meet the increased demand for places in the university and industry's needs for skilled manpower at the least possible cost, there was a conscious ministry policy of encouraging the rapid expansion of private universities—with disastrous consequences for the quality of education.[11]

The Ministry of Education also shapes the development of higher education through selective granting of requests for new chairs, faculties, institutes, and campuses to existing institutions. For example, the number of chairs in the Faculty of Engineering at the University of Tokyo increased rapidly after the ministry changed its science policy in response to Sputnik. The University of Tokyo was able to take advantage of this policy to maintain its position of eminence in higher education, but at the expense of the previous balance between the humanities and pure and applied sciences.

The degree of discretion the Ministry of Education can exercise over the budget is limited and is largely related to the support of new institutions it charters and to the establishment of new chairs, faculties, institutes, and campuses at older institutions. The Ministry of Education is beholden to the more powerful Ministry of Finance for approval of item changes before the budget is sent to the National Diet. Most of the funds for higher education are recurring expenses with regular annual increases.

The power of the Ministry of Education to approve university-recommended staff promotions and appointments of faculty members, deans, and presidents can influence the university choices of candidate, although the ministry almost never exercises a veto.

CHARACTERISTICS OF DECISION MAKING: CONSENSUS AND THE CONTAINMENT OF CONFLICT

A simple description of the formal levels of organization tells us less about how decisions are made in Japanese universities than in the universities in other countries treated in this book. The reason is that the attempt to get a broad consensus *between levels* is a central characteristic of decision making in Japanese universities and informal intermediary levels play an important role in this. Every attempt is made to avoid open conflict. In this pattern of decision making it is often difficult to locate the main sources of a decision.

First, this process will be examined in the case of establishing a new chair at a national university. Proposals for new chairs come from the chair holders or departments (Level 1). All requests are then discussed in the faculty councils of each faculty (Level 2) and their priority listing is taken to the dean's meeting for discussion (Level 3). The dean's meeting then makes its priority listing of new chairs to be requested from the Ministry of Education (Level 6). The merits of each proposed chair and the probability that the Ministry of Education will grant the request are discussed, but the crucial factor in setting priorities within deans' meetings is "whose turn it is," based on the granting of previous requests. After the priority list is decided, the president (Level 3) sounds out the Ministry of Education on what new chairs are likely to be granted. The president then proposes these chairs to the university senate; the senate officially requests them; and they are normally granted.

Certain distinctive characteristics of the consensus-formation process become clear:

1. Leaders from each level of organization must join in making important decisions. Leaders on each level forge consensus *on their level.* Then they join with the leaders of the other levels to form a consensus *between levels.* Seniority and position in the organization dictate the extent to which an individual participates in the decision making and insists on his own viewpoint. In the end, ideally, all participants support the leader, and the leader takes all participants into account according to their different

status in the group. However, students are not considered to have an independent role in university decision making. They are viewed as apprentices of individual faculty members or as clients of a faculty committee on student affairs. Student self-government associations are officially for student affairs, not for university affairs.

2. Each unit filters all its requests through *one* unit above it in the hierarchy.[12] The unit above harmonizes all requests from below. Again, students have no formal part in this process.

3. Achieving a consensus *between levels* is greatly assisted by sending the proposal up and down the line (*ringi*).[13] The ringi may occur when a proposal is initiated, when the decision is being made, or after the decision has been made as a confirmation of consensus.

4. Informal units such as the dean's meeting work out the consensus and prepare formal proposals for smooth passage by the official bodies. Informal negotiations (*nemawashi*) between official representatives, such as those between university presidents and officials of the Ministry of Education, are also important.[14]

5. Formal decision-making bodies such as the university senate ratify the consensus that has already been achieved.

There is little communication between different units on the same level of organization except through leaders who meet to resolve differences between the units they represent, for example, in the dean's meeting. Units on the same level of organization are competing with one another for favorable treatment by the unit above. Thus cleavages and conflict within the university usually follow faculty and departmental lines. Often, however, cleavages based on generational or ideological differences (which overlap somewhat) cut across faculty and departmental lines and threaten the usual mechanisms of consensus formation. The traditionalists (usually senior professors in positions of responsibility) aim at unanimity (formalism of ends) by including only the most senior people on each level in the consensus making between levels. The modernists resist the traditional value of unanimity on the grounds that their concerns are not given due consideration. They press for the use of formal democratic procedures (formalism of means) such as written agendas, open meetings, and majority votes—mechanisms that could destroy the present consensus-formation process, based as it is on agreement between the leaders of units on each level of organization. In practice, the traditionalists often accommodate the modernists on substantive issues in order to avoid procedural changes that would undermine their control. The New Left radicals on the faculty reject piecemeal reforms and often refuse to participate. The modernists have gradually gained in numbers and influence during the postwar period; the active constituency involved in decision making has gradually broadened.

Conflict Control Mechanisms

Several important mechanisms exist for controlling conflict while consensus is sought. First, lower levels of organization, after being consulted, are expected to conform to the consensus. Groups unlikely to conform, such as students, can be isolated from the decision-making process. Second, informal negotiations up and down the hierarchy provide a means for ironing out differences between units.

Third, the devision of labor between informal and formal decision-making bodies eliminates the strains that would ensue if the same unit both resolved differences and legitimized the decisions. The informal units, free of public scrutiny, harmonize differences and present a unified proposal. The formal bodies enact the proposals they receive and give them official sanction. In Western systems, informal consultations are usually held on an ad hoc basis between individuals rather than in regularized group meetings. In the Japanese university the usual practice is to combine formal decision making with regularized informal group consultation on various levels.

Finally, in order to minimize conflicts of interest, personality clashes, and ideological differences, attempts are made to adhere to established criteria for decisions. These criteria exhibit deference to traditional authority. Precedents applicable to a particular situation are respected, and senior members of a faculty are in the best position to know and apply these precedents. The principle of "fair share" also helps control conflict; each unit has an equal claim to its share (not necessarily an equal share) of the available resources, and merely has to wait its turn to get it. The seniority and prestige of a group play a part in determining its fair share and when it will receive it. Consultation is carried on according to established procedures in order to prevent opposition on procedural grounds. However, customary procedures differ according to the occasion. Again, senior members of the group are likely to make the most convincing case for the relevant precedents.

The consensual style of decision making in universities has functioned well in encouraging communication, participation, and a sense of solidarity on the part of the teaching and research staff. Trusted leaders from each level have been able to work out consensus between levels. At the same time individual units have had considerable autonomy to decide their own affairs, to the extent that they did not interfere with others. The consensual style has also been important, though it has functioned less well, in relationships between individual universities and the Ministry of Education.

The consensual decision-making process has serious shortcomings as well. From the standpoint of efficiency, it is very time-consuming. Furthermore, the timing and even the content of decisions depend more on the complex needs of the group process than on the needs of the situation for which a decision is required. From the point of view of effectiveness, the bias against specialization and division of labor, and against reliance on the technical expertise of outsiders often leads to poorly grounded decisions. From the point of view of broad participation, although all involved parties are consulted before a decision, in the end it is the leaders at various levels who determine the consensus. Once a decision has been made, public expressions of dissent are considered disloyal.

Stresses on the consensus-formation process can be illustrated by the University of Tokyo dispute of 1968-69.[15] There was strong sentiment among faculty and students, and also in the press and public, that President Kazuo Okochi had not attempted to deal with the students and their grievances in good faith. After he was forced to resign, the new acting president, Ichiro Kato, promised to meet the students and include them in the settlement. He accepted the consensus ideal, which put him in the position of having to try to satisfy the demands of the students and also those of the Ministry of Education. Kato first approached the Zenkyoto, a left-wing student group. Their demands had the broadest student support and they had fewer off-campus political ties that could influence their negotiating position. A settlement with the Zenkyoto would undoubtedly split their weak organization and have the additional advantage of weakening the influence of a rival left-wing student organization, the Minsei, because they would be left out of the settlement. However, the Zenkyoto refused to compromise. This left Kato with no alternative but to accept the Minsei offer of a moderate solution: the election of student representatives from each faculty to work out with the university a compromise to be ratified in a public meeting. The Minsei carried through their plan, an agreement was signed by student representatives and the president, and after a few days the president called in the police to clear the campus of the Zenkyoto students. The Ministry of Education refused to accept the agreements between student representatives and the university as binding. The president strongly and publicly defended the agreements. But gradually enormous loopholes became apparent. Superficially, all the major parties got what they wanted, but there was less to the settlement than met the eye. The Zenkyoto held out to the end in order to spread the struggle to other schools, but the defeat and arrests at Todai were very costly. The Minsei got credit for arranging the compromise, but they won few concessions in the end. The president settled the dispute, but later could not translate this into university reform. The Ministry of Education counteracted the Minsei thrust for more influence on campus, but gained no influence itself. Nothing had been solved, but the consensus form of decision making had been saved.

CRISIS AND CHANGE

The previous example illustrates some of the stresses on the consensual decision-making process that have aggravated its weaknesses. Other such strains are the overloading of administrative machinery, facilities, and educational programs; insufficient financial resources; student and faculty dissatisfaction; and the constant activities of the student movement.

In the late 1960s students born in the first postwar baby boom descended in droves on the campuses, fresh with new democratic ideals and high expectations.[16] In contrast to their immediate predecessors they had no direct experience of the devastation and humiliation of defeat in World War II. They were educated in the postwar educational system by teachers who renounced the wartime regime or remained silent. Optimism and hope for change were fed by unflagging rapid economic growth.[17] Thus many students were sensitive to the vestiges of "feudalism" they found in their professors and in the responses of university administrators to their demands. By the late 1960s, the major cities had large numbers of dissatisfied university students. Students with a bent toward activism could channel their anger and hope for change through any one of three left-wing student movements differing in style and opposed in ideology: the Minsei, various New Left militant sects spawned about the time of the anti-Security Treaty struggles of 1960, and the Zenkyoto.[18]

Campus disputes highlighted many long-term complaints against the universities. In the beginning there was considerable public sympathy with the aims of striking students. Many faculty members were also sympathetic with the students' critique of the universities. The campus disputes gave reform-oriented faculty members an opportunity to work for basic changes. Already the ministry's Central Council of Education was working on its model of university reform.

By the end of 1970, more than 300 reform plans had been produced, most of them by university reform committees established for that purpose.[19] However, the enthusiasm for creating plans was not matched with implementation, for several reasons. First of all, public opinion shifted against the striking students in favor of restoring order first, and thinking of reforms later. Second, the settling of campus disputes and exhaustion, fragmentation, and defeat of the New Left student movement took away the urgency of reform. The government pushed the first postwar university control law through the National Diet on August 3, 1969. The law, called Provisional Measures Concerning University Administration, called on universities to solve their disputes or to face intervention by the Ministry of Education—initially with a warning; then, if the dispute was not settled in six months, by directly administering the university; and finally, by dissolving the university.[20] The immediate response to the law was an increase in campus disputes, but the threat of ministry intervention was by itself sufficient to spur university officials to bring in the police and most disputes were settled within a few months.

Third, there were basic disagreements between the interested parties concerning the goals of university reform. The political hawks saw their chance to get the universities under control. The overwhelming majority of the faculty members hoped for more efficient administration that could lighten the everyday burden of university management. Many students, on the other hand, saw the real problems as being those of more relevant education and greater student participation in university decision making. University administrators feared that granting broader participation would play into the hands of the Japan Communist Party and its strategy of advocating moderate reforms. Fourth, many reforms would involve closer relations with the Ministry of Education and there was little enthusiasm for that.

Yet some reforms did take place.[21] Minor changes in the consensus-oriented decision-making process were speeded up by the outbreak of "reform fever" in the late 1960s. Some bureaucratization of university administration has occurred along with an increase in administrative support staff. Administrators are more carefully selected and trained, particularly at the private universities. Also, university deans and presidents are relying much more on the executive skills of advisory cabinet groups they form to assist in administration. New offices for public relations and information gathering have been established at most universities.

A new breed of campus politician has appeared in this increasingly difficult situation to provide much needed help in achieving consensus: they could be called facilitators. Sometimes the facilitator is a member of an ad hoc task force appointed by the president or a dean and sometimes he has no official designation, but the role is nevertheless similar: gathering and analyzing information for decision making, communicating across genera- tional and ideological gaps, negotiating behind the scenes with a certain anonymity.

Increasing bureaucratization has added to the responsibilities of indi- vidual professors since it is they who are assigned to the most important administrative tasks. In fact, one of the most notable changes has been the proliferation of faculty committees with expanded participation of junior faculty members and a consequent increase in the time it takes to make decisions.

Increased student participation in decision making was an important issue for faculty and students in Japan as in the other countries treated in this book. However, except for some cases of peripheral involvement in the election of university presidents, there has been almost no increase in participation. In addition to the usual lack of faculty enthusiasm for further complicating the decision-making process by including students, and student doubts about the effectiveness of their participation, the Ministry of Education has opposed it. Moreover, university administrations hesitate to deal with the various politically motivated student groups because they are unrepresentative and any attempt to deal with one group will rouse the active opposition of the others. Most administrators attempt to limit such groups' influence by restricting participation in the decision-making process largely to professors and associate professors.

In June 1971, the Central Council on Education produced a set of *Basic Guidelines for the Reform of Education.*[22] The main proposals dealing with the structural reform of higher education met with almost universal opposition from the universities because they appeared to be designed to increase Ministry of Education control over the universities at the expense of university autonomy. The result has been a deadlock on structural reform. The "big bang" of the university disputes threw the university into disorder, but as soon as the disputes died down, the universities returned to predispute patterns.

Because the government was unable to institute basic reforms in the structure of higher education, it has taken other steps. Finally forced by the university disputes to recognize the financial plight of the private universities, the Ministry of Education, supported by the Ministry of Finance, agreed to subsidize half of the salary costs of the teaching staff at private universities. Later they agreed eventually to support half of the current operating expenses of the private universities. This support is administered by the Private School Promotion Foundation, a quasi-governmental agency that includes substantial private university representation. Undoubtedly a pattern of slanted resource allocation will develop that will help maintain the present prestige hierarchy of institutions. However, since the government is providing the money, it also may increase its control, including stricter quality standards for those that receive the highest sums.[23]

By far the most important of several new academic institutions started by the ministry is an academic city at Tsukuba outside Tokyo. It will include many research institutions including some related to the United Nations University. The central component of the academic city is Tsukuba University, founded in October 1974. Tsukuba University is a result of the initiative of some of the leaders of Tokyo University of Education who wanted to move from the narrow confines of their Tokyo campus and create a new type of university. Although the controversy over moving split the faculty, the Ministry of Education gave strong support to those advocating the move. The organization of Tsukuba University includes many of the experimental reforms that the Ministry of Education failed to introduce at existing universities. There is strong central administration with no semiautonomous faculties. The university is organized with various flexible research and educational clusters that are coordinated by committees of faculty members on the model of U.S. cluster colleges.

If traditional semiautonomous faculties protect the interests of faculty members too much, the committee method being experimented with at Tsukuba would seem to protect them too little. Many of the dissenting faculty members, particularly in the humanities and social sciences, are resigning after Tokyo University of Education is phased out in 1978. Tsukuba University has failed to attract high-quality faculty members in large numbers. There has been a widespread negative reaction against what is considered a violation of the consensus norm in the decision to establish

Tsukuba University, and the weakened influence of traditional faculty authority there.

Among its other efforts the ministry initiated the University of the Air, which will offer a B.A. degree. The ministry plans to grant charters to new medical faculties in order to have at least one faculty of medicine in each of the 47 prefectures by 1980. It plans to establish several new teacher training institutions but will face strong opposition from the Japan Teacher's Union. However, in 1975 the ministry pushed through a law to limit the founding of new institutions and faculties of higher education and to limit the expansion of student bodies in the private sector. This reflects the desire of the conservative party to limit its subsidies to private institutions, but also the desire to improve the quality of education.

The ministry is now considering proposals from the University of Tokyo and other prestigious schools to allow them to set up graduate schools that would be administratively separate from the present faculties. This could be done without special legislation simply by granting charters to new faculties, setting up new chairs, and giving the funds. The interests of several groups coincide on the desirability of this proposal. The Ministry of Education and many faculty members want to upgrade research and graduate education. Also, many faculty members would like to be free of undergraduate teaching. This proposal has the advantage of not requiring the restructuring of any existing faculties, which would be almost impossible.

Despite the deadlock on basic structural reform, as William Cummings points out, "the University crisis marked a turning point in Japanese higher education."[24] It was clear that the government could not make basic structural changes without the cooperation of the universities. The confrontation had nevertheless exposed many flaws in higher education. The financial crisis pointed to the need either to stop the phenomenal growth of higher education or to provide a rationale for it and improve the quality. The attention given to the university problem created a general awareness of need for change in the examination system and admissions policy, improvement of educational quality, internationalization, more flexibility in transferring and accepting credits from other institutions, and adaptation of the curriculum to changing societal needs.

Significant changes in personnel in the Ministry of Education under Cabinet Minister Michiya Sakata, during the university disputes of 1968-69, paved the way for the reshaping of policies in the direction of those liberal reforms. Also, the confrontation between conservatives and progressives over higher education policy lessened.[25] After it became clear that radical restructuring was not forthcoming, the leadership of former Vice Minister Isao Amagi in a new (1972) consultative body, Higher Education Roundtable, contributed greatly to the detente, as did the appointment of Dr. Michio Nagai, a former professor and a "dove," as minister of education from 1974 to 1976.

The subsidies to private universities have steadily increased, a standardized entrance exam for national universities (for the first screening) was carried out in 1976, and significant steps toward internationalization of the curriculum (language study, foreign visiting scholars) are being encouraged by the ministry. Although these are minor gains that could be lost, the present detente and the continuation of reform are encouraging.

In summary, the Japanese university system has been evolving gradually from more traditional patterns to more modern ones (in terms of increased efficiency and participation), as well as from an elite to a mass enrollment system. However, the basic patterns of control and decision making have changed little. The universities have been able to resist intrusions by the Ministry of Education,[26] but many needed reforms have not taken place. Frustrated in its attempts to introduce structural reforms in existing universities, the Ministry of Education has turned more to the use of incentives to accomplish its aims, and it has established some new institutions on its own initiative. In the long run, these are likely to have considerable influence on the shape of Japanese higher education.

NOTES

1. This analysis was developed with assistance from Professor Ikuo Amano of Nagoya University. See also Herbert Passin, *Society and Education in Japan* (New York: Teachers College Press, 1965), Michio Nagai, *Japanese Higher Education: Its Takeoff and Crash* (Tokyo: University of Tokyo Press, 1971), and Herbert Passin, "Japan," in *Higher Education: From Autonomy to Systems,* ed. James A. Perkins and Barbara Baird Israel (New York: International Council for Educational Development, 1972), p. 221.

2. Michio Magai, *Higher Education in Japan: Its Take-off and Crash* translated by Jerry Dusenbury (Tokyo: University of Tokyo Press, 1971), p. 21, taken from the Imperial University Ordinance of 1886.

3. Robert M. Spaulding, *Imperial Japan's Higher Civil Service Examinations* (Princeton: Princeton University Press, 1967). For the present system see Akira Kubota, *Higher Civil Servants in Postwar Japan: Their Social Origins, Educational Backgrounds, and Career Patterns* (Princeton: Princeton University Press, 1969).

4. Koya Azumi, *Higher Education and Business Recruitment in Japan* (New York: Teachers College Press, 1969); Morikazu Ushiogi, "A Comparative Study of the Occupational Structure of University Graduates," *The Developing Economies* 9, no. 3 (September 1971).

5. See Ulrich Teichler, "Some Aspects of Higher Education in Japan," in *KBS Bulletin,* July 1972 (published by the Kokusai Bunka Shinkokai). Teichler gives an excellent analysis of the examination system.

6. William K. Cummings describes the chair in his Ph.D. dissertation "The Changing Academic Marketplace and University Reform in Japan" (Ph.D. diss., Harvard University, 1972).

7. Ivan Hall: personal communication.

8. Kazuo Kawai, *Japan's American Interlude* (Chicago: University of Chicago Press, 1960), Chs. 10 and 11.

9. John E. Blewett, ed., "Higher Education in Postwar Japan—The Ministry of Education's 1964 White Paper," *Monumenta Nipponica Monograph 22* (Tokyo: Sophia University Press, 1965).

10. William K. Cummings, Ikuo Amano, and Donald F. Wheeler, eds., *Changing*

Japanese Higher Education (New York: Praeger, forthcoming). See chapters by Cummings and Amano.

11. T. J. Pempel, "The Politics of Enrollment Expansion in Japanese Universities," *Journal of Asian Studies* 33, (November 1973):67–86.

12. Chie Nakane, *Japanese Society* (Berkeley: University of California Press, 1970), pp. 40–41.

13. Albert M. Craig, "Functional and Disfunctional Aspects of Government Bureaucracy," in *Modern Japanese Organization and Decision-Making*, ed. Ezra Vogel (Berkeley: University of California Press, 1975), pp. 23–30. Craig gives a useful analysis of how the ringi system works. Recent research has cast doubt on how much the system is used in deciding *important* matters.

14. Ibid., pp. 22–23.

15. A more complete analysis can be found in Donald F. Wheeler, "The Japanese Student Movement: Value Politics, Students Politics and the University of Tokyo Struggle" (Ph.D. Diss., Columbia University, 1974).

16. Although the Ministry of Education set maximum limits on enrollments based on the number of teachers and other factors, they were not enforced. Private universities enrolled more in order to get tuition and fees. National universities had no similar incentive since they received no extra government subsidy for students above the limit and tuition rates were so low it did not pay to add students just to get their fees. For statistics see Japan, Ministry of Education, *Educational Statistics in Japan: Present, Past, Future* (August 1971), pp. 38–41.

17. For an analysis of the relationships between economic growth and changes in youth attitudes, see Wheeler, "The Japanese Student Movement," pp. 94–118.

18. For an analysis of the different styles of student movements see Wheeler, "The Japanese Student Movement," pp. 162–94.

19. Kazuyuki Kitamura analyzes university reform plans in "Daigaku Kaikaku no Dōkō ni Kansuru yobi Chōsa: 1968–1970" [Analytical Survey of Reform Plans in Japanese Higher Education: 1968–1970]. *Refurensu* [Reference of the National Diet Library], 245, June 1971, pp. 85–121. See also Michiya Shimbori and Kazuyuki Kitamura, *Higher Education and the Student Problem in Japan* (Tokyo: Kokusai Bunka Shinkokai, 1972).

20. Government of Japan, *Law No. 70 on Provisional Measures Concerning University Administration, promulgated in August, 1969.* Translated in *Minerva* 8-1, January 1970 ("Coping with Student Disorder in Japan"), pp. 129–35.

21. For evaluations of university reform see William K. Cummings, "Japanese Education and Politics in the Seventies," in *Japan: The Paradox of Progress*, ed. Hugh Patrick and Lewis Austin (New Haven: Yale University Press, 1976), and Cummings, Amano, and Wheeler, *Changing Japanese Higher Education.* For the results of a sample survey on decision making in Japanese higher education see IMHE Project Team, Research Institute for Higher Education, *Japanese Patterns of Institutional Management in Higher Education* (Hiroshima: Research Institute for Higher Education, 1975).

22. The final report was published in English in 1972 by the Ministry of Education. An abridged version of the higher education sections of the report appears in *Minerva* 11, No. 3 (July 1973).

23. Cummings, "The Japanese Private University," *Minerva* 11, (July 1973):348–71.

24. Cummings, "The Aftermath of the University Crisis," *Japan Interpreter* 10, No. 3-4 (Winter 1976):353.

25. Cummings, "The Aftermath of the University Crisis," p. 354.

26. Cummings, "Japanese Education and Politics in the Seventies," in *Japan: The Paradox of Progress*, ed. Patrick and Austin (New Haven: Yale University Press, 1976).

PART II
CONCLUSIONS

9
SYSTEMS OF HIGHER EDUCATION
Dietrich Goldschmidt

The analysis of changes in structures of power and decision making in the higher education systems of seven industrialized countries proceeds from the general observation that, under the pressure of basic social, economic, and political forces, higher education has developed from relatively small, selective, and loosely coordinated groupings into massive systems of great socioeconomic significance.

The chapters focus on the balance of power between the teaching staff and their academic institutions on the one hand and the state authorities, interest groups, and market forces on the other. These relations determine the extent of the universities' autonomy. They also determine the degree to which government and society can supervise and hold the universities accountable, plan their development, and stimulate innovation.

CHARACTERISTICS OF THE NATIONAL SYSTEMS

International relations in science and scholarship, as in other areas of public life, have become increasingly interwoven. Yet the movement toward mass higher education in the past 30 years underlines the uniqueness of each national system of higher education. The particular historical features of each country are manifested in their educational systems, which serve to introduce each succeeding generation to the nation's cultural and economic systems. In contrast to the international nature of science, the functions of higher education are nationally determined, increasingly so as systems lose their elitist character. National histories, cultures, and economic systems, as well as varying authority structures and processes of informal communication, lend different weight to certain common features that are present in all of the countries analyzed, such as relative professorial independence, state supervision, and comprehensive planning.

Federal Republic of Germany: Politicized Legalism

German higher education manifests much legalism and politicization. Constitutional provisions and their interpretation by the federal constitutional court are frequently invoked in political debate, and the use of legal regulations to manage tension and conflict within institutions is widespread. The constitutional articles granting fundamental rights, which are expressly excluded from any amendment, include the guarantee of freedom of research and teaching, which is central to the controversy over the expansion of participation in the university, and the right of free educational and occupational choice, which has direct implications for the thorny problem of university admissions. Moreover, in the past decade, all aspects of higher education policy and structure have been subjected to extensive legislation and ministerial regulation at both the state and the federal levels. And large numbers of court cases have grown out of the legislation.

The effectiveness of these new regulations in dealing with perennial political and ideological tensions remains to be seen. Altogether the state has emerged stronger than before, exercising increasing supervision over the universities' capacities, staffing, and curriculum.

Italy: Patrimonial Politics

All of the countries studied have historically accorded substantial influence to the full professor and have frequently taken the German Ordinarius as a model. However, nowhere have the professors dominated all levels of higher education so completely and in such patrimonial and political fashion as in Italy. In the style of barons, the professors have made decisions on research, teaching, and personnel in the universities. To be sure, the universities are under the central ministry of education in Rome, but there too the professors have dominated policy making as members of central committees. Their influence is reinforced by their strength in Parliament, as well as by the weakness of the state as a whole. Political feuding undermines Parliament and the executive alike, and the financial crisis hinders any expansion of facilities already overburdened by skyrocketing enrollments.

Yet incremental changes have begun in the 1970s that move toward a more diverse and adaptive system and transfer some power from the traditional academic oligarchs to other groups within and outside the system. Change in Italy is often subtle and indirect, brought about mainly by intricate political negotiation leading to piecemeal adjustments, rather than through broad legislation, as in Germany, or grand plans, as in France.

France: Administrative Centralism

Some tendency toward centralized control of expanding systems of higher education is present in every one of the countries studied. But nowhere is the principle of centralized, national administration so firmly rooted in traditional attitudes toward the state as in French *étatisme*, or statism. Paris is the absolute political and administrative fulcrum of France.

The 1968 Orientation Act attempted to meet the need for organizational and functional diversification of the expanding system of higher education through decentralization, restructuring of the universities, and broadened participation of regional and university groups. Nonetheless, significant elements of central control remain, such as the fragmentation of higher education into vertically distinct sectors, including universities, grandes écoles, and research institutes, and the national competitive examinations (concours), which entail standardized curricula. Psychologically and socially the prestige of Paris remains, along with the expectation that decisions will be made there. Meanwhile, the representatives of the universities confront a technocratic bureaucracy.

Sweden: Consensus and State Planning

Governments in all these countries (but least of all in Italy) now undertake some sort of planning for higher education, whether at the national or state level. But Sweden, the smallest and the most homogeneous, has developed planning most extensively, earlier than other nations, and has carried it forward with greater continuity—with so-called rolling reform—than elsewhere.

Two aspects are central to the Swedish planning process. First, basic policies and reforms are adopted by Parliament or the executive after extensive consultation with concerned interests, usually on the foundation of a broad consensus, and are implemented by a central administrative bureaucracy with unchallenged authority. Second, planners and policy makers seek to link higher education ever more closely to the needs of the employment system. Nowhere do higher studies so directly serve professional and occupational training as in Sweden, and no other country plans so thorough a transformation of traditional university institutions into a general system of tertiary education. The Swedes have refined planning for higher education to a point that contrasts vividly with the hypertrophy of professorial power in Italy, at the opposite extreme.

Despite general acceptance of these measures, some students and professors remain skeptical. Such planning not only limits the autonomy of individual institutions, but by dividing functions among them, separating research from teaching, it also restricts the traditional academic freedom of students and professors.

The State Systems of Continental Europe

The four nations summarized thus far all possess state systems of higher education. It is true that the other countries provide the bulk of funds for higher education from governmental sources: from the states in the United States, and from the national government in Britain and Japan. Yet, with the exception of Japan's national universities, the institutions in these countries enjoy the status of legally independent corporations with full authority in financial and personnel matters, and draw funds from a variety of sources.

In contrast, the continental European institutions are fundamentally under governmental authority, however much the modalities may vary. Their funds come almost exclusively from governmental sources, which facilitates central planning and guidance. Moreover, the separate institutions conventionally receive these funds directly according to line-by-line budgets, which together with the state's particular authority in matters of personnel, permit detailed state supervision. Thus the comparative perspective shows the relative meaning of university autonomy—an autonomy which in Germany has been particularly stressed historically. This autonomy must be understood as an area of freedom that the various countries have permitted for the development of academic science and scholarship, to a varying and yet well defined extent according to their historical situations.

Changes since World War II have partly restricted this autonomy and partly maintained it. The state increasingly controls the curriculum, in terms of overall organization and general programs; often only substantive details are beyond such external control. As they become more costly, research and the training of researchers are affected by closer financial supervision, but otherwise they preserve a certain amount of relative autonomy.

In particular, state influence on the curriculum goes beyond formal supervision where training prepares mainly for admission to the civil service, including public education, and therefore is subjected to detailed substantive control, although often with the involvement of academics as members of state examination boards. This government influence is all the more significant in that the systems of continental Europe, in accordance with their historical function as state institutions, have hitherto sent a much higher proportion of their graduates into public service than have institutions of higher education in the other three countries. To deliberately overstate the matter: The state institution is traditionally an enterprise of the state dedicated to the welfare of the state, and especially to the needs of the public service and of the publicly acknowledged professions. The explosion of student enrollment in all four states, however, and recent structural

changes in such countries as Sweden and France—participation of representatives of public service, of industry, trade unions, etc.—do seem to
suggest an impending opening to the broader needs of society.

Great Britain: Autonomy within a National System

British universities are independent corporations under royal charter
and traditionally have enjoyed a great degree of autonomy. The autonomy
of the universities rests largely on the ability of representatives of universities
and government to negotiate pragmatic policies on the basis of their
common understanding of what constitutes the public interest. Shielded by
such tacit understandings, teaching staff traditionally have had great independence, free from government or university bureaucracies.

However, growth and rising costs, economic crisis, and budgetary
restrictions have led to government limitations on autonomy through
increasing central planning and financial oversight. Nevertheless, academics
make the decisions about selection of students, appointment of teaching
staff, curricula, and examinations. New universities have been founded to
absorb expansion of the system, helping to keep all universities and their
internal units small. Since the mid-1960s the nonuniversity, or public, sector
of higher education has been expanded and upgraded to form (with the
universities) the controversial binary system, provoking considerable tension.

Some are skeptical of the autonomy, the elitist tradition, and the
academic, theoretical orientation of the universities. Others—especially in
the universities—suspect socialist inclinations behind the expansion of
locally oriented colleges devoted mainly to professional training and oppose
the financial priority given the nonuniversity sector by the government,
claiming the polytechnics are costly and have not reached the standards
expected of them. Increasingly, the Department of Education and Science
has taken on the role of a national ministry of education, undermining the
traditional conventions on which university government had been based.

United States: Dispersed Control and Market System

Colleges and universities in the United States are controlled by dispersed and disparate authorities and are very susceptible to market forces.
Market influence as a social and economic regulator has a much more direct
effect than in Europe on the supply of and demand for student places, on the
adjustment of curricula to the employment opportunities of graduates, and
on the system of research grants.

Precisely because they are not tied together under a single administrative organization, the individual institutions can pursue their own

initiatives—as long as these do not collide with state-level plans for higher education—or adjust to shifting demands and expectations, whether from politicians or public opinion, from student applicants, from the employment market for graduates, or from the research community. At the same time this can create difficulties for long-term enterprises. Economic crises threaten institutions that are financially weak or have failed to adjust to market conditions.

To a large extent the institutional bureaucracy of the university takes the place of government administration. Individuals on the teaching staff generally have less security of tenure than in Europe, although as long as supply and demand are balanced, the chances for mobility between institutions are greater, thanks to the size and relative elasticity of the academic labor market. The diversity of administrative structures in U.S. postsecondary education has promoted the development of a great variety of pedagogical approaches. However, recent trends point to an increase in centralization and political influence.

Japan: Institutional Hierarchy and Dual Structure of Control

Japan has many highly stable social and institutional hierarchies and the system of higher education is one of them. Within a structure of dual public and private control, universities and colleges are hierarchically ordered according to prestige and status. A meritocracy based on postsecondary certification (largely independent of actual achievement) has developed, making an individual's social and employment opportunities overwhelmingly dependent on the prestige of the institution attended.

The state administers the national universities. Like the elite grandes écoles in France, the national universities train recruits for the civil service and for elite positions in private business and industry. These universities serve as models for the private universities.

The great majority of students attend the private universities, which themselves are hierarchically ordered but are generally much lower in prestige than the national universities. The private universities are entirely dependent on the market of student applicants and on the employment opportunities for their graduates.

Concepts of university autonomy developed in the West are difficult to apply to Japan. The relationship of private institutions to the government is ambiguous, while the Japanese procedure of group-based informal agreements derived through unwritten structures of authority, a process that generally precedes formal decision making, appears to be more significant than elsewhere.

Since the crisis in higher education at the end of the 1960s, changes are occurring. The national government has begun to exert greater influence. National policy makers are beginning to reduce the drastic educational, financial, and social inequities of the hierarchical system, while ensuring that the system functions more effectively as a whole.

COMPARISONS

There are several specific policy areas to be considered in a comparison of shifts in the distribution of power in the seven systems of higher education in recent decades.

Overall Planning and Policy Making

In principle, long-term general planning, whether for the system of higher education as a whole or for individual institutions, involves general, basic decisions rather than specific ones. However, the planning process can greatly affect specific policy areas, such as personnel, curriculum and research, and it is often closely linked to budgetary decision making. The salience of planning for the material and intellectual development of higher education has increased since the explosive growth of student numbers and costs, as well as the increasing importance of the universities as a political and economic factor. Administrative authorities in Europe, Japan, and the United States have strengthened their planning efforts, in some cases by establishing distinct planning bureaus and by limiting the jurisdiction of decision-making authorities within the universities.

At the state and national levels (Levels 5 and 6), the organizational structures responsible for overall planning vary according to the degree of centralization and bureaucratization (with the United States at one end of the scale, as the most decentralized, and Sweden at the other); the extent of integration of the different sectors of postsecondary education (France, Great Britain, and Japan are the most segmented, whereas Sweden is the most integrated); and the concentrations of government planning authority at the central level, or its distribution between federal government and the states.

Even systems with a strong tradition of autonomy, such as Britain's, are forced to yield to central planning authorities in the course of expansion. In this situation, the universities (with the exception of the private sector in the United States and Japan) are left with leeway only to submit proposals as inputs to the planning process and to undertake detailed planning to the extent it is left to them, making decisions within the limits of the overall budget or within curricular or personnel guidelines.

As the universities have lost autonomy, particularly in the realm of curriculum, government authorities must seek ways to legitimate their policies. This has been the primary function of the specially appointed expert planning commissions in Sweden, and both Sweden and France are attempting to involve interest-group representatives in decision-making bodies at a number of levels on a continuing basis.

To counterbalance increased centralization and bureaucratization, certain nations, such as Sweden and France, have introduced a limited degree of decentralization. The objectives are to gain local and regional support and to stimulate the cooperation of those involved in the system. Increased emphasis on local and regional decision making also represents an attempt to democratize the systems, although the jurisdiction of the democratized organs is usually limited.

Such developments have largely bypassed the private, market-oriented sectors of higher education in the United States and Japan, where overall planning and policy making remain basically prerogatives of the individual private institutions. They remain autonomous, and their progress or decline is determined not by government planning but by their distinctiveness and desirability in the market.

Budget and Finance

Most of the funds available to universities under various budgetary categories, such as current expenditures, capital expenditures, and research funds, are earmarked for relatively routine, continuing tasks. The budgetary decision-making process ordinarily concentrates on marginal increases in continuing programs, one-time expenditures, or temporally limited programs. There is frequent tension between the individual scholar or institute seeking additional funds and whichever higher levels of administration are responsible for overall institutional planning and coordination of all activities. Supplementary funds from external sources can often serve as instruments of interventionist policies, especially in systems that consist of legally independent corporations and are open to market forces. The federal government and the large foundations in the United States as well as the Japanese national government often employ such means for influencing policy.

In state systems of higher education, the development of research and teaching is determined in practice by the priorities established in the budget of the national government (or states). The independence of the individual institution in the allocation of its means is likely to be greater in those cases where the funds come from several sources and where the institutions, as legally independent corporations, manage their own financial resources. It is this which distinguishes the public and private institutions of higher education in the United States and the universities (not the polytechnics) of Great Britain from the state institutions of continental Europe and Japan. The income from student fees in the Anglo-Saxon countries and in Japan plays a significant role, while in continental Europe the fees have been abolished. Such fees—attracting some applicants while deterring others—represent a market force that affects such policy areas as curriculum and personnel planning.

The real basis for financial independence, the income from capital endowments, which traditionally played a significant role in the Anglo-Saxon countries and in the private sector of Japan, today is so much reduced that its function remains important only in the U.S. private colleges and universities, and even there it is diminished.

As enrollments and institutions have expanded, budgets have grown as well. To avoid losing overall budgetary control, central accounting procedures have been introduced, mainly at the level of the university, but sometimes at higher levels. At the same time, in order to overcome bureaucratic alienation, attempts have been made (especially in France and Sweden) to delegate authority for lower-level budget allocation to those units.

Access and Student Admissions

In their admissions procedures, the seven systems of higher education can historically be divided into two groups: the Continental European countries, and the Anglo-Saxon nations together with Japan.

In the Continental systems, all graduates of the academic secondary school traditionally have possessed the right to enter the university of their choice and to plan their course of study relatively freely. The length of studies was virtually unregulated, and the institutions themselves possessed no right of selection. In all cases, student fees were kept very low, and today a substantial proportion of students—with the exception of Italy—receive government grants in support of living costs. Thanks to the free and flexible course of studies—especially in the humanities and social sciences—which is even today often based largely on lectures, the capacity of the individual institutions was relatively elastic. Only the grandes écoles in France traditionally selected a sharply limited number of entrants each year from a large applicant pool on the basis of competitive examinations for each institution.

The extraordinary growth of student numbers has brought the traditional systems to the point of crisis. With the exception of Italy, all of the Continental countries are introducing a system of government-determined enrollment capacities and controlled access and admissions. Free access for all individuals possessing an academic secondary-school-leaving certificate still exists formally in Italy and France; but Sweden and the German Federal Republic are controlling access through a government-administered process of admission and assignment to individual institutions. For some "hard" subjects (mainly medicine, dentistry and pharmacy), a numerus clausus is in operation.

In Sweden, such measures had gone furthest. However, the surprising decline of enrollment figures since 1970 has enabled the government to make the admission procedures fairly flexible on the basis of two principles: fairly open admission to the unrestricted fields in humanities and social sciences; and centrally controlled admission to the "restricted" fields such as natural sciences, technology, and medicine with favorable provisions for students with professional experience, thus providing an opportunity for students who had not applied or were not admitted on graduation from high school.

In the Federal Republic of Germany, institutional capacity is now planned jointly by the federal and state governments. More than any other country, Germany has a large and steadily growing group of applicants who have no prospect of admission to the hard subjects until after a waiting period. Although solutions for this problem are still under discussion, the federal government's recent role as a mediator between the states in this area and as a policy initiator in its own right has significantly contributed to the growth of its influence on overall policy for higher education. In France, as in Italy, there is no general limitation on access to the universities; however, French secondary schools have begun to establish selective counseling procedures.

In Japan and the Anglo-Saxon countries, individual institutions retain the right to select applicants freely according to their own criteria. Each institution—especially the U.S. private colleges—attempts thereby to maintain its special character, educational orientation, and academic distinction. Institutions in Britain, Japan, and the United States require student fees, although in greatly varying amounts, even from students who receive grants or scholarships. The extensive grant system in Britain keeps fees from significantly restricting access, but the ability of the individual to pay influences access in the United States and in Japan. The less prestigious the institution, the more it must cater to potential applicants in order to attract them. As for the student applicants, their origin, achievement, preferences and—to a minor extent in Great Britain—degree of affluence determine their success and therefore their distribution among the diverse, hierarchically ordered set of institutions of higher education.

Curriculum and Examinations

The distinction between state systems and systems in the rest of the countries is again useful for analysis. Among the state systems, France and Italy traditionally have set uniform national guidelines for the curriculum, whereas Germany and Sweden have allowed the universities greater freedom. Recently, however, governments in the latter two countries have begun to regulate study programs more closely, reducing students' options. Therefore, although academics are in charge of implementing the programs at the level of the institute or the department, their academic freedom consists merely of a modest amount of leeway within the guidelines. For the cases in which the state conducts examinations for entry into certain professions and the civil service, most notably in Germany and France, freedom of learning and teaching are reduced even further. These trends are directly related to the growing tendency to separate advanced or graduate studies from basic courses, much as the Anglo-Saxon countries have always done. Thus individual freedom of learning, teaching, and research in the traditional sense is increasingly concentrated at the graduate and postgraduate stages of study, and here the units at Levels 1 and 2 retain much of their traditional power.

British and U.S. institutions of higher education, on contrast, still possess significant control over curriculum and examinations, exercised primarily at Levels 1 and 2. (The state may regulate standards of entry into certain professions.) Undergraduate courses are highly structured and limited in length, although substantial options for the individual student usually remain. In place of state regulation, the British system of external examiners (or the Council for National Academic Awards, or CNAA—for the nonuniversity sector) and, much more minimally, accrediting associations in the United States serve as checks on standards. Japan takes a middle position: curriculum and examinations are organized largely on the U.S. pattern, but state regulation is strong. Advanced work is even more restricted to the postgraduate level than it is elsewhere.

Academic Appointments

Decision-making processes for academic appointments are difficult to compare. For junior or nontenured positions, the process is likely to take place largely within the department or equivalent unit, which usually makes the effective decision, even if a higher organizational level must formally authorize the appointment.

Appointments to senior, tenured positions seldom fall under the primary control of the lowest organizational level. Departments in high-status U.S. universities and colleges represent perhaps the major exception. Most often, a body at Level 2, the faculty or school, effectively controlled by senior professors, assesses the candidates and proposes one or more names, whereas the actual appointment is made at a higher level.

Here a distinction can be made—although with important qualifications—between the state systems and the others. In the state systems, Level 3 or 4 university organs play a minor role, and the formal appointment is made by government officials at the national level (at the Land level in Germany). In Italy, elected committees of professors at the national level effectively control appointments, whereas in France such committees generally provide supplementary opinions, thus potentially providing the ministry a genuine choice. The senior-appointments process in the state systems remains cumbersome and inflexible, a hindrance to interinstitutional mobility, and often subject to the wishes of powerful peer professors.

In contrast, the Anglo-Saxon countries and, to a lesser extent, Japan endow their university-level authorities with more power. Generally the process of making appointments is more flexible than in the state systems; it is oriented primarily to the interests of the departments although it may also consider concerns of the university as a whole. Market factors, such as the latest academic fashions, can easily play a substantial role, but the barriers against direct government intervention are strong.

Everywhere, therefore, a two-step procedure tends to prevail, with academics at the lowest levels making proposals and authorities at some higher level fulfilling a function of review. However controversial some review procedures may be, they appear to be essential. This is evident from the Italian system, which provides few effective checks on appointment decisions made by professorial committees at the center.

Research

Along with the separation of undergraduate and postgraduate education, research is increasingly separated from teaching. A particular manifestation of the separation is the familiar case of research programs or institutes within universities but without links to any departments.

As long as research does not require special resources and can be financed from the regular budget, the individual researcher and institute are relatively free in their choice of projects. Such regular financing may favor basic research. However, many fields require more extensive research resources. Such funds come from a variety of sources, such as governments at different levels, national research organizations, foundations, and business corporations. Grants usually must be applied for, are program- or project-oriented, and are given most often for applied research. The relative significance of such funds varies greatly among the countries studied, with the United States having used them most extensively. On the other hand, in Italy—although comparatively very short of research funds—the National Research Council coordinates and finances most research.

Two consequences for decision making are evident. First, as research demands more extensive resources and becomes increasingly important in political, economic, and military policies, there is a tendency toward more systematic cooperation and planning, notably at the institutional level, which partially supplants the traditional system of individual negotiations between the researcher and funding sources.

Second, the various grantors exercise growing decision-making authority, particularly when they pursue policies of their own. To the extent that scientists and academics serve as experts on the advisory bodies of the funding organizations, they serve as mediators between scientific and public interests. The autonomy of individual institutions thus finds its limits in the growing societal relevance of scientific research.

CHANGES IN THE PATTERN OF DECISION MAKING

A review of the process of decision making in various policy areas over the past three decades demonstrates in almost every case a shift of power from lower to higher levels. The role of government, whether national or state, has become more important. Within the universities (and sometimes at the multicampus level), bureaucracies devoted to administration and planning, staffed by full-time academic administrators, have expanded, assuming considerable responsibility for preparing and implementing policy decisions. Although much initial work is still done at lower levels, the actual locus of decision making has tended to rise. There is simultaneously a contrary trend toward the delegation of responsibility for detailed decisions and implementation to lower levels. The policy process has become increasingly formalized, especially in the larger institutions. Other changes include the participation of junior staff, a shifting role for students, and the inclusion of laypersons in policy making. The changes in the decision-making patterns and structures of the seven national systems are summarized below.

As higher education has grown, so has its administrative structure in all countries. Full-time academic administrators, long influential in the U.S. system, are playing an increasingly important role. In France and Germany university presidents have been instituted. This development has been related to another: older personal and informal forms of communication and decision making have been supplanted by formal arrangements. Formal arrangements are especially necessary where "clubs" in which senior professors enjoyed automatic membership have been replaced by representative bodies to which professors, and others, must delegate their spokesmen.

The expansion of administrative structures has been accompanied by attempts to decentralize decision making in certain policy areas. Such decentralization may be considered a functional necessity in enlisting the active cooperation of staff at the lower levels. Sweden and France have undertaken such measures in connection with regionalization of their systems. In Germany, curricular reforms have been undertaken primarily by junior staff. Nevertheless, despite the evident need and demand for decentralization and the attention given to structural changes intended to achieve it, cases where a real shift of power from a higher to a lower level of organization has taken place are still very rare.

Decentralization is usually associated with the extension of participation to groups hitherto uninvolved in decision making. In the traditional state systems, faculty and university organization was collegial in a negative sense, for it tended to exclude staff below the full professor and to protect professorial interests. Organs for inclusive decision making were relatively weak, and for the most part the constituent units—faculties within the university, and chairs or institutes within the faculty—pursued their own goals. Under particular circumstances, certain fields fared well, but for the most part these structures have favored the status quo within traditional disciplines. New fields have remained subordinate, and interdisciplinary cooperation has been inhibited.

Among the new groups participating in decision making, the junior academic staff have generally been the most important, especially at the lowest organizational level, the institute or department, as for example in Germany and Sweden. Traditionally, a junior teacher or researcher on the Continent was treated merely as an adjunct of the senior professor who carried sole responsibility for his discipline within the university. Subordinate staff took no part in decision making and remained dependent on the senior professors for career advancement. Today, junior staff virtually everywhere have been granted some participation in university government. In certain cases, particularly in Germany and Italy, substantial numbers of junior staff have been granted professorial rank. With ever-increasing professional specialization and enlarged student enrollment, junior staff must contribute heavily to research and teaching.

The position of the senior professors, who have traditionally dominated decision making within the university (with the partial exception of U.S. institutions), has thus been weakened through expanded participation by other university groups, and the power structure within the university and most of its constituent units has become flatter and less hierarchical than before.

The broadening of participation has not been restricted to junior staff; it has also benefited students and nonacademic personnel. Nonacademic personnel have been admitted to decision-making organs primarily in France, Sweden, and the Federal Republic of Germany, although only in token proportions, and they have not had any clear impact on policy making. The role of students has been somewhat greater. They have been admitted in substantial numbers to policy organs in France and the Federal Republic, and in small numbers elsewhere. Everywhere, however, students are either in a minority (together with the other nonprofessorial groups) relative to the senior professors, as in Germany, or excluded from decisions in certain areas, usually appointments and research, as in France and Sweden. Although the Anglo-Saxon countries and Japan increased student involvement to some extent, they have also kept the number of student representatives very low or restricted them to an advisory role or to areas of direct student concern.

In all countries, structural change in higher education, including the broadening of participation, received a distinct impetus from the student protest movement of the late 1960s. This was clearest in France and Germany. Elsewhere, student protest has affected the administration less directly. Student demonstrators tended to voice sweeping demands. They wanted a new, "critical" university, with its forms and curricular content derived from critical analysis of society and committed to changing it. The actual trend of development, toward bureaucratic rationalization and large-scale administrative systems, is contrary in every way to the radicals' ideals. The degree of student participation, in particular, has certainly not met the high-flown expectations of its radical advocates, but where it has not faded for lack of interest it has become routine, contributing unspectacularly yet constructively to decision making.

Student influence in a broader, latent sense has also become more important. Shifts in the social situation and background of youth in general and students in particular, including the lowering of the age of majority, have significantly influenced higher education, stimulating, for example, the growing orientation of the curriculum to vocational requirements. In the United States and Japan, the role of the student as client, choosing suitable curricular offerings, has become more crucial with the stagnation of enrollments. Generally, the transition from elite to mass higher education has led to a formalization of study programs, making the success of a curriculum more than ever dependent on involving the students in determining its objectives, content, and structure. Such involvement is perhaps best exemplified by the course critiques prepared by students in many U.S. colleges.

The British universities, U.S. institutions of higher education, and Japanese private colleges are governed by boards or councils consisting primarily of outside laypersons and, sometimes, representatives of interest groups. In the United States, business people have traditionally played the leading role on boards of trustees, at least in private institutions, whereas the boards of public universities often include a greater range of groups. In every case, the lay boards at Level 3 (sometimes Level 4 in the United States) provide a channel of influence for outside interests, whether political, social, or economic, in institutional policy making.

The state institutions of continental Europe and Japan traditionally have not had formal provisions for direct representation of outside groups in policy making. Outside groups have attempted to exercise influence either through government or through grants supporting particular projects and researchers. In recent years, reformers from all political camps have urged a redistribution of social values, emphasizing the social responsibility of science. Sweden, and France have responded by taking measures to include outside groups in policy making for higher education. Sweden is the only Continental European country in which societal representatives have begun to play an important role, particularly in increasing the professional orientation of the curriculum. In Germany and France, there has been widespread resistance—mainly from the Left—to the involvement of employers in academic policy making.

CONCLUDING PERSPECTIVES

The changes in decision-making structures and processes have not been caused merely by the growth of the institutions and systems as a whole, nor by the need for efficient administration. In varying degrees social, economic, and political factors have influenced the directions of higher education in each country. Governments have advocated their own policies, interest groups have made demands, especially for changes in curriculum that would relate more effectively to employment opportunities and to the need for trained manpower. More broadly, there is increased emphasis on the social accountability of higher education.

To a great degree, specific measures of structural reform have been forced on higher education institutions from outside. This has occurred through government-drafted legislation, as in Sweden, France, and the Federal Republic of Germany; through ministerial policy making, as in the establishment of the binary system in Great Britain; or through market forces, as in the United States. The more absolutely the professors controlled research and training, and the more directly they resisted long overdue reforms, identifying their responsibility for the maintenance of excellence and academic freedom with the retention of their traditional academic prerogatives and powers, the sharper the eventual conflicts became and the more drastic were the measures finally taken.

The state systems, in particular, were historically not so much exposed to direct government influence as they were (and in some cases still are) shielded against societal forces that might have induced change. This is demonstrated as much by the conflicts and extensive legislation in France and Germany as by state measures against student unrest in Japan and the continued frustration of reform attempts in Italy. The diversified, market-exposed U.S. system is more flexible, if only because it must continually adapt to outside forces. Even the national system of Great Britain appears to adjust relatively effectively to modern challenges, by increasing the number and variety of institutions rather than simply letting existing institutions grow.

The greater flexibility of the nonstate systems, and the greater institutional autonomy they provide, do not, however, ensure that their teachers and researchers will enjoy greater academic freedom. Both state and nonstate systems are accountable and subject to oversight, whether by government bureaucracies or by representatives of various political, economic, and other social interests.

A more fundamental point is that research and teaching apparently suffer either when they are entirely autonomous activities or when they are rigidly supervised. Academics as decision makers need a partner to which they are accountable. It may be a state bureaucracy, or their own university administration, or a foundation—any authority to which they must periodically demonstrate the scientific and social relevance of their activity and which in turn grants them the necessary autonomy and resources while mediating social demands. The lack of such accountability is particularly evident in Italy, whereas Sweden may be approaching the other extreme, endangering its scientific progress through restrictions on the freedom of teaching and research.

This study has raised certain organizational problems which all of the systems still face. Two are of particular significance. First, the transition from elite to mass higher education raises the issue of the place of the traditional universities within the larger system of postsecondary education. The elaborate institutional hierarchies of the United States and Japan contrast with the European systems, where tradition leads governments to promote formal parity of status within groups of institutions and even among them. Except perhaps in the United States, no permanent solution has been found to the problem of reconciling the need to provide postsecondary programs for large numbers of students with the necessity of concentrating resources for research and scholarly training in a relatively small number of institutions.

As the systems of higher education expanded, the individual institutions also grew in size; this among other factors gave rise to many of the changes analyzed here. But this raises a second issue: What are the scientific, social, and economic consequences of such large-scale institutions? If they are necessary, that might in turn imply that bureaucratization and formalization of the policy-making process, with the shifting of decision loci from lower to higher levels of organization, are unavoidable. Yet in Great Britain, where institutional growth has been slower than elsewhere, partly due to the establishment of new universities, decision making continues to be relatively informal, and the expansion of academic administration has been held in check. A more systematic comparative study should clarify the relationships between the size of individual institutions and their communication and decision-making structures.

Comparative studies such as the present one are indeed capable of providing practical findings for policy makers in higher education. Knowledge of the strengths and weaknesses of decision-making structures in other national systems can give insight into one's own system and its problems. At the same time, analyses of individual national systems demonstrate that each one must ultimately confront its problems with measures suited to its own national situation and context.

10
ACADEMIC POWER: CONCEPTS, MODES, AND PERSPECTIVES
Burton R. Clark

In this volume, the basic structure of academic authority in each of seven nations has been characterized by identifying important levels of organization, estimating group influence and the nature of authority at each level, and locating areas of policy making by levels in order to determine what groups have primary influence and by means of what forms of control. There are important differences in the way that authority is distributed in the seven academic systems, and in the very nature of the authority exercised at each of various levels of organization. Modern national systems of higher education are among the most complex social enterprises ever evolved. Researchers need all the conceptual help they can get to penetrate that complexity and disentangle the strands of control. What, then, is the minimal vocabulary for discussing the prime ingredients in various compounds of academic authority? Starting from the bottom of national systems of higher education and working our way up to the highest levels, as has been done in the seven countries, what different types of legitimate rule can be observed? The ten concepts set forth below offer a battery of possibilities that may apply heavily, moderately, lightly, or not at all to a particular case. They represent starting points for the analyst.

CONCEPTS OF ACADEMIC AUTHORITY

Personal Rulership (Professorial)

All modern organizations, usually characterized as impersonal and bureaucratic, nevertheless seem to contain much personalized and arbitrary rule by superiors over subordinates.[1] Systems of higher education are saturated with this form of rule. Individual professors exercise extensive supervision over the work of students and often that of junior faculty. And their judgment is not closely circumscribed by the bureaucratic rules of the institution. The personal rule of professors has many sources. It is historically linked to the dominance of the master in the early academic guilds; it is ideologically supported by doctrines of freedom in teaching and research, which in practice have been interpreted to mean that senior professors should be free to do largely as they please; and it is functionally based in expertise and the need for conditions that would promote creativity and scientific advance. Moreover, as professors have acquired fixed slots in institutional and state bureaucracies, they have achieved rights that strengthen personal rule—an outcome opposite to the intention of bureaucratic order. Personal rule has been extremely high in chair-based academic systems, especially where collegial supervision is nominal and state supervision too remote from academic operations to be effective. It exists in lesser degree in department-based systems, such as that of the United States where power is formally held by an impersonal unit and spread within it among a number of permanent professors. But even there it exists, most noticeably in advanced research and teaching—for example, in the supervision of the graduate student in dissertation research. Although personalized authority is always potentially subject to abuse, systems of higher education apparently cannot function effectively without it since it is involved in the conditions of freedom for individual initiative in research, individual freedom in teaching, and personal attention to students as a basic method of advanced training. Hence it would have to be invented if it did not already exist.

Collegial Rulership (Professorial)

Collective control by a body of peers is a classic form of traditional authority, within the fundamental Weberian typology of traditional, bureaucratic, and charismatic authority.[2] Like personal rulership, it has been widespread in the academic world from the twelfth century to the present; it has had exceedingly strong ideological support in the doctrines of "community of scholars" and "freedom of teaching and research." It is also congenial to the expression of expert judgment; and the growth of specialization in recent decades, outside of as well as inside higher education, has increased the influence of collegial control in the form of peer review and decision in ever-increasing numbers of occupational fields. In chair-based academic systems, collegial rule has often been the sole mechanism for coordination at faculty and university levels of organization. Central to its strength is the election of a head from within a body of peers—"appointment" from below instead of appointment from above by a superior official or chief (the bureaucratic mode). With election from below, amateur administration results, but so too does a close connection between administration and faculty. At the same time, political action within the voting group is often encouraged, since the consent of a majority must be obtained in various divisions, and senatorial courtesies and other tacit agreements are needed that allow collective governance to keep order and get the work done. Collegial rule is also strong in department-based systems; it is the professors' preferred way to run a department and, if possible, the larger units of college, school, and university.

Guild Authority

This type of authority is a compound of the first two, blending collegiality with autocracy. The individual master has a personal domain within which he controls subordinates; the masters come together as a body of equals (one person, one vote) to exercise control over a larger territory of work.[3] This combination never disappeared from certain sectors of society, preeminently academic systems. Such systems have continued to be guild-like at the lowest levels; and the combination of personal rulership and collegial authority commonly dominates the substructure of even fully nationalized universities. The academic guilds simply moved completely inside the bureaus created in modern nation-states. The capacity of guild authority to survive inside large governmental agencies—in the case of higher education, in ministries and departments of education—now seems surprising mainly because of two prevalent misconceptions: that guilds have always been largely independent of government and that governmental agencies are bureaucracies. Historically, guilds have had varying degrees of connection to state authorities, including being located virtually inside government;[4] and agencies vary greatly in the strength of the bureaucratic tendency. There are modern government tendencies that run counter to bureaucratic impartiality—tendencies that are linked to conceptions of guild and community.[5]

In the blending of autocracy and collegiality in groups of experts, one element or the other can sometimes predominate. For example, in the guilds of Italian academic life, personal rule has tended to dominate collegiality, whereas in Great Britain, collective control has generally been stronger than personal rule. The dominance of personal rule means virtually full personal control over a private fiefdom; collective rule dampens that tendency by locating decision making in a body of the whole which attempts to monopolize control over a larger domain of work, even if that work territory is increasingly a formal part of the apparatus of government and thereby subject in theory to the control of general public policy.

Professional Authority

Bureaucracy and profession have been widely identified as the two primary forms of organization of modern occupational activity in and out of government. Professional authority is supposedly rooted in universalistic and impersonal criteria, as is bureaucratic control, but its standards are drawn from the profession rather than the immediate formal organization. It is then viewed as based on "technical competence," on expertise, rather than on "official competence," which derives from position in a formal hierarchy.[6] But the classic literature on professional authority has been unduly idealistic, assuming that altruism is the dominant characteristic of professional life, under doctrines of service and the limitation of professional rule to expert judgment alone. In practice, however, professionals exercise authority in a host of ways, through personal rule, collegial control, bureaucratic position, and political struggle. In such professions as medicine and law, as in the case of the academic occupation, authority began in guild organization; and still today guild forms persist in these fields even when their practitioners become located within large public and private complex organizations. Within a large profession overall control is typically weak, with discretion radically decentralized to operating levels where it tends to take autocratic and collegial forms. The actual expression of professional authority is thus problematic: taking different forms, professional authority may be particularistic as well as universalistic, oriented to personal profit as well as to service in society, and used to subordinate clients and allied personnel as well as to serve ideals.[7]

Thus, the concept of professional authority needs to be put in reserve at this time; it may be useful in the analysis of academic power but only if broken down into more specific forms of rule. There are vast differences in the professional rule of academic experts, with that rule considerably more universalistic in the United States than in Italy, and in Great Britain than in Japan. These variations are not a function of the degree of professionalization. They are related to differences in institutional structures and the way the position of the academic professional within the structure affects the exercise of power. It is often said in accounting for the uses of power in government that "where one stands depends upon where one sits"—that organizational position determines one's posture in organizational politics and power. One can add that different sites affect not only perspectives but also provide for different ways of engaging in politics and exercising power. Because systematized ways are often deeply engrained in a sector of society, and possibly in the whole of a society, professionals have different patterns of influence in such a sector as higher education in different societies.

Charismatic Authority

The concept of charismatic authority refers to the willingness of a group of people to follow a person and accept his or her dictates because of unusual personal characteristics—in the extreme, "a gift of grace."[8] The authority of the leader thus derives not from position in an administrative structure or from established right in a traditional line of descent, but from personal qualities. However, the exercise of charismatic authority is commonly compounded with bureaucratic or traditional position. In U.S. higher education, for example, charisma has been noted most often in the college or university presidency, with the leader thereby drawing authority from both personal and structural sources. And, like all other forms of authority, charismatic authority is directly situational; the personal qualities of the leader must be perceived and valued by actual or would-be followers and subordinates. The authority disappears when followers are disillusioned and turn away.

Guild authority strongly opposes charismatic authority in the administration of faculties, universities, and systems. At the same time, strong personal rulership within the guild form encourages charismatic authority at the operating level of chair, institute, and department, The chair holders' ability to elaborate and accumulate roles, as well as the magnitude of the gap in status between chair holder and subordinates, encourages the assumption of personal superiority, evokes a steady stream of deference, and leads toward the adoption of a commanding presence.[9] The office of chair holder itself has had elements of charisma in many societies, similar but in lesser degree to that of priest in the Catholic Church. This relation between guild and charismatic authority indicates how much one form of authority can displace the expression of a second form from one level of organization to another. To permit personal authority systematically at one or two levels is to push back the boundaries of routine authority that normally control the intrusion of charisma.

An important opening for charismatic authority at the institutional level occurred in U.S. higher education during the late nineteenth and early twentieth century. Traditional rule by amateur trustees was then giving way to more systematic direction from the top, faculty guild forms were not yet elaborate, and some presidents were given the responsibility of building entire institutions—administrative staff, faculty, and all. In comparison, present-day U.S. higher education seems lacking in such openings, except that crises as well as situations of new organization occasionally beckon the person with gifts of leadership. Even stable established contexts sometimes open up to such personal intervention, as when a college or a professional school or a department becomes ambitious to do better or become different and invites in a builder, a specific agent of change.[10]

Although charismatic authority still occurs in higher education, serving needs for leadership, mission clarification, and change, it is hemmed in by more entrenched forms in a societal sector that has become more dense with organizations. It seems likely to occur infrequently at regional and national levels, because key positions there require trained managers of complex systems. The greatest degree of openness to its occurrence at administrative levels, which is not very great, still attaches to the headship of campuses in those systems, such as the American, British, and Japanese, that have provided some independent power to parts of the strata located between professors and central state officials.

Trustee Authority (Institutional)

Trusteeship has been a common form of legitimate authority in Anglo-Saxon higher education and parts of such other systems as the Japanese. Traditionally, it refers to general stewardship and supervision of an enterprise by a board of outsiders (laymen in U.S. terminology), essentially unpaid and part-time, whose primary commitments and roles are elsewhere. The outsiders are supposed to represent a large interest, that of the general public in a public institution or a more specific constituency and supporting group in a private institution, or some combination of the two. They are the long-run caretakers, to be held finally responsible for the fate of the enterprise, and, as a body, are generally the legal owners or legally established managers.

In the United States the current trend toward control of institutions by higher levels of state and national government makes problematic the continued strength of trustee authority at the institutional level. At the same time, European systems, in which institutional trusteeship has been absent, are now searching for new modes of participation of outside groups in institutional decision making, in order to break the old guild-bureaucracy control and to give higher education better connections to other sectors of society.

Because of this search, it is important to begin to consider the difference made by the presence or absence of trusteeship, how it conditions other forms of authority and blends or conflicts with them. Its continued pervasive exercise in the American system is a fundamental part of what is different about that system from nearly all others. It has served as an instrument of institutional aggrandizement, linking the participation of influential citizens and the interests of specific constituencies and publics to the welfare of the individual college or university. It helped make the middle levels of the national system in the United States relatively strong.

In its many variations of public and private boards, trusteeship may be considered as a form of dispersed public control, with specific publics, as narrow as a few families or as wide as the population of a state, represented in different instituions. In nontrustee systems, the general public participates more diffusely and indirectly but more globally in the control of a whole set of institutions, by means of elected representatives in the legislature and elected executives, their policies, and the policies of the bureaus of the executive branch of government. The public interest, and the interest of publics, proceed via regular government and its tendencies toward even development across a subsystem such as higher education. In contrast, the fragmented public control of little groups of trustees allows for much ad hoc, uneven development, and for the particularisms of small-group preferences.

Bureaucratic Authority (Institutional)

As the best-known idea in the twentieth-century analysis of organization, the concept of bureaucracy needs little explanation. It refers to formal hierarchy, formal delegation of authority to positions, formal written communication and coordination, and impersonality in recruiting personnel, judging individual worth, and deciding what will be done. Bureaucratic authority is the antithesis of personal rule and collegial control among professors, as well as of lay control and charismatic authority at the institutional level. In the bureaucracy the expert manager draws power solely from an explicitly defined position. Of course, as is true of other conceptions, there are, in practice, degrees of bureaucracy. Thus it is useful to speak of a bureaucratic tendency and to ascertain its strength in various settings rather than to assume that organizational personnel follow bureaucratic dictates.

This study of seven systems has made clear the importance of distinguishing who the bureaucrats are, which comes down largely to where they are located in large structures. In the chair systems of the Continent, administrators subject to the bureaucratic tendency are found largely in central ministries, there devoted to the tasks of systemwide allocation and coordination. In these systems bureaucratic authority at the university or campus (or institutional) level has been weak and sometimes nonexistent; in contrast, in the U.S. system, bureaucratic authority has been strong at the institutional level and until recently much weaker at ministerial levels of governmental coordination. For a century, the U.S. pattern has put bureaucratic authority in the service of local ambition and institutional aggrandizement. Even more than professors, campus officials become boosters of their own institutions, because job rewards and career successes depend directly on the apparent success of the whole. Their perspectives and interests can thus be fundamentally different from those of officials in central offices, as they increasingly are from those of faculty and students. Where large numbers of campus administrators interact largely with one another, a quasi-autonomous administrative culture will form alongside the faculty and student cultures of the campus.[11]

In short, it is not the case that a bureaucracy is a bureaucracy is a bureaucracy. Bureaucratic authority can be coupled to different chariots; it functions in different ways in systems depending in part on the organizational level at which it operates. Future research and understanding will be aided greatly by a clear séparation in analysis between bureaucratic authority at the institutional level and the play of bureaucratic tendencies at higher levels of system coordination.

Bureaucratic Authority (Governmental)

Whenever government assumes some responsibility for the provision of higher education, certain agencies are likely to become the loci of administrative implementation. However, the involvement of agency staffs can vary widely, depending on the historical relation of the state to higher education and how that relationship has been expressed in recent policy. High administrative involvement has been presupposed and exercised in the European systems that used ministries of education as embracing frameworks, whereas, for example, low involvement occurred in Great Britain throughout the first four decades of the existence of the University Grants Committee (1920-60). Even though the national treasury became increasingly the main means of financial support, the UGC, as mediating mechanism, was not under the jurisdiction of a regular governmental department, had only a small staff of its own, and was controlled largely by persons from the universities.

The older British pattern was atypical; the Continental pattern has been widespread and increasingly so. The British, American, and Japanese systems are evolving toward the Continental model of bureau administration, the British and Japanese at the national level and the American at both the state and national levels. Recent governmental policies in these countries have induced a buildup of central administrative staffs as public officials have responded to problems of growth, equity, accountability, and duplication by enacting laws that require larger central offices to disperse funds, set uniform requirements, check compliance, and otherwise implement public policy. Reform has brought administrative accretions, including the addition of more levels of administration as well as the augmentation of permanent staffs.

If systems of higher education are to be understood, the behavior of the central administrative staffs must be approached in terms that go beyond those of the classic concept of bureaucracy. The staffs of governmental bureaus apparently are conditioned by national cultures, especially as those cultures are expressed in the styles of politics and public administration. For example, there may be a particular French style of bureaucratic behavior, one that leads unduly to rigidity and stagnation, a thesis proposed by Michel Crozier that has stimulated a debate in comparative politics and public administration about the character of French bureaucracy and government and national differences generally.[12] The central staffs will also develop a somewhat separate administrative subculture of their own, which will condition the uses of their authority, as against the various subcultures within the operating institutions. And it has been increasingly perceived in the study of modern public administration that central administrative staffs are not neutral tools of higher policy but rather are strongly inclined to become interest groups within government—groups with privileged access, vested rights, and self-sustaining points of view, often agency by agency, in a fragmented fashion.[13] Each staff battles for its own interest. A staff in a central educational agency, in need of allies and supportive exchanges, will develop tacit agreements with key legislators and staffs of legislative committees, political appointees in executive agencies, staff peers in bordering agencies, trustees and administrators at lower levels, and professors. Internally, in European systems, the ministerial staffs have had to trade principally with the most important senior professors within the system. That has not been the case in the U.S. system; the central staffs operate at several removes from the professors and deal directly with institutional bureaucracies and trustees. The nature of the authority of such staffs, as of governmental bureaucratic authority generally, needs now to be seen as problematic; intensive research is needed to dissect the mixture of bureaucratic, guild, and political elements.

Political Authority

From the beginnings in Bologna and Paris some eight centuries ago, European higher education has faced the problem of relating to the larger controls of state and church. As the nation-state increased its strength in the last several centuries, it became the dominant framework, and throughout most of the world today, higher education is primarily an organizational part of national government, there conditioned by the nature of the legislative, executive, and judicial branches and affected by the exercise of political authority in each government. For example, coalitional governments, as in Italy, are hard put to enact major reform legislation, but rather must move by studied indirection and incremental adjustment in order to safeguard a precarious ruling consensus; a more dominant state authority, as in France under DeGaulle in 1968, can push through a big bill promising extensive reform of higher education, even if implementation is later slowed and attenuated by countervailing resistance in the universities.

Due to traditions of private-sector institutions, campus-level control, and institutional autonomy, in the United States there has been a strong reluctance until recently to recognize higher education as a part of government and to study it as such. Appropriate conceptualization has also been restrained by the long-standing differentiation between the study of public administration, located in political science departments and schools of administration, and the study of college administration, which if done at all, has taken place mainly in schools of education. Of all the social sciences, political science remains the least involved in the study of educational organization. In all countries, the lack of careful research on the role of political authority in the governance of higher education has left a near vacuum that invites easy speculation on the dominance of particular elites: for example, leftists charging that conservative cabals of ministers (or trustees) and administrators rule the campuses.

Such stereotypes of academic power will be corrected only as the intricate webs of political relationships found at the highest levels of state and national systems, as well as the distribution of authority at lower levels, are considered in the analysis of authority. Such analysis will be aided considerably by concepts drawn from comparative public administration and comparative politics—concepts such as bureau Balkanization, bureaucratic clientelism, and the distinction between political centralization and central administrative concentration.[14]

Systemwide Academic Oligarchy

In European systems of higher education, professors have been capable of transferring local oligarchical power to the national level. Operating as the major professional group within a ministry of education, they have had privileged access to central councils and offices and have been the most important constituency for top bureaucratic and political officials. In the British mode of national organization of higher education, a few senior and influential members of the academic profession have served on the important central bodies that have allocated resources, until recently dominating decision making to the virtual exclusion of central bureaucratic staff. In the United States, systemwide academic oligarchy has been relatively weak, because the power base of professors has been weaker and higher levels of coordination have been occupied by trustees, institutional administrators, and governmental administrators. Even here, academics sometimes have imposing, if fragmented, influence. The leaders of national academies and associations of scientists advise government; science advisory committees operate within the White House; committees of professors and scientists exercise peer review, which has become standard operating procedure in major governmental agencies that dispense funds for different segments of research and education.

Thus, even in the American system relatively small numbers of professors may play systemwide roles. Those roles vary greatly according to a host of such factors as the traditional prestige of academics, the guild strength of senior professors, and the countervailing power of other interested groups. But there is no neat unilinear trend toward diminished influence of professors in control at the highest levels; everywhere the need to seek and use the judgment of experts increases, and among those who gather to whisper words of advice into the ears of the modern-day prince—the chief executive, committee chairman, or bureau chief—are notables based in academe.

These ten forms of authority can be more closely specified, and more forms identified, in further efforts to escape the ambiguity of such general concepts as bureaucracy and profession with terms that are closer to reality and more helpful in research. But greater specification at this point would lead toward the incoherence of a laundry list. Generated by this effort to review side by side the distribution of authority in seven countries, these ten forms may at least serve as sensitizing conceptions, bringing together many of the leading ideas about modern authority as they apply to observed blends of academic authority at many levels of academic organization.

MODES OF ACADEMIC AUTHORITY

The play of these various types of authority may be seen in broader perspective in an examination of the modes that have emerged in academic organization. Four such modes are identified below: the European, the British, the American, and the Japanese.

The European Mode

The basic structure of academic organization in the countries of the European continent has combined faculty guild and state bureaucracy. From the beginnings in the twelfth century until now well into the twentieth, guild-like authority has predominated in the understructure, the first three of the six levels used. The chair-holding professor has been the master of a teaching domain and, in the last century or so, a research domain, exercising personal control over assistants and students in a field of study. Groups of masters have exercised collegial rule over faculties and universities, essentially monopolizing decision making in determining curriculum, membership in the teaching corps, and the direction of research. State bureaucracy has been located in the superstructure of control, generally at the level of national government, as in Italy, France, and Sweden, following upon the placement of all or nearly all universities and colleges under one or more ministries of central government. Thus, the European mode has a nationalized variant, the most common subtype. But there is also a federal variant, as in the Land structure of Germany, with the embrace of the government occurring traditionally at a subnational level.

The national-federal distinction is an important one, since the national system is a single-system monopoly while the federal structure has multiple systems and some competition. But it remains useful to lump them together as subtypes of a general European mode, in order to emphasize a common structure that expresses primarily the interests of two groups—senior professors and officials located in a state ministry.[15] In contrast, efforts in comparative higher education to lump West Germany, the United States, and Canada together as federal systems obscure crucial differences among them in the amount of influence that the primary structure of authority gives to different groups. Viewing organizational structure as a mobilization of bias, systematically sustaining the values of certain groups to the exclusion of others, it is found that the European mode has provided such mobilization primarily for the points of view of professors and of officials of a particular ministry within government, two relatively small interest groups in the vast conglomeration of political and bureaucratic interests found in modern nations.[16]

Thus, the main contest for power in the understructure and especially in the superstructure has been between these two groups. Professors generally control the understructure, but not everywhere and continuously; for example, the minister, using formal powers inherent in the office, may sometimes intrude in the appointment system to make his own choices of chair holders.[17] State officials tend to have primacy in the superstructure, but senior professors, as the most powerful constituency, seem to have important rights of advice and consultation in central decision making, and, as in Italy, they may devise and elaborate procedures for ensuring their primacy in the exercise of centralized control.

The European mode, particularly in comparison with that of the United States, exhibits weak administration at the levels of the university and its constituent faculties. The professors have not wanted a separate administrative class; the distant ministry has preempted overhead services. This mode has also minimized institutional competitiveness and distinctiveness, dampening the incentives for the individual units to compete for talent or to emphasize special approaches. The unitary system located within government commonly attempts to equalize institutions; for example, degrees are awarded by the system as a whole and not the individual university; all faculty members are appointed to the same civil service; and one or more central offices or collective bodies are engaged systematically in the application of uniform standards across the entire system or major segments within it.

Thus, in vertical profile, the European structure places strong authority at the bottom, in guild forms; secondarily at the top, in ministerial bureaucracy that accommodates to the faculty guilds; and only weakly provides for authority at middle levels of the state system in the form of institutional administration. Trustee control is entirely absent or extremely weak. In horizontal profile, the European mode typically exhibits little differentiation of sectors: a private sector is forbidden or kept small, and the university form of organization dominates the public sector. (The most important exception here is the special role of elite training that has been assigned to a small nonuniversity sector, the grandes écoles, in France.)

The European mode faces reform in two directions: the strengthening of administration at the middle levels (stronger deanships, stronger rectoral and presidential offices, stronger regional administration), while weakening the powers of both chaired professors and central ministerial staffs; and the differentiation of types of institutions, or greater internal differentiation of existing types, in response to the widening variety of demands inherent in modern mass higher education.

The British Mode

The British style of academic organization has combined faculty guilds with a modest amount of influence from institutional trustees and administrators. The individual colleges and universities have been chartered corporations responsible for self-management, each to admit its own students, arrange its own courses, hire its own faculty, raise its own income (at least in part), and pay its own bills. In this context, guild authority has flourished, especially in the many colleges of Oxford and Cambridge. But trustee authority and some administrative authority (the vice-chancellorship) have also been present, interfused with the guild forms at the local levels.

Since the British did not early develop the continental devices of placing institutions under a governmental bureau and the teachers within a civil service, there has not been a formally organized system either nationally or at provincial levels. Even as the national treasury became the main means of financial support, the device of the UGC kept primary influence in the hands of senior professors and university administrators. Compared with the Continent, a high degree of institutional autonomy has encouraged some institutional competitiveness and dictinctiveness. But the status and influence of Oxford and Cambridge and a resulting imitation of their style by other institutions have dampened such tendencies considerably, compared with the United States. In place of officially mandated similarity, voluntary convergence has been much in evidence.

Thus, in vertical profile, the British mode has placed strong authority at the bottom, in guild forms, as on the Continent; it has given some strength to middle levels of coordination, providing systematically at the institutional level for a modest degree of administrative leadership and for the participation of laymen, as well as for collective faculty rule. Governmental bureaus and other components of state administration traditionally had little power, with national coordination provided instead by a body of academic oligarchs. In horizontal profile, there has been a modest differentiation of sectors, with teacher training colleges and technological colleges historically separated from the universities and generally more influenced by government, local and national, than were the universities.

Until recently, the main contests for power were located within the understructure—the university itself—and were largely contained by an elaborate web of tacit agreements among faculty clusters, each of which had primacy in its own domain, and between those clusters and all-university administrative staff, trustees, and faculty bodies. The contest was not faculty versus state officials, as on the Continent; the subordination of a ministerial superstructure has been central to the British mode.

The British mode faces reform that has one basic direction of effort: to strengthen coordination at the national level. Between 1965 and 1975, British higher education moved firmly into a de facto national system, with the Department of Education and Science (DES) taking on some of the attributes of a continental ministry, able, for example, to tell some formerly autonomous units that they must consolidate with other units, or even that they must cease to exist; with the UGC relocated within the government so as to answer directly to the DES and itself made more bureaucratically competent; and with the legislature and the top political councils of the executive branch more determined to have explicit national policies in higher education and to use the DES and the UGC as central instruments to carry out those policies. With this current thrust, the power contest moves toward the European mode of professors versus the state apparatus.

The American Mode

The American mode of academic authority, like the British, has combined faculty guilds with institutional trusteeship and institutional administration. But in comparison with the British, faculty rule has been weaker and the influence of trustees and administrators stronger. The mechanism of the chartered corporation has been used heavily by many hundreds of independently established units, with separate boards of trustees each fully in charge of its own institution and, sooner or later, creating its own administrative staff, from president to assistant dean, to "run" the place. With faculty authority developing late, within the context of the established powers of trustees and administrators, the faculty forms of personal and collegial authority did not achieve the influence they had in the European and British modes. Notably, the chair did not become the building block; instead, the department emerged as an operating unit that both damped personal authority and blended internal collegial order with external relations in a university structure that, within itself, was decidedly more bureaucratic than that found within the European and British modes.

Thus, the U.S. mode localized bureaucracy. No national bureau had an important role; even the departments of education of the separate states, where public responsibility for education became lodged, often had little influence in the face of chartered autonomy. And no one had any important degree of control over the differentiation of institutions and sectors, as private groups went their own way in founding colleges and the public sector operationally became 48 (and now 50) sectors. As a result, this highly atypical national structure tended to promote institutional competitiveness and distinctiveness. And, although "Ivy League" institutions were once prestigious pacesetters, no one or two institutions have dominated the rest as much as Oxford and Cambridge have in England. Voluntary divergence has been as much in evidence as voluntary convergence.

Thus, in vertical profile, the U.S. academic structure has emphasized a strong middle, in the forms of institutional administration and boards of trustees. A modest amount of authority has been available at the lower levels of the department and the multidepartment college or school, in a blend of guild and bureaucratic forms. Authority has been modest to nonexistent at the governmental levels. In horizontal profile, there has been an unparalleled differentiation, with such major sectors as the private college, the private university, the state university, the state college, and the community college each containing a variety of institutions.

Reform has had one main thrust: to bring more administered order into what is the most disorderly of all major advanced systems of higher education. The drift of authority for a quarter-century has been steadily upward toward ever stronger campus administration and, especially, an elaborate, greatly strengthened superstructure consisting of multicampus administration, state superboards, state government planning and control, regional compacts, and more frequent and increasingly systematic interventions by national government.

The Japanese Mode

In Japanese academic organization, significant elements are found that are similar to the European, British, and U.S. modes, in a unique mixture. The greatest likeness is to the European mode, because the system as a whole has been dominated for a century by the handful of leading national Imperial Universities which exhibit the classic pattern of faculty guilds located within a national state bureaucracy. In the imperial sector, the chair holder possesses a high degree of personal control over subordinates; chair holders exercise strong collegial control within faculties and universities; and the superstructure consists of a bureaucratic staff in a national ministry. There are no trustees, and middle management is relatively weak.

But other sectors have been organized differently. A large private sector, unlike anything in Europe, has important similarities to the U.S. private sector: trustees, strong campus administrators, and departmental organization. Since the private institutions must struggle individually to stay alive and viable, like poorly endowed private institutions in the United States, there is some struggle in a market of academic firms. Both the private and public sectors exhibit much internal variety; Japan is second only to the United States among the seven countries in the degree of institutional differentiation.

Finally, however, because of the towering prestige of one or two institutions, the Japanese mode, like the British, includes a strong tendency for imitation. Tokyo and Kyoto have effected elite placement of their graduates, on a scale superior even to Oxford and Cambridge or France's grandes écoles, having developed guaranteed and closely specified links to leadership levels of government and business for relatively large cohorts of graduates. With prestige, power, and resources concentrated accordingly, voluntary convergence on a single model has been stronger than the counterpart process in the United States.

Thus, the Japanese mode is a fascinating mixture of varied forms of organization and authority. The mixture allows for diverse adaptiveness, but it also is a structural source of conflicts and cross-purposes that appear dysfunctional to many, especially to central state officials held responsible for the welfare of the whole. The course of reform is toward nationally administered order: the private institutions have to be upgraded, it seems, given standards and guidelines as well as money by a national bureau and made somewhat more regular members of a formal national system.

The direction of reform in authority structure in each of the countries is set by the basic weakness of each mode. In the Continental mode, reform seeks to pull authority from the top and the bottom to strengthen the historically weak middle levels of administration in "ministerized" systems. In the German federal variant of this mode, reform has also been attempting to move authority upward to an explicit national level of coordination (a stronger Level 6), while simultaneously strengthening coordination below the Länder ministries. In the British mode, reform seeks to develop a superstructure responsive to politically and bureaucratically determined central policy, to strengthen the top level of coordination in what was previously, in formal terms, a nonsystem of autonomous institutions. Similarly in the American mode, the name of reform is administered order, but in a more complicated arrangement of at least three levels of coordination (multicampus, state, national) in the superstructure, to strengthen coordination and direction in what was historically the nearest thing to a large laissez-faire system ever developed in the history of higher education. In Japan, also, authority is drifting upward, but at the national level as in Britain and not in such a fractured manner as in the United States.

ANALYTICAL PERSPECTIVES

The approaches of this book to the complex reality underlying concepts of academic power have not focused on the psychology of leadership, the decision-making process per se, and the economics of resource allocation, but rather on the organizational structure of power, the authority rooted in the organizational positions occupied by groups of people. That structure is as important as it is hard to uncover, and its study requires a number of analytical probes. Four approaches that developed strength in the course of this study and that seem necessary and promising for useful description and cogent conceptualization in future research are set forth below.

Levels Analysis

Comparative analysis of educational systems reveals the necessity of systematic attention to levels of organization. For example, to what units of organization in France and Germany does one compare the American department? To what governmental level in the United States does one compare the operations of a ministry of education in a German Land? Even a minimal awareness of levels can help analysts avoid such simple mistakes as comparing higher education in France with higher education in California, a comparison that ignores the extensive interchange the California system has with other subsystems in a national complex characterized by institutional competition and high personnel mobility. The six-level schema imposed in each of the country chapters in this volume permitted a view of the counterpart subsystems, where they exist, in each country. This approach also ordered the empirical materials in a way that forced attention to the bottom and the middle as well as the top of national structures. In forcing attention to the bottom tiers, the schema prevented an easy overview of system as solely a matter of top-level coordination, while encouraging attention to the authority of those in lower operating units—at the chair, department, faculty, and institutional levels. Such attention has been increasingly lacking as the growth of large systems has led to specialized attention to planning and general management.

Levels analysis locates areas of decision making, forms of authority, and the interaction between the two, on a vertical plane. Decision making in such areas as finance, admissions, curriculum, and faculty selection commonly takes place at different levels and is thereby differentially shaped by the forms of authority characteristic of the levels. Faculty selection commonly remains the prerogative of lower levels, thereby influenced heavily by the collegial rule of professors, whereas budget determination has increasingly gravitated upward, influenced even more than in the past by governmental bureaucracy and political authority. Thus, even relatively simple analysis by levels may provide insights into hierarchical specialization in academic control; different levels not only have different functions but also specialize in different types of decisions and in exposing decisions to different forms of authority. Even rudimentary attention to levels helps to clarify contradictions in global perceptions and characterization, for example, the contradiction between the American perception of the French system as a monument to bureaucracy and the French perception of the U.S. system as one saturated with administrators and hence even more bureaucratic than their own. As has been seen, administrative machinery in the French case is heavy at the top but relatively weak in the middle tiers and especially at the bottom, whereas in the American structure the administrative apparatus has been most strongly located at the campus and within-campus levels.

Integration and Differentiation Analysis

Although organized social systems, large and small, vary greatly in degree and form of integration, research on organizations has had great difficulty in grappling with those that are not tightly ordered. Analysts have preferred to study individual governmental agencies or business firms, rather than networks thereof, and to approach the apparently unified system as a problem in bureaucratic and hierarchical coordination. These analytical biases have been particularly inappropriate for the study of academic authority, because, even within the single college or university, hierarchy may be flat, coordination inordinately loose, and the exercise of power decidedly nonbureaucratic. Fortunately, recent organizational studies have recognized increasingly the problems of coordination and exchange among units that are loosely connected. From an interest in relating the individual organization to its environment, there has developed research on relations among organizations and on whole sets or fields of organizations as the units of analysis themselves.[18] This new literature is increasingly pertinent to the study of complex state and national systems of higher education, offering, for example, schemes that help one go beyond such arguments as whether the university is really a bureaucracy or a community or a political system. As indicated in the Introduction, a useful typology has been set forth by Roland Warren, who identifies contexts in which organizational units interact in making decisions.[19] His four types, containing six dimensions, range roughly along a general continuum from tight to loose connection: a unitary context, in which the units are parts of an inclusive structure; a federative context, in which the units primarily have disparate goals but some formal linkage for the purposes they share; a coalitional context, in which disparate goals are so paramount that there is only informal collaboration among the parts; and a social-choice context, in which there are no inclusive goals, and decisions are made independently by autonomous organizations. The latter three types—federative, coalitional, and social-choice—are found frequently in systems of higher education. A university that is complex and internally fragmented may actually operate more like a federation than a hierarchical bureaucracy; a higher education association, such as the American Council on Education, may operate largely as a coalitional organization; and autonomous private universities and colleges, freely competing and interacting with one another and with public campuses, may constitute an interorganizational field that is mainly social-choice or market-like, but perhaps with some subtle systematic linkage provided by tacit agreements that develop over time and edge the whole set of organizations toward coalitional and federative arrangements. These four types can be used in dissecting the nature of authority as systems become tighter or looser, more centralized or more decentralized. What is already known about federations and coalitions from analysis of political systems can be mined for potential applications to higher education subsystems.

In the country chapters of this volume an attempt was made to specify the nature of integration of authority at various levels, pointing, for example, to the federative and coalitional character of fragmented collegial clusters in the substructures of national systems. Even in closely organized social systems there is a tug of war between forces of fragmentation and forces of integration. The fragmenting forces include the personal preferences of those in charge of the operating units, their adaptation to local interests, and the difficulties they encounter in translating general directives into appropriate actions at the local level. The tools of modern administrative integration, on the other hand, include budgetary and rule-making techniques for "pre-forming" the decisions of lower officials, methods of reporting and inspecting that detect and discourage deviation from uniform rule, and ways of socializing the personnel of a complex agency to common viewpoints that lead to similar judgments and responses.[20]

The modern world is so dense with organizations, and relations among these primary social actors in many sectors are such a jungle of connections, that some organizational analysts are attempting to devise whole new ways of thinking about "organized social complexity."[21] Given the growing variety of tasks assumed by systems of higher education and the increasingly complex structures of authority they possess, the study of higher education should draw upon such emerging perspectives and in turn contribute to their development. Systems of higher education can provide important leads on characteristics of organizational networks that are staffed with diverse experts. They reveal much about authority rooted in expertise, the personal and peer relations that are congenial to expert judgment, the flattening of hierarchies that thereby follows, and the capture of slices of public power by professional interest groups that have privileged access by virtue of location within public bureaus.

One broad perspective that will be particularly useful in future research on academic systems comes from general sociological thought on structural differentiation as a response to growth in size and function. This approach has received a useful first application to higher education in Neil Smelser's research on public higher education in California.[22] That research details a set of six possible structural responses to rapid growth, identifies three that actually took place, and then suggests that the mix of responses led to a university system more "ripe for conflict, because its structure was producing some significant groups with intense feelings of deprivation and disaffection."[23] Faculty growth did not keep pace with that of students; the number of teaching assistants and research personnel expanded rapidly, producing large groups who did crucial work but did not receive the rewards of full citizenship. As these ancillary personnel staffed more classrooms, faculty partially withdrew from undergraduate teaching, which increased the sense of deprivation among undergraduate students. In the research for this volume, a similar process was observed in systems in other countries, usually in sharper form than that found in California; the senior faculty typically held on to traditional prerogatives within limited-membership guilds of chair holders, while growth in size and functions produced large cadres of junior faculty, who did much of the work with small rewards, and swarms of students more distanced from the chair holders. The lack of structural change contributed to a work overload, the creation of a large gap between responsibilities and rewards among subordinate personnel, and the growth of feelings of deprivation among all groups, including in time the senior professors themselves.

Differentiation analysis leads directly to questions about the fate of authority and coordination in growing, or contracting, social systems. For example, in a growing system, there is an increase of persons and units over which coordination must be exercised and hence there is a greater authority workload which can either be distributed and shared more equitably or increasingly concentrated. As noted in the chapter on the United States, there can be simultaneously an increase in faculty authority at one level, administrative authority at another, and trustee and/or political authority at still another. At the same time, in the growing system, the struggle between centralization and decentralization becomes wider and more elaborate, as authority is pulled upward to higher levels of larger systems, in order to meet systemwide problems and maintain integration, and is simultaneously segmented and retained at lower levels to have effective decision making in specialized operations. Groups that formerly were in close contact become more distant from one another by domains of specialization as well as levels of organization, producing for more groups a sense of remoteness from where the decisions on issues appear to be made. A "we-they" separation then leads to more formal articulation of interests by such forms as collective bargaining between management and unionized personnel.

The integration-and-differentiation topic is so large in itself that it may be broken down into discrete research problems: forces of fragmentation, techniques of integration, differences in integration among sets of organization, differentiation of structure and authority in growing systems. Levels analysis could also be included as a specific concern within this broad approach, one that points to vertical differentiation of authority within institutions and systems. Clearly, even simple mapping projects can be helpful in the study of academic power if they are organized around the concept of differentiation. Differentiation may occur vertically as well as horizontally, among institutions and within them. These four dimensions of differentiation may be applied in the study of organizational tasks. For example, how much and in what form is graduate education, the most advanced training, separated from undergraduate education, the first level of training in higher education? There are wide variations among university and country structures in vertical differentiation of such programs, with fundamental consequences for the handling of such problems as that between open and selective admissions. In a two-tier structure, as in the United States, the lower tier can have a veritable open door while the second tier remains heavily selective, a combination not readily available in a one-tier structure, as in many Continental systems, where entry to professional school is simultaneous with entry to higher education. The dimensions may also be applied to organizational personnel and their preferred forms of control. For example, does a single faculty maintain jurisdiction over all levels of training, or does it differentiate into essentially two faculties for different levels? Or does the administration control more of the basic training while the faculty controls primarily the advanced training? Dissections of academic power can be aided greatly by schemes that compare national structures systematically on dimensions of differentiation and integration.

Developmental Analysis

Everyone agrees that one should learn from history, to avoid repeating the errors of the past and to sense better what road one is on. But systematic approaches to that task are hard to come by. The study of academic organization is badly split between a small historical literature that makes little connection to the present and a much larger outpouring of reflections on current issues, which have little or no historical depth. What can usefully be done to improve this state of affairs?

One way to proceed is to analyze the historical origin and development of the major forms of organization and control that at present comprise the structure of higher education. In this approach the units of analysis are current components. The search is for a developmental answer to several questions. Why did the present-day form originate? Once it was initiated, why did the form persist into the present, often enduring over decades and even centuries of marked turmoil and change? How did earlier forms condition later ones as they emerged? The question of persistence seems the central one. Persistence may be rooted in apparent effectiveness; a given type of organization or form of control seems to remain a more efficient tool than its possible competitors. Or, persistence may stem from lack of competition; the form in question may have developed a protected niche in higher education and never had to face an open battle against other forms that may be equally or more effective. Or, persistence may follow basically from a set of sociological forces that turn an organizational form into an end in itself, a social institution. Participants perpetuate a form that serves and protects them and as they develop legitimated rights, become a vested collective interest, developing appropriate ideologies that justify the traditional ways and the vested interests.[24] These sociological phenomena are seemingly at the heart of organizational persistence. They help a form to establish protection against possible competitors and thereby make irrelevant the rational question of comparative effectiveness. They help give certain types of colleges and universities and certain forms of academic control a stubborn capacity to survive all types of pressure, including the efforts of powerful reformers.

The institutionalizing forces are bolstered by the monopoly position so typical of forms of public organization, including those involved in public higher education. In most countries, all of higher education is under the aegis of the national government. In many of these cases, the government traditionally used only one form, the university. In others, there was a minor division of labor between the university form and one or two other forms such as the teachers training college and the technological institution, each with a monopoly over a respective function. Appearing most deeply in the European mode of academic organization, the public university financed by national government has had such dominance in role that it has acquired overwhelming dominance in prestige. Thus the words university and higher education are used interchangeable. In the interaction between such monopoly of domain and normal institutionalizing forces may be found basic causes of the great persistence of forms of organization and control in higher education.

Developmental analysis needs also to include research on the international transferring and borrowing of organizational forms. In new nations, or nations newly turning attention to the development of higher education, organizational forms commonly are brought from elsewhere, not independently invented, and the establishment of these older forms in a new setting raises intriguing questions of the intentions of their native or colonial founders.[25] Whatever those reasons, the transferred forms must be adapted to survive in a different context, and in time the adapted form becomes traditional, a focus of organized interests and the subject of a supporting ideology. This topic connects to that of modernization, the development of modern social institutions.[26] In the present work, the borrowing and adapting of forms seemed especially significant in Japan. Officials of the modern Japanese state explicitly sought to speed modernization in the late nineteenth and early twentieth centuries by reaching to Western societies for modes of organization as well as technology. In higher education their chair organization and control was partly imported from the Continent, particularly from Germany, as was in part national-ministry control, particularly from France. Private colleges were clearly an import from the United States and Britain, often initiated by foreign missionaries. The Japanese conditions resulted in an unusually steep hierarchy of institutions—affected by the concentrated investment of the national government in the Universities of Tokyo and Kyoto as training places for governmental cadres and pace setters for the rest of the system—amidst a differentiation of sectors, public and private, second only to the United States among the countries considered.

Questions of international influences—weighing, transferring, borrowing, and adapting organizational forms—might well be more deeply explored for older countries as a part of developmental analysis. Nations, sometimes in response to ambitions, often in response to a worsening international position or defeat in war, may question the efficacy of their institutions, including higher education, and look abroad for solutions. International comparative evaluation is then a partial, long-run way of challenging monopolies of form and group control at home. Of course, certain functions, preeminently scientific research, lend themselves more readily than others (such as teaching) to comparisons among nations, and have been considered more directly involved in the national welfare. For cultural and institutional reasons, nations vary greatly in their willingness to look to the outside; Spain, for example, was apparently closed off to a great degree during the nineteenth and twentieth centuries. And finally, what is imitated or borrowed across national lines is subject to extensive bending and twisting as it is blended into a different configuration of interests and beliefs.

Interest Analysis

In understanding authority and power in modern life the key questions remain those of who governs and by what means. The who and the means are increasingly determined by the location of groups in a structure. And so it is in higher education—its structure represents a mobilization of bias that gives certain groups primacy in the determination of what will be done.[27] That primacy is established only in part by participation and leverage in decision making. It ensues also in the established beliefs and patterns of action that limit what is put on the organizational agenda for explicit decision. There is so much about the exercise of academic power that is a matter of course, of assumption of the right way by the right people.

In line with this understanding, the structural approach in this volume has entailed much analysis of group control of the sites and means of power. In the basic European mode of academic organization, two groups have been depicted, chair-holding professors and ministerial administrators, as having primary location; the structure has expressed best their self-defined interests.[28] In the American mode, in contrast, trustees and campus administrators have had primary sites, along with tenured faculty. This structural approach is a realistic way of assessing whether new claimants to power, however noisy and newsworthy, actually achieve power. Do they gain a location in the organizational structure that is central rather than peripheral, becoming involved in such crucial areas as long-range planning of overall development, the allocation of resources, and the determination of permanent appointments? Out of all the student protests of the 1960s, as noted, students have made at best only small gains in such areas in most countries, compared to the gains realized by junior faculty, campus administrators, and administrators in the superstructure.

To focus on group interest and its embodiment, then, is to marry the analysis of organizations to the analysis of politics. In a time when groups express their interests by occupying and penetrating administrative agencies, especially those of national government, nothing short of this approach will do. Those who analyze organizations without regard to how authority becomes distributed among groups fail to face the basic question of who has power. Those who seek power differentials in modern institutions without regard to the location of groups within organizations fail to grasp that rooted position determines stabilized power. It is around the solid organizational position of a group that traditions develop and interests are made legitimate. As put by Arthur Stinchcombe in looking at organizational development, "The problem is to specify who it is that carries 'tradition' and why they carry it, whose 'interests' become 'vested,' under what conditions, by what devices, whose 'folkways' cannot be changed by regulation, and why. This problem is at the very center of sociological theory."[29] The analysis of group interest in educational structures will permit research to relate problems of academic power to the core issues of political as well as sociological theory.

NOTES

1. Cf. Guenther Roth, "Personal Rulership, Patrimonialism, and Empire-Building in the New States," *World Politics* 20, 1968, pp. 194–206; and Max Weber, *The Theory of Social and Economic Organization*, trans. A. M. Henderson and Talcott Parsons (Oxford: Oxford University Press, 1947), pp. 346–54.

2. Weber, *Social and Economic Organization*, pp. 392–407.

3. Sylvia L. Thrupp, "Gilds," *International Encyclopedia of the Social Sciences* (New York: Macmillan and the Free Press, 1968), Vol. 6, pp. 184–87; John W. Baldwin, "Introduction," in *Universities in Politics: Case Studies from the Late Middle Ages and Early Modern Period*, ed. John W. Baldwin and Richard A. Goldthwaite (Baltimore: Johns Hopkins Press, 1972); Burton R. Clark, *Academic Power in Italy: Bureaucracy and Oligarchy in a National System of Higher Education* (Chicago: University of Chicago Press, 1977), Chapter 5, "Guild."

4. Cf. Thrupp, "Gilds"; and Max Weber, *General Economic History*, translated by Frank H. Knight (Glencoe, Illinois: The Free Press, 1950), pp. 136–37.

5. See, for example, the analysis of the executive branch of U.S. government by Seidman which portrays agencies as self-governing professional guilds, with relations among them so Balkanized around expertise and constituencies as to constitute a system of "cooperative feudalism" instead of cooperative federalism; and the analysis of British government by Heclo and Wildavsky in terms of the nuclear family, village life, kinship and culture, within a small society of civil servants. Harold Seidman, *Politics, Position, and Power: The Dynamics of Federal Organization* (New York: Oxford University Press, 1970); and Hugh Heclo and Aaron Wildavsky, *The Private Government of Public Money: Community and Policy Inside British Politics* (Berkeley and Los Angeles: University of California Press, 1974).

6. Talcott Parsons, "Professions," in *International Encyclopedia of the Social Sciences* (New York: Macmillan and The Free Press, 1968), Vol. 12, pp. 536–47.

7. Eliot Freidson, *Professional Dominance* (New York: Atherton Press, 1970).

8. Edward Shils, "Charisma," in *International Encyclopedia of the Social Sciences* (New York: Macmillan and The Free Press, 1968), Vol. 2, pp. 386–90; Weber, *Social and Economic Organization*, pp. 358–73, 386–92.

9. For a discussion of role elaboration and its outcomes in the case of Italian chair holders, see Clark, *Academic Power in Italy*, Ch. 3,"Oligarchy." For an insightful discussion of the rewards of "role accumulation" generally, see Sam D. Sieber, "Toward a Theory of Role Accumulation," *American Sociological Review* 39, August 1974: 567–78.

10. Cf. Burton R. Clark, *The Distinctive College: Antioch, Reed, and Swarthmore* (Chicago: Aldine, 1970), passim, and especially pp. 237–45.

11. On academic administrative culture, see Terry F. Lunsford, "Authority and Ideology in the Administered University," in *The State of the University: Authority and Change,* ed. Carlos E. Kruytbosch and Sheldon L. Messinger (Beverly Hills, Calif.: Sage Publications, 1970), pp. 87–107.

12. Michel Crozier, *The Bureaucratic Phenomenon* (Chicago: University of Chicago Press, 1964); Michel Crozier, *The Stalled Society* (New York: Viking, 1970); and Ezra N. Suleiman, *Politics, Power, and Bureaucracy in France: The Administrative Elite* (Princeton: Princeton University Press, 1974).

13. Seidman, *Politics;* Heclo and Wildavsky, *Private Government;* Francis E. Rourke, *Bureaucracy, Politics, and Public Policy,* 2d ed. (Boston: Little, Brown, 1976).

14. Cf. Seidman, *Politics;* Heclo and Wildavsky, *Private Government;* Rourke, *Bureaucracy;* Ezra N. Suleiman, *Politics, Power, and Bureaucracy in France: The Administrative Elite* (Princeton: Princeton University Press, 1974); Henry W. Ehrmann, "Interest Groups and the Bureaucracy in Western Democracies," in *State and Society,* ed. Reinhard Bendix (Boston: Little, Brown, 1968), pp. 257–76; Joseph LaPalombara, *Interest Groups in Italian Politics* (Princeton: Princeton University Press, 1964); John Creighton Campbell, "Japanese Budget Baransu," in *Modern Japanese Organization and Decision Making,* ed. Ezra F. Vogel (Berkeley: University of California Press, 1975), pp. 71–100.

15. On academic structure as an expression of group interest, see James S. Coleman, "The University and Society's New Demands Upon It," in *Content and Context: Essays on College Education,* ed. Carl Kaysen, a report prepared for the Carnegie Commission on Higher Education (New York: McGraw-Hill, 1973), pp. 359–99.

16. On the mobilization of bias through "nondecision" as well as decision-making, see Peter Bachrach and Morton S. Baratz, *Power and Poverty: Theory and Practice* (New York: Oxford University Press, 1970), Ch. 1, "Two Faces of Power," pp. 3–16.

17. As happened in Prussia under a forceful minister of education, even during years when the prestige and power of German professors were second to none in the world, much to the dismay of Max Weber. See *Max Weber on Universities: The Power of the State and the Dignity of the Academic Calling in Imperial Germany,* trans., ed., and with an introductory note by Edward Shils (Chicago: University of Chicago Press, 1974).

18. Cf. James D. Thompson and William J. McEwen, "Organizational Goals and Environment," *American Sociological Review* 23, 1958, pp. 23–31; Sol Levine and Paul E. White, "Exchange as a Conceptual Framework for the Study of Interorganizational Relationships," *Administrative Science Quarterly* 5, 1961, pp. 583–601; Burton R. Clark, "Interorganizational Patterns in Education," *Administrative Science Quarterly* 10, 1965, pp. 224–37; James D. Thompson, *Organizations in Action* (New York: McGraw-Hill, 1967); Shirley Terreberry, "The Evolution of Organizational Environments," *Administrative Science Quarterly* 12, 1968, pp. 590–613; and Merlin B. Brinkerhoff and Phillip R. Kunz, eds., *Complex Organizations and Their Environments* (Dubuque, Iowa: William C. Brown, 1972), Section 5, "Organizational and Environmental Interaction," and Section 6, "Interorganizational Analysis."

19. Roland L. Warren, "The Interorganizational Field as a Focus for Investigation," *Administrative Science Quarterly* 12, December 1967, pp. 396–419.

20. See the superb elucidation of tendencies toward fragmentation and techniques of integration in Herbert Kaufman, *The Forest Ranger: A Study in Administrative Behavior* (Baltimore: Johns Hopkins Press, 1960).

21. For example, Todd R. LaPorte, ed., *Organized Social Complexity* (Princeton: Princeton University Press, 1975); and Harry Eckstein and Ted Robert Gurr, *Patterns of Authority: A Structural Basis for Political Inquiry* (New York: Wiley, 1975).

22. Neil J. Smelser, "Growth, Structural Change, and Conflict in California Public Higher Education, 1950–1970," in *Public Higher Education in California,* ed. Neil J. Smelser and Gabriel Almond (Berkeley: University of California Press, 1974), pp. 9–141.

23. Smelser, "Growth," p. 111.

24. Arthur L. Stinchcombe, "Social Structure and Organizations," in James G. March, *Handbook of Organizations* (Chicago: Rand McNally, 1965), pp. 142–93, especially pp. 153–69.

25. The most important study to date of international transplanting of forms of higher education is Ashby's study of the transference of British models to India and Africa. See Eric Ashby, *Universities: British, Indian, African* (Cambridge, Mass.: Harvard University Press, 1966).

26. On modernization and education generally, see James S. Coleman, ed., *Education and Political Development* (Princeton: Princeton University Press, 1965); and John W. Hanson and Cole S. Brembeck, eds., *Education and the Development of Nations* (New York: Holt, Rinehart and Winston, 1966).

27. For the conception of organization as a mobilization of bias, see E. E. Schattschneider, *The Semi-Sovereign People* (New York: Holt, Rinehart and Winston, 1960), p. 71.

28. On the basis primarily of experience in the U.S. system of higher education and secondarily the British, James S. Coleman has depicted the two groups of faculty and university administrators as most strongly rooted in academic structure. But even for these systems it is useful to distinguish between administrators and trustees at the institutional level; and, in Europe and Japan, as has been seen, ministerial officials predominate over institutional administration. Coleman, "The University," especially pp. 361–66.

29. Stinchcombe, "Social Structure," p. 167.

STATISTICAL APPENDIX

ABBREVIATIONS FOR STATISTICAL APPENDIX

CNAA   Council for National Academic Awards

GNP   Gross National Product

n.a.   not available

OECD   Organisation for Economic Co-operation and Development

UNESCO   United Nations Educational, Scientific, and Cultural Organisation

INTRODUCTION

This statistical summary of quantitative changes in the postsecondary systems of the seven countries aims simply to illustrate certain of the basic forces presented in the introduction and the country chapters as being at the root of changes in patterns of authority.

A number of developmental characteristics and trends are systematically juxtaposed, both to permit rough comparisons between countries and to identify characteristic traits of particular countries. The selection is obviously limited; it was made in part according to the quantifiability of factors, and also in view of the availability of data already prepared in comparative form, notably by the Organisation for Economic Co-operation and Development (OECD). The data permit, therefore, no more than simple statistical comparisons of a descriptive kind, with little indication of complex contextual factors. The presentation is highly condensed, to simplify the reader's comparative task as much as possible.

Even straightforward statistical comparisons of this sort, however, are problematic, despite the fact that the seven countries were originally chosen as relatively similar in terms of their level of social and economic development. Their systems of high education differ significantly in various aspects, and recent efforts to develop schemes for systematically classifying types and levels of education confront substantial difficulties. National statistics may reflect their particular systems faithfully, but some of the subtlety is inevitably lost when data are forced into a standard classification system for comparison with other countries. Therefore, the figures presented here allow only the crudest kind of comparative statements about similarities or differences between systems, and only the roughest characterization of developmental patterns.

The bulk of the data deal with student enrollments, and these are classified according to the scheme developed by OECD. This scheme specifies formal criteria for distinguishing among different sectors of postsecondary education, assuming that the sectors so identified in different nations are in fact equivalent. Although this assumption is questionable, the OECD classification is the one that has been most widely used by far (see Technical Comments).

The most significant distinction in this scheme, which can serve to illustrate the difficulties in its use, is the division between university-type and nonuniversity-type higher education. The former is defined as involving relatively long programs of study, as requiring a secondary school leaving certificate, and as permitting access to a doctorate. Typically, university-type higher education involves academic study of a traditional sort. Nonuniversity-type higher education, on the other hand, entails short-cycle programs with flexible admissions requirements and is ordinarily practical or vocational in orientation.

This two-fold division, however, is fully applicable only to countries in which a binary structure actually exists. Among the seven countries this is the case only in Great Britain, and even there the distinction is not unproblematic, for students on CNAA degree courses in polytechnics are classified by OECD as in university-type higher education. In the case of the United States, students in two-year community courses are inevitably classified as belonging to the nonuniversity sector, although a substantial portion transfer to four-year colleges (the long-cycle sector); in contrast, students in four-year colleges are counted as part of the university sector, although many are in vocationally oriented programs of a standard well below that of universities in most countries. In all countries, the distinction becomes increasingly fuzzy as universities adapt to the leveling off of enrollments by instituting shorter courses with more technical or vocational content. A further problem in statistical comparisons is the internal consistency of time series data, especially in a period of substantial structural changes such as that covered here.

Statistics on expenditures for higher education also are problematic. Here again, data prepared by international sources are used (chiefly UNESCO). The sources have the disadvantage that they do not specify the classification used in aggregating the data. Table A.2 includes only current or operating expenditures, omitting capital or investment costs. The extent to which ancillary services (such as student residences) play a role in the various systems and are included in the data varies, and the same is true of research costs. The expression of expenditures for higher education as a percentage of GNP represents a means of partially compensating for problems of comparability.

THE TABLES AND FIGURES

Table A.1 presents, in highly condensed form, certain demographic and economic data on the seven countries, as well as data on key characteristics of the national higher education systems. In this table particularly, the material has been highly compressed to facilitate rough comparisons and should not be used for any other purpose.

Per capita gross national product (GNP), in row 2 of the table, serves as a basic indicator for the level of economic development of the countries, as do the figures in row 3 on the distribution of employment among the three basic sectors of the economy: The agricultural or primary sector; the industrial or secondary; and the service or tertiary. On all measures, Italy clearly ranks lowest, while the United States and Sweden rank highest; otherwise the order is not entirely clear. Row 3 gives the proportion of university graduates employed in the labor force, which tends to be related to enrollment ratios in higher education (Figures A.1 and A.3). This is most obvious for the case of the United States, reflecting the fact that its enrollment ratios have been high for decades.

The problem of employment opportunities for university graduates has considerable significance for the planning of higher education. From the beginning, the expansion of higher education was accompanied by warnings of a possible saturation of the labor market for academically-trained manpower. However, if the rate of unemployment among graduates of postsecondary institutions is compared with unemployment in the total labor force, as in row 5, it is clear that graduates run a lower risk of unemployment than persons without a higher education diploma, with the sole exception of Italy—probably a further indication of problems with the Italian economy and with the coordination and curriculum of the Italian universities. These figures, it should be noted, predate the recent worldwide recession, and it is possible that the situation of graduates has deteriorated relative to that of their compatriots without postsecondary credentials. In any case, the more fundamental question as to whether economic development will lead in the longer term to an increase or decrease in the demand for academically trained manpower is still highly controversial.

Equality of opportunity for higher education was one of the most important reform goals of the 1960s, and rows 6–9 in Table A.1 provide pertinent data.

As has been mentioned, the expansion of short-cycle, practically-oriented programs was intended both to relieve the pressure of expanding enrollments on the universities and to adapt to the varying background and preparation of new student cohorts. However, it is evident from row 6 that such programs have generally *not* attracted a larger share of enrollments from 1960 to 1970. In France and the Federal Republic of Germany, admissions requirements and quotas may have restricted numbers. As for Italy, the continued dominance of the (unreformed) universities is symptomatic of the system's failure to undertake any meaningful diversification. In the United Kingdom, the figures do reflect the strength of the nonuniversity half of the binary system, which of course since the end of the 1960s has been strengthened by creation of the polytechnics. If all of their students are included, nonuniversity higher education is now at least holding its own with the universities.

Row 7 shows that the demographic factor (larger age cohorts) played only a minor role in the expansion of the 1960s, relative to the growth of enrollment rates. This was most extreme in the Federal Republic of Germany, where the demographic trend alone would have meant a *reduction* in student numbers. In contrast, the United States was the only country of the seven where growing cohorts played a relatively significant role. In Europe, an essential factor associated with the growth of higher education was the recent expansion of secondary schools, especially those providing university access; this expansion at the secondary level has begun much earlier in the United States, and led in turn to relatively early growth at the tertiary level.

Row 8 gives direct measures—although highly approximate—of the growth of educational opportunity from 1961 to 1970. Despite substantial improvement, disparities remain large, above all in the Federal Republic of Germany and in France.

The last row in Table A.1, finally, portrays the proportion of women enrolled in university-type and nonuniversity institutions. United States women have relatively broad access to both sectors, while inequality between men and women is greatest in the Federal Republic of Germany and above all Japan; in the latter case it is evident that a large share of junior colleges are overwhelmingly female institutions, while the more prestigious universities remain predominantly a male domain.

THE FINANCING OF POSTSECONDARY EDUCATION

Financial data are important in the context of this study, for they reflect the priority which governments assign to higher education. Tables A.2 and A.3 give figures only for operating expenditures, since the inclusion of capital costs would have complicated the picture. Levels of expenditure have risen dramatically, in response to expanding enrollments and other factors. The availability of funds plays a major part in determining the degree of leeway that the various governing authorities possess in determining policy. As budgets grow less rapidly or even stagnate, as has occurred widely since 1970, policy options are severely restricted.

Looking at Table A.2, if the growth rates of public expenditures on higher education has generally increased both as a proportion of the enrollments in the same period, it is clear that expenditures have grown faster than enrollments. This permits the general conclusion that units costs per student have risen substantially, as was noted in the introduction.

From rows 3 and 4 of Table A.2, it is evident that public expenditure for higher education has generally increased both as a proportion of the educational budget as a whole and as a share of GNP. In other words, public funds allocated to higher education have grown at a faster rate than both funds for other sectors of education and the GNP. This reflects the relatively high priority assigned to higher education by policymakers, both in relation to other national needs in the various countries and within the education system; in the latter arena, postsecondary enrollments were generally growing faster than other types of enrollments. Italy represents the most significant exception to this pattern, which probably reflects again the relatively low priority of reform efforts in that country.

Turning to Table A.3, which shows the source of funds spent on higher education, it is evident that the higher education budget in Europe is financed almost entirely from public monies, while in Japan (and also in the United States) a distinct proportion comes from private sources. Since higher education is dependent in large part on public funds, and demands an increasingly share of those funds in terms both of the budget as a whole and the GNP, it naturally tends increasingly to be affected by public priority-setting and resource planning.

The proportion of funds from public sources is even greater than indicated by the figures, since tuition and other fees are often born to a large extent by the government; this is true notably of France and the United Kingdom.

To properly gauge the relative significance of private funds in Japan and the United States, one must note that the proportion of students in United States private higher education has decreased to 25 percent since World War II, while that proportion has *risen* to 75 percent in Japan. Per student expenditures for private higher education are extraordinarily low, amounting to roughly one-third of per student expenditures by government universities (cf. Table A.2, note f to row 1). Thus the bulk of the expansion in Japanese higher education has taken place in private institutions that are run very cheaply; this may explain why the proportion of the overall education budget spent on higher education in Japan has increased only slightly (row 3 of Table A.2) and higher education's share of the GNP is relatively low (row 4).

Table A.2 represents the financial condition of higher education through the end of the 1960s; since then, the situation has changed drastically. In virtually all countries, costs continue to rise, while the funds allocated to higher education have stagnated, and most institutions have faced budget cuts at one time or another. If this development should prove to be a long-term one, as seems likely, the effects on decision-making structures will be significant; criteria of rationality and managerial efficiency will play an increasing role in policy debates.

THE GROWTH OF ENROLLMENTS

The data in Table A.4 provide a vivid portrayal of the expansion of higher education in the past two decades. Enrollments in all countries have multiplied severalfold, requiring extensive structural changes. The figures also document the relative monopoly of university-type higher education in 1950, which has since been attenuated in most countries by the somewhat faster growth of nonuniversity institutions, which provide alternative programs to those of the universities. Universities must increasingly compete with other sectors of higher education for scarce resources, and it is becoming ever more rare that they can do so from their former position of strength.

Table A.5 shows clearly that higher educational growth rates differ significantly between countries and over time. In France, Sweden, and the United States growth rates are already decreasing by the mid-1960s or soon thereafter. In the other countries, with the exception of the Federal Republic of Germany, the strongest growth took place in the second half of the 1960s and started to fall off by 1970. The Federal Republic of Germany is the only one of the seven countries in which the growth rate continued to climb after 1970. This can be ascribed partly to the steadily growing number of secondary school leavers, some 90 percent of which saw no alternative but to apply for higher education, and also to the lengthening time which students spent at university. From 1970 to 1974 alone, the time spent by the average student in his program increased from 5.7 to 6.5 years. Sweden represents the opposite case: the absolute number of students has actually dropped. This may be partially explained by the introduction of restrictions on the length of studies in 1960 and the drop in entrants since 1968.

Data on the growth of entrants to higher education, as presented in Table A.6, provide further clues to enrollment trends. In general, these figures confirm the picture gleaned from Table A.5, although the variations from year to year and from country to country are stronger, rendering deviations more visible. Since entrants to higher education fluctuate, perhaps in response to short-term demand factors, so sharply, trends can be ascertained only over a relatively long period. The continental European nations manifest strong variations in the annual growth rate of entrants between 1965 and 1970; from 1970 on there is a distinct decline. The United States experienced an actual drop in admissions between 1970 and 1973, which hit private institutions especially hard, due to their dependence on tuition fees. In contrast, the number of entrants has quite recently increased again in Japan and in the United Kingdom.

ENROLLMENT AND ADMISSIONS RATES

The three figures show the development of relative attendance in higher education in the seven countries, by presenting enrollments as a proportion of the relevant age group of cohort. The age range which is taken as a base is related to the age structure of the student body and the average length of studies.

Attendance at university-type institutions is shown in Figure A.1, demonstrating that the student quota has doubled in most countries between 1950 and 1970. The United States started from a much higher level than the other countries in 1950, and only Sweden had passed that level in 1970. Furthermore, despite accelerated expansion, in most countries only a small minority of the age group attended university in 1970. If one adds short-cycle higher education the United States reached nearly 40 percent attendance, but Sweden just surpassed 20 percent and the rest of the countries had not gone beyond roughly 15 percent. The low enrollment rate in the

United Kingdom is striking, but here nearly half of the students are in nonuniversity programs; thus the figure does not give a valid picture of the overall attendance in British higher education.

Figure A.3 shows the proportion of students entering university-type programs, in relation to their age cohort. This quota gives a rough comparative indication of the average chance of attending higher education for individuals within the cohort. Above all, in the 1960s the admissions quotas rose rapidly in all of the seven countries except the United States. As was evident from row 7 of Table A.1, demographic factors were generally much less significant in this development than the increasing demand for higher education, encouraged by reforms aimed at easing access.

Enrollment rates for 1970 by single years of age are presented in Figure A.3, which gives an idea of the age structure of the study body and the average length of studies. In the Federal Republic of Germany, France, and Sweden, there are relatively high proportions of older students. Especially in the Federal Republic of Germany and France, this can be attributed to the relatively long period of time spent at the university by most students, while the Swedish data probably already show the consequences of recurrent training courses attended by adults. In Japan, the United Kingdom, and the United States, there is a clear disjuncture between undergraduate and graduate enrollments, with a sharply lower quota for the latter.

TECHNICAL COMMENTS

The OECD Conversion Key

All data on student enrollments are classified according to the OECD conversion key, although not all enrollment data are from OECD sources. The key was published in 1972–73 for 19 member nations in the series *Classification of Educational Systems.*

The enrollment data for the Federal Republic of Germany present particular difficulties. For years after 1970, figures could not exactly be classified according to the OECD conversion key. In respect to the nonuniversity-type higher education sector, the figures do not comprise students enrolled in courses of advanced technical schools (*Höhere Fachs-chulen*) that have not been transformed into higher technical colleges (*Fachhochschulen*) which have been in existence since about 1970 though they are classified by OECD as nonuniversity higher education. In national statistics there is no distinction made between the remainder of these advanced technical schools and specialized secondary technical schools. For the years prior to 1970, an adjustment is made for the enrollments of the former advanced technical schools, the predecessors of the higher technical colleges, provided by the source used. Enrollment data are comprised of total full-time and part-time students except for the Federal Republic of

Germany, where until 1970 only fulltime students are included. For later years there is no specification available.

Parttime students are reported as follows. University-type higher education: United Kingdom: 34,700 students in 1970; United States: 1,644,000 students (degree-credit) in 1971. Nonuniversity-type higher education: United Kingdom: Further education courses leading to recognized qualifications: 109,500 students in 1970; United States: 795,000 students (degree-credit) in 1971. Enrollment data on new entrants are organized according to the same classification used for total enrollments. Generally, new entrants are considered to be students enrolled for the first time in the first year of a given program; i.e., not including repeaters. A student is counted each time he changes from one faculty or university to another. However, a student who was given a years's dispensation and who entered directly into the following year would not be considered as a new entrant.

The figures are intended to include both fulltime and parttime except for the United Kingdom where only fulltime students are included.

Enrollments in University-type Higher Education

Federal Republic of Germany: The statistics cover students following degree level courses in universities and equivalent establishments (*Wissenschaftliche Hochschulen*): universities, technical universities, institutes of theology and philosophy, church schools (*Kirchliche Hochschulen*) and teacher training colleges (training of primary and lower secondary teachers).

Italy: The data include students enrolled in courses leading to a first degree (*Laurea*) and students above first degree level studies provided by universities, university institutes, postgraduate schools and schools of specialization (*Scuole di Perfezionamento*). The first university degree (*Laurea*) confers the title of *dottore* in the chosen field.

France: The statistics cover universities, university institutes and *grandes écoles* excluding double registration of students enrolled in grandes écoles and university courses, and excluding students working for the proficiency certificate in law (*la capacité en droit*).

Sweden: The data include students enrolled in universities and specialized institutions recognized as providing university-type higher education and training in particular fields of study; i.e., technology, agriculture, economics, social work and public administration, journalism, domestic sciences, etc.

United Kingdom: University-type higher education corresponds to degree level courses. Most of these students are enrolled in the university sector and in the further education sector following advanced courses leading to a university first degree or university higher degree, and to a CNAA first degree or CNAA higher degree including also students enrolled in other postgraduate and research courses. Most of the advanced courses in further education are provided by polytechnics and other major establishments of further education.

United States: The data cover enrollments in degree credit courses leading to the following degrees: bachelor's degree, masters's degree, first professional degree, and doctorate. The courses are provided by universities, liberal arts colleges, teachers colleges, professional schools and colleges.

Japan: The data cover students enrolled in regular undergraduate and postgraduate courses, advanced and short-term courses leading to a first degree (*Gakushi*), to the postgraduate diploma (*Shushi*), and to the doctorate (*Hakushi*). Correspondence courses are omitted because they are difficult to classify. The courses are provided by universities (*Daigaku*).

Enrollments in Nonuniversity-type Higher Education

Federal Republic of Germany: The figures comprise students enrolled in institutions of fine arts, music and sports (*Kunst-, Musik- und Sporthochschulen*), and higher technical colleges (*Fachhochschulen*), with *Fachhochschulreife* as entrance requirement.

Italy: The data cover courses for the training in physical education and training of primary school supervisors. (Regular training of primary teachers takes place in schools of secondary level.) Furthermore, enrollments in certain specialized schools that provide courses in specific scientific and technical subjects and in academies of fine arts are included. These courses prepare for the awarding of the *Licenza* and other diplomas.

France: The statistics mainly cover students working for the proficiency certificate in law (*la capacité en droit*), students enrolled in the university institutes of technology (*Instituts universitaires de technologie*), enrollments in the higher technician's section of the technical *lycées*, the preparatory classes for the *grandes écoles* in *lycées*, and the teacher training colleges for primary teachers.

Sweden: The figures cover advanced vocational and technical education (i.e., agriculture, health services and administration, social services, economics and commerce, public and state enterprise, arts, military, etc.), enrollments in teacher training for primary school teachers, comprehensive school teachers for the first to the sixth grade, to mention only the quantitatively most important types of training.

United Kingdom: Nonuniversity-type higher education corresponds to below degree level courses and to other advanced level courses. The data mainly comprise students enrolled in teachers' training colleges (initial training, excluding postgraduate courses) and enrollments in further education courses leading to *Higher National Diplomas* (HND), and equivalent diplomas and certificates offered by polytechnics and other major establishments.

United States: The figures cover degree-credit students following courses leading to a semiprofessional degree (*Certificate or Associate Degree*) provided by two-year institutions.

Japan: The figures are comprised of the junior colleges including regular courses, advanced and short-term courses; correspondence courses have been omitted.

SOURCES FOR THE TABLES AND FIGURES

Table A.1

Rows 1 and 2 (population and GNP per capita): OECD, *Economic Surveys: France, Germany (FRG), Italy, Sweden, United States* (Paris: OECD, 1975), p. 1. For United Kingdom and Japan: *The OECD Observer*, 11 (1975), no. 74, pp. 1–4. Row 3 (employment by sectors): *The OECD Observer*, 11 (1975), no. 74, p. 2. Row 4 (university graduates): Manfred Tessaring, "Bildungsexpansion und Arbeitsmarkt für hochqualifizierte Arbeitskräfte im internationalen Vergleich", *Die Deutsche Universitätszeitung/Hochschuldienst*, 11 (1975), p. 435. Sweden 1973. Row 5 (unemployment): Manfred Tessaring, "Expansion," p. 436. FRG = 1974; UK = 1971; Japan = 1970. Row 6 (nonuniversity-type enrollments): See Table A.4. Row 7 (age group versus enrollment ratio): OECD, *Towards Mass Higher Education* (Paris: OECD, 1974), Table 10, p. 26. Row 8 (social bias): OECD, *Towards Mass Higher Education*, Table 13, p. 31. Row 9 (women in higher education): Calculated from: For FRG, Italy, France, and United Kingdom: OECD, *Educational Statistics Yearbook*, vol. II, Country Tables (Paris: OECD, 1975), pp. 132–133, 172–173, 232–233, and 380–381. For Sweden, United States, and Japan: Calculated from sources provided by the European Foundation, Institute of Education, Paris. France = 1965.

Table A.2

Row 1 (per student expenditures): UNESCO, *Statistical Yearbook 1973* (Paris: UNESCO, 1974), Table 5.4 pp. 468–471, 474–476; UNESCO: *Statistical Yearbook 1972* (Paris: UNESCO, 1973), Table 5.3, p. 566. Row 2 (growth rates): UNESCO, *Hochschulbildung in Europa, Schlussbericht und Arbeitsdokumente der von der UNESCO vom 26. November bis 3. Dezember 1973 in Bukarest veranstalteten 2. Konferenz der europäischen Erziehungsminister* (Pullach bei München: Verlag Dokumentation, 1975), p. 232. Rows 3 and 4 Operating expenditures): For European countries: UNESCO, *Hochschulbildung in Europa*, pp. 298–302. For United States and Japan (row 3): UNESCO, *Statistical Yearbook 1972*, Table 5.2, pp. 537, 540, and UNESCO, *Statistical Yearbook 1973*, Table 5.2, pp. 442, 444, Row 4: Calculated from sources to row 3 and OECD, *Economic Surveys: United*

States, Japan (Paris: OECD, 1974), pp. 42, 69. Sources of footnotes to Row 4: For Japan: Ministry of Education, *Educational Standards in Japan* (Tokyo: Ministry of Education, Government of Japan, 1971), pp. 235, 242; for United States: Carnegie Commission on Higher Education, *Higher Education: Who Pays? Who Benefits? Who Should Pay?* (New York: McGraw-Hill, 1973), p. 30.

Table A.3

For Federal Republic of Germany: Bundesministerium für Bildung und Wissenschaft and Statistisches Bundesamt, eds., *Bildung im Zahlenspiegel* (Bonn and Wiesbaden: Kohlhammer, 1974), p. 164. For France: OECD, *Towards Mass Higher Education*, p. 204. For Sweden: Information provided by the Chancellor of the Swedish Universities (UKÄ) For United Kingdom: University Grants Committee, Department of Education and Science, *Statistics of Education 1972*, vol. 6, *Universities* (London: HMSO, 1975), pp. 68-71. For Japan: Ministry of Education, *Educational Standards in Japan*, p. 160.

Table A.4

All data for 1950: OECD, *Towards Mass Higher Education*, Tables A–C, pp. 54–55. Federal Republic of Germany: For 1960–70: Bundesministerium für Bildung und Wissenschaft and Statistisches Bundesamt, eds., *Bildung im Zahlenspiegel*, p. 179. For 1971: Der Bundesminister für Bildung und Wissenschaft, *Grunddaten* (Bonn: Klüsener, 1974), p. 26. For 1972 and later: Der Bundesminister für Bildung und Wissenschaft: *Informationen—Bildung—Wissenschaft*, 9 (1975), p. 131. Italy: For 1960–70: OECD, *Educational Statistics Yearbook*, vol. II, Country Tables, p. 232. For 1971 and later: Data provided by the European Foundation, Institute of Education, Paris. France: For 1960–65: OECD, *Educational Statistics Yearbook*, vol. II, Country Tables, p. 134. For 1970 and later: Data provided by the European Foundation, Institute of Education, Paris. Sweden: For 1960–65: OECD, *Towards Mass Higher Education*, p. 54; for nonuniversity-type higher education, and for university-type higher education: OECD: *Educational Statistics Yearbook*, vol. II, Country Tables, p. 356, and corrections for 1965 provided by the European Foundation, Institute of Education. For 1970 and later: OECD, *Educational Statistics Yearbook*, vol. II, *Country Tables*, p. 356, and corrections for university-type higher education provided by the European Foundation, Institute of Education, Paris. United Kingdom: For 1960: OECD, *Towards Mass Higher Education*, p. 54. For 1965–70: OECD, *Educational Statistics Yearbook*, vol. II, *Country Tables*, p. 380. Later: Data provided by the European Foundation, Institute of Education, Paris. United States: For 1960–70: OECD, *Educational Statis-*

tics Yearbook, vol. II, *Country Tables*, p. 406. For 1971 and later: Data provided by the European Foundation, Institute of Education, Paris. Japan: For 1960–73: Data provided by the European Foundation, Institute of Education, Paris.

Tables A.5 and A.6

For average growth rates 1960–65: OECD: *Development of Higher Education 1950–1967: Analytical Report*, p. 44. For 1965 to 1973–74: Calculated from sources to Table A.4.

Figure A.1

For 1950–55: OECD, *Development of Higher Education 1950–1967: Analytical Report*, p. 81. For 1960–70: Calculated from sources to Table A.4 (higher education enrollments) and OECD, *Towards Mass Higher Education*, Table 9 and Tables A and B, pp. 25, 54.

Figure A.2

For 1950–55: OECD, *Development of Higher Education 1950–1967: Analytical Report*, p. 86. For 1960 (Italy, France, United States, Japan): Calculated from: OECD *Educational Statistics Yearbook*, Vol. II, *Country Tables*, pp. 146, 237, 259, 411, and OECD, *Towards Mass Higher Education*, Table 17 and Table D, pp. 37, 55. For Federal Republic of Germany (1960): Calculated from source to Table A.6 and OECD, *Towards Mass Higher Education*, pp. 37, 55. For Sweden (1960): Calculated from: OECD, *Development of Higher Education 1950–1967: Analytical Report*, pp. 86, 235, and OECD, *Educational Statistics Yearbook*, Vol. II, p. 360. For United Kingdom (1960): OECD, *Development of Higher Education 1950–1967: Analytical Report*, p. 86. For 1965–70 (FRG, Italy, France, United States, Japan): Calculated from sources for Table A.6 and OECD, *Towards Mass Higher Education*, pp. 37, 55. For Sweden and United Kingdom (1965): Calculated from: OECD, *Development of Higher Education 1950–1967: Analytical Report*, pp. 86, 235, and sources to Table A.6. For Sweden (1970): OECD, *Educational Statistics Yearbook*, Vol. II, p. 360. For United Kingdom (1969): Calculated from: OECD, *Towards Mass Higher Education*, pp. 37, 55, and sources for Table A.6.

Figure A.3

Except for Federal Republic of Germany, see OECD, *Educational Statistics Yearbook*, Vol. II, pp. 148, 260, 361, 387, 412. For Federal

Republic of Germany: Bundesministerium für Bildung und Wissenschaft and Statistisches Bundesamt, eds., *Bildung im Zahlenspiegel*, p. 127.

NOTES TO THE TABLES AND FIGURES

Table A.1

a. Japan, Sweden, United Kingdom: Gross Domestic Product.

b. Including forestry and fishing.

c. Including mining, manufacturing, construction and utilities (electricity, gas and water).

d. USA: Estimated figures.

e. Data for England and Wales only.

f. Excluding graduates of nonuniversity-type higher education (except for France).

g. Data are calculated on a comparable basis.

h. Data for Great Britain.

i. Sweden: For 1965/1972.

k. Considering the lack of comparability of social origin statistics, the data presented can only give very crude information on general trends in the different countries. For more information about the classification of students by socioeconomic groupings applied here, see OECD, *Group Disparities in Educational Participation and Achievement* (Paris: OECD, 1971), pp. 89–102.

l. France: For 1959/1968.

m. Sweden: For 1960/1968; the classification used is not fully comparable with the other countries.

n. Data for England and Wales.

o. France: Figures for the *grandes écoles* are incomplete.

Table A.2

a. Public expenditures include educational expenditure by all governmental levels; they comprise, if not otherwise indicated, public education and, where applicable, subsidized private education.

b. France: Data for the Ministry of National Education only.

c. National expenditures per student have been converted to US dollars in order to compare the different amounts in rough terms. The exchange rates are from UNESCO, *Statistical Yearbook 1973*. Since they do not normally represent comparative purchasing power the figures presented do not reflect actual per student expenditures.

d. For England and Wales only.

e. US: For *private* higher education, operating expenditures per student (from public and private sources) in 1970 were 4,041 U.S. dollars.

f. Japan: For *private* higher education, operating expenditures per student (from public and private sources) in 1970 were 415 U.S. dollars.

g. Sweden: Gross Domestic Product.

h. United States: If *private* expenditures are included, total operating expenditures for higher education as a percent of GNP were 1.5 in 1965 and 2.0 in 1970.

i. Japan: If *private* expenditures are included, total operating expenditures for higher education as a percent of GNP were 0.5 in 1965 and 0.5 in 1968.

Table A.3

a. The table covers essentially expenses which are part of the ordinary budgets. Reliable and comparable figures on external funds, mainly for research (from governments, research councils, foundations, endowments, donations or industry) are not available.

b. Federal Republic of Germany: The figures include university clinics; they cover public expenditures only, but non-public expenditures are negligible. (Student fees were abolished statewise in the course of the late 1960s and early 1970s.)

c. United Kingdom: The figures cover universities only. The figure in row 1 (central government) included exchequer grants as well as grants and payments for research and other specific purposes from government departments.

Table A.4

a. Italy: Excluding postgraduate courses and schools of specialization ("Perfezionamento"). For 1972: 15,000 students are estimated.

b. Sweden: Data for 1972.

c. Japan: Excluding the training at technical colleges of which the last two years are considered as nonuniversity-type higher education.

Table A.6

a. France: Students in the first year, including repeaters and excluding *grandes écoles* and university institutes.

b. United Kingdom: Students in the first year, including repeaters and excluding further education courses in Northern Ireland and graduate students in the university sector.

c. United States: Degree credit students only.

d. Japan: Regular courses only.

Figure A.1

a. The figures for 1950 and 1955 are in many cases uncertain. The age span covered is the same as generally in OECD figures, encompassing at least three-quarters of the students. The age spread varies from country to country depending on the age structure of the student population and the length of studies. Age group considered: Federal Republic of Germany, 20–25; Italy, 19–25; France, 18–23; Sweden, 20–24; United Kingdom, 18–22; United States, 18–23; Japan, 18–22.

Figure A.2

a. The rates of admission are percentages of an average age cohort; the age groups considered for entrants are Federal Republic of Germany, 20–22; Italy, 19–21; France, 18–20; Sweden, 19–21; United Kingdom, 18–20; United States, 18; Japan, 18–19. The figures for 1950 and 1955 are not always comparable to those for later years because of uncertainty in classification of entrants. The calculation of admission rates from different sources is based on the assumption that the demographic data implicitly included in the applied sources correspond. See also notes to Table A.6 (growth rates of entrants).

Figure A.3

a. For France: Excluding the *grandes écoles* and university institutes; including holders of the proficiency certificate in law (capacitaires). For Federal Republic of Germany: Data for 1971. For Sweden: Data for 1972. For Japan: Data are estimated. No figures are available for Italy.

TABLE A.1:
Basic Comparative Data

	FRG	Italy	France	Sweden	UK	USA	Japan
1. Population (1973 or 1974; in Millions)	62	55	53	8	56	213	108
2. GNP per Capita (1973 or 1974; in US Dollars)	6200	2507	4905	6830[a]	3100[a]	6571	3760[a]
3. Per Cent of Civilian Employment in Agriculture[b] / Industry[c] / Other (1973)	7/50/43	17/44/39	12/39/49	7/37/56	3/42/55	4/(32)[d]/(64)[d]	13/37/50
4. University Graduates as Per Cent of the Total Labour Force (1970 or 1971)	3.8	3.2	3.0	6.1	3.9[e]	12.5	6.5
5. Per Cent Unemployment among: Higher Education Graduates[f] / Total Labour Force[g] (1972 or 1973)	1.0/2.4	4.3/3.8	1.8/2.2	1.0/3.2	1.0/3.3[h]	2.1/5.2	0.9/1.4
6. Per Cent of Non-university Enrollments in Higher Education (1965/73)	19/19	3/2	17/17	21/16[i]	50/46	15/23	14/16
7. Relative Effect on Higher Education Enrollments of Changes (1960-70) in: Size of Age Group / Enrollment Ratio	-27/127	2/98	38/62	24/76	26/74	60/40	n.a.
8. Chance of Entering University for Upper Stratum Compared to Lower Stratum Youth (1961/70)[k]	58:1/12:1	n.a.	84:1/28:1[l]	9:1/5:1[m]	8:1/5:1[n]	n.a.	n.a.
9. Per Cent of Women in: University / Non-university-type Higher Education (1970)	31/12	38/49	41/35[o]	37/n.a.	27/40	42/42	18/83

TABLE A.2:
Public Expenditure on Higher Education [a]

	Year	FRG	Italy	France[b]	Sweden	UK	USA	Japan
1. Operating Expenditures for Public Higher Education per Student (in US Dollars)[c]	1970	1469	640	864	2179	2323[d]	2302[e]	1747[f]
2. Average Annual Growth Rate in Per Cent of Public Expenditure on:								
--All Education	1960–70	13.5	14.5	14.3	15.2	11.0	n.a.	n.a.
--Higher Education	1960–70	17.3	11.6	25.3	22.3	19.3	n.a.	n.a.
3. Public Operating Expenditures for Higher Education as Per Cent of Expenditures for All Education	1960	13.2	11.4	8.3	8.0	13.8	18.9	12.4
	1965	18.8	7.7	17.6	9.2	21.5	27.8	11.0
	1970	17.7	8.8	21.3	14.5	26.3	29.5	12.7
4. Public Operating Expenditures for Higher Education as Per Cent of GNP	1960	0.3	0.3	0.2	0.3[g]	0.5	0.7	n.a.
	1965	0.5	0.3	0.5	0.5[g]	0.8	1.3[h]	0.4[i]
	1970	0.5	0.4	0.6	0.9[g]	1.2	1.7[h]	0.4[i]

TABLE A.3:

Sources of Income for Higher Education [a] (in percent; Italy and United States Omitted)

	FRG[a] (1971)	France (1968)	Sweden (1973)	UK[b] (1971)	Japan (1968) Public	Japan (1968) Private
1. Central Government	16.7	95.0	97.0	84.0	88.6	3.1
2. State or Local Government	83.3	–	–	1.0	7.9	0.1
3. Fees	–	5.0	–	6.0	3.5	48.0
4. Endowments and other Private Sources	–	–	–	1.0	–	48.8
5. Not Classifiable	–	–	3.0	8.0	–	–
Total	100.0	100.0	100.0	100.0	100.0	100.0

TABLE A.4:

Higher Education Enrollments in Selected Years (in thousands)

	Year	FRG	Italy	France	Sweden	UK	USA	Japan
All Higher Education	1950	147*	241	185*	27	n.a.	2297	240[c]
	1960	296	284	282	49	n.a.	3583	710[c]
	1965	373	425	525	85	433	5526	1085[c]
	1970	528	710[a]	805	151[b]	599	7920	1670[c]
	1973	733	847[a]	924	138[b]	634	8520	1907[c]
	1974	788	--	943*	--	--	8491*	--
1950 = 100	1973	499	351	499	511	n.a.	371	795
University-type Higher Education	1950	122	236	156*	17	115*	2079	225
	1960	239	275	234	37	147*	3131	626
	1965	304	412	434	67	209	4685	938
	1970	410	695[a]	679	123[b]	312	6290	1407
	1973	594	830[a]	767	115[b]	343	6598	1597
	1974	628	--	783*	--	--	6563*	--
1950 = 100	1973	487	352	492	676	298	317	710
Non-university-type Higher Education	1950	25*	5	29*	11	n.a.	218	15[c]
	1960	57	9	48	12	n.a.	451	84[c]
	1965	69	12	91	17	224	841	148[c]
	1970	117	16	126	28[b]	288	1630	263[c]
	1973	139	17	157	23[b]	290	1922	310[c]
	1974	160	--	160*	--	--	1928*	--
1950 = 100	1973	556	340	541	209	n.a.	882	2067

* Estimate

TABLE A.5:

Growth Rates of Enrollments in University-type Higher Education, 1960–1974 (in percent)

Growth Rates:	FRG Annual / Avg.	Italy Annual / Avg.	France[a] Annual / Avg.	Sweden Annual / Avg.	UK[b] Annual / Avg.	USA[d] Annual / Avg.	Japan[b] Annual / Avg.
1960–65	4.2	8.7	13.8	14.7	7.6*	8.4	8.3
1965–66	7.6	12.1	10.0	17.0	14.1	6.4	11.7
1966–67	3.1	9.7	13.5	22.1	9.8	6.8	10.8
1967–68	6.2	10.4	15.6	18.3	8.0	5.9	9.5
1968–69	5.0	12.0	4.6	-0.4	5.9	5.6	6.7
1969–70	9.0	10.8	3.8	8.5	4.3	5.6	3.8
1965–70	6.2	11.0	9.5	13.1	8.4	6.1	8.5
1970–71	13.7	11.3	6.5	-1.3	4.1	1.6	4.4
1971–72	15.1	2.6	5.1	-5.3	2.9	1.3	4.1
1972–73	10.6	4.7	0.8	--	2.6	1.9	4.5
1973–74	5.9	--	2.1*	--	--	-0.5*	--
1970–	11.3	6.2	3.6	-3.3	3.2	1.1	4.3

* Estimate

TABLE A.6:

Growth Rates of Entrants to University-type Higher Education, 1965–1973 (in percent)

Growth Rates:	FRG Annual / Avg.		Italy Annual / Avg.		France[a] Annual / Avg.		Sweden Annual / Avg.		UK[b] Annual / Avg.		USA[d] Annual / Avg.		Japan[b] Annual / Avg.	
1965–66	26.2		13.2		4.3		22.7		5.9		-5.0*		17.2	
1966–67	-7.8		6.5		16.7		29.3		8.5		0.3*		6.7	
1967–68	22.5		12.1		-12.9		18.0		6.1		8.5*		4.1	
1968–69	2.3		23.5		-9.3		-7.1		4.7		2.9		1.2	
1969–70	3.4		11.2		36.3		-2.3		2.9		1.7		1.1	
1965–70		9.3		13.3		7.0		12.1		5.6		1.7		6.1
1970–71	13.2		10.6		1.0		-11.9		5.5		-2.7		7.4	
1971–72	15.3		-0.5		-10.1*		2.0*		2.2		-2.8		5.1	
1972–73	5.3		2.1		1.5*		--		1.5		6.2		--	
1973–74	2.6		--		1.6*		--		--		--		--	
1970–		9.1		4.1		-1.5*		-5.0*		3.1		0.2		6.3

* Estimate

FIGURE A.1

Enrollment Rates for University-Type Higher Education, 1950-70 [a]

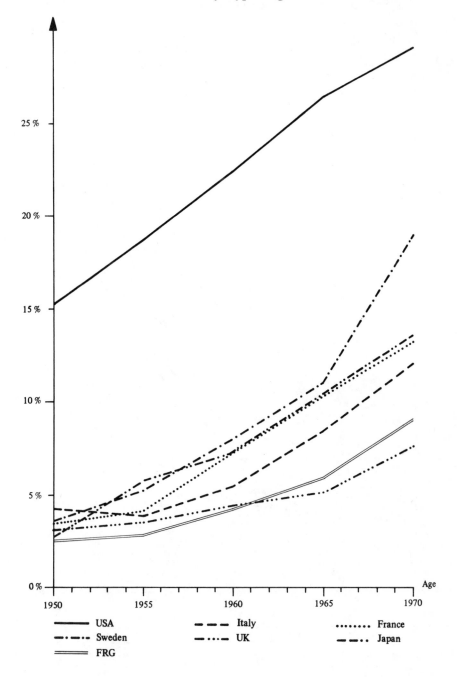

FIGURE A.2

Rates of Admission to University-Type Higher Education, 1950–70 [a]

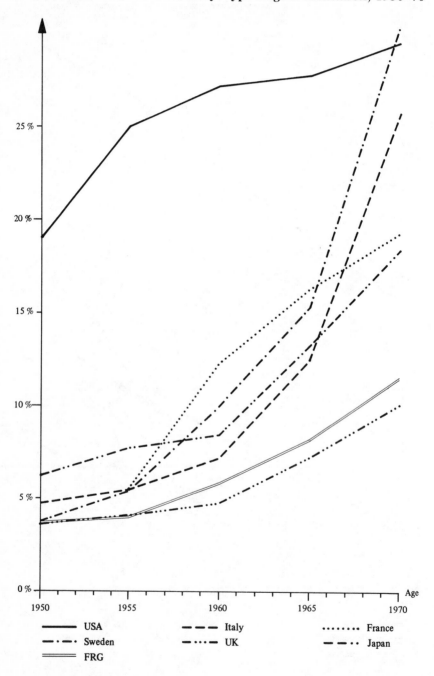

FIGURE A.3

Full-Time Enrollment Rates by Single Years of Age, University-Type Higher Education, 1970 [a]

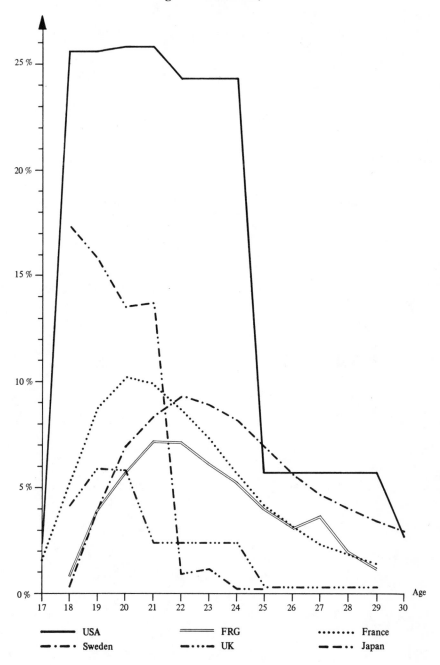

ABOUT THE AUTHORS

JOHN H. VAN DE GRAAFF teaches in the Department of Educational Foundations, University of Calgary. He has been a Postdoctoral Fellow in the Higher Education Research Group at Yale University and a Program Officer at the Unesco Institute for Education in Hamburg, where he edited the *International Review of Education.* He is co-editor of *Relevant Methods in Comparative Education* and author of articles in *Comparative Education Review* and *Higher Education.* Dr. Van de Graaff holds a Ph.D. from Columbia University.

BURTON R. CLARK is Professor of Sociology and Chairman of the Higher Education Research Group (within the Institution for Social and Policy Studies) at Yale University. He has previously been a Scholar-in-Residence at the Aspen Institute for Humanistic Studies and a Visiting Scholar at the Japan Society for the Promotion of Science, Kyoto and Tokyo, Japan; at the Institute for Higher Education and Science, Warsaw, Poland; and at the Institute of Education, European Cultural Foundation, Paris, France. Dr. Clark's extensive list of published works includes *The Problems of American Education* (editorship), *Academic Power in the United States* (with T.I.K. Youn), and *Academic Power in Italy: Bureaucracy and Oligarchy in a National University.* He holds a Ph.D. from the University of California at Los Angeles.

DOROTEA FURTH is Head of the Higher Education Programme in the Education and Training Division of the OECD, Paris. She has published several articles on problems of higher education in the Western industrialized countries and was editor and main author of the OECD publications *Short Cycle Higher Education* (1973) and *Selection and Certification in Education and Employment* (1977).

DIETRICH GOLDSCHMIDT is Director at the Max-Planck-Institut for Educational Research in West Berlin and teaches sociology at the Free University Berlin. From 1971 to 1973 he headed an official German commission collaborating with its Swedish counterpart in studying the democratisation of German and Swedish education. In 1973/74 he was Visiting Professor in the Institution for Social and Policy Studies and the Department of Sociology at Yale University. Outside Germany Dr. Goldschmidt has published articles in Higher Education, in Comparative Education Review and in UNESCO publications.

DONALD F. WHEELER is Assistant Professor of Sociology, School of Intercultural Studies, Ramapo College of New Jersey. Previously Research Associate and Lecturer in Sociology at the Institution for Social and Policy Studies, Yale University, Dr. Wheeler has lived and taught extensively in Japan and has written on Japanese student movements. He earned his Ph.D. at Columbia University and is Visiting Scholar at the university's East Asian Institute.